In ... collection ...

David Ives creates a hilarious collection of scenes, each one exploring *Variations on the Death of Trotsky.*

A brother and sister deal with life after parents in **Daisy Foote's** *Farley and Betsy.*

No Skronking, by **Shel Silverstein,** illustrates how rules were truly made to be broken.

Plus a host of other engaging scenarios and memorable moments from some of the country's top writers.

M. Jerry Weiss is a distinguished professor of communications emeritus at New Jersey City University. He currently lives in Upper Montclair, New Jersey.

THE SIGNET BOOK
OF SHORT PLAYS

EDITED BY

M. Jerry Weiss

SIGNET CLASSICS

SIGNET CLASSICS
Published by New American Library, a division of
Penguin Group (USA) Inc., 375 Hudson Street,
New York, New York 10014, USA
Penguin Group (Canada), 10 Alcorn Avenue, Toronto,
Ontario, Canada M4V 3B2 (a division of Pearson Penguin Canada Inc.)
Penguin Books Ltd, 80 Strand, London WC2R 0RL, England
Penguin Ireland, 25 St Stephen's Green, Dublin 2,
Ireland (a division of Penguin Books Ltd)
Penguin Group (Australia), 250 Camberwell Road, Camberwell, Victoria 3124,
Australia (a division of Pearson Australia Group Pty Ltd)
Penguin Books India Pvt Ltd, 11 Community Centre, Panchsheel Park,
New Delhi - 110 017, India
Penguin Group (NZ), cnr Airborne and Rosedale Roads, Albany,
Auckland, New Zealand (a division of Pearson New Zealand Ltd)
Penguin Books (South Africa) (Pty) Ltd, 24 Sturdee Avenue,
Rosebank, Johannesburg 2196, South Africa

Penguin Books Ltd, Registered Offices:
80 Strand, London WC2R 0RL, England

Published by Signet Classics, an imprint of New American Library,
a division of Penguin Group (USA) Inc.

First Signet Classics Printing, December 2004
10 9 8 7 6 5 4 3

*(Author copyrights and permissions and publishers note can be found on
pages 369–70.)*

SIGNET CLASSICS and logo are trademarks of Penguin Group (USA) Inc.

Library of Congress Catalog Card Number: 2004056493

Printed in the United States of America

Dedicated to Helen S. Weiss,
my lifetime theatergoing companion and great love

Contents

Acknowledgments

My editor, Tracy Bernstein
My very good friends: Dan Lundy, ArtsPower,
Gary Blackman, Mark Blackman, Patricia
Reilly Giff, Jeff Mathis, Eileen B. Weiss,
Michael S. Weiss, and the many agents and
playwrights who assisted with this project.

Introduction

I am an avid playgoer and play reader, and perhaps my best reason for editing this book is a hope of sharing my enthusiasm for the theater with others. To do this, I have searched through dozens of plays to find the ones that I think best show the power and purposes of the short play.

Each play has a theme or central idea that the playwright hopes to get across through dialogue and action. A few characters are used to create a single impression growing out of the theme. It is not my intent to point out the central theme of each of the plays in this volume, for that would, indeed, spoil the pleasures of reading, discussing, and thinking about the plays and the effectiveness of the playwright. However, a variety of types is represented here. These include comedy, satire, and poignant drama. Most were written expressly for the stage, but one was originally written for television and one is an adaptation of a prizewinning children's novel.

A biography for each of the playwrights appears at the end of this volume and will show the numerous awards all of these playwrights have won. These writers are among the most prestigious in America. Some have written novels, nonfiction, and poetry as well as dramas, both short and full-length.

To get the most out of reading these plays, try to picture the play being performed on a stage, with you, the reader, in the audience. The house lights dim. The curtains are about to open, and in a few minutes, the action and dialogue will tell you the story.

Enjoy!

—M. JERRY WEISS

LIFE BY ASPHYXIATION

by Kia Corthron

CHARACTERS

JOJO, a black man, 54

CRAZY HORSE, a Native American man, 35

NAT TURNER, a black man, 31

ANDY, a white man, fifties

KATIE, a white girl, 15

LUCY, a black woman, fifties

PARAMEDIC

Death Row, the present. Three adjacent cells. They are divided by walls but these need not be represented literally so long as they are clearly defined. Cell doors, or bars, should be invisible so as not to hinder sight lines.

Andy's chuckle is soft, not a snicker, and often more to himself than to the others. He is good-natured, and while his laughing habit may at times seem inappropriate, there is never any intention of cruelty.

SCENE 1

[Jojo *sleeps. Suddenly his eyes open.*]

JOJO: Hey! I got company.

[*He taps on the wall between the cells.*]

JOJO: I'm Jojo. Grew up with Isaiah, he says, "Let's go on a adventure ride." Seen them hitchhikers, one in jean shorts frayed one in black pants, their car stalled. They ask for a lift to the gas station, we took 'em the other direction. Raped 'em, strangled 'em. One was fifteen, one was seventeen. I was twenty-two. I'm fifty-four.

CRAZY HORSE: I'm thirty-five. All rests on the decoys, the timing, when to let them see us, when to

3

move. They think they're trapping us, if they suspect otherwise, it's over. I was the decoy leader. Winter battle, they followed like clockwork like clay we molded the outcome Fetterman's Soldiers we led them to their deaths a hundred! And Stanley's soldiers under Long Hair Custer, and later, later when I feared all was lost came the Rosebud. I charge, and behind a few fall in, then twice that many behind them, twice that many behind them mighty triangle we form spirit not broken!

NAT TURNER: Crazy Horse!

[Jojo *rushes to the other side of his cell.* Crazy Horse *smiles: recognition.*]

JOJO: Somebody else! [*no answer*] Hey! Jojo. Rape-murder. Fifty-four.

NAT TURNER: Thirty-one. I drew blood only once, one battle, a woman. Beat her to death. Rest of the war I was the general, organizer, the hands-off orchestrator. The enemy was everything white: "Do not spare age nor sex," I commanded. Men, women, down came the ax, throng of schoolchildren we tossed their headless bodies in a pile, and that's just the abridged version of what we did to them. What they did to us was worse. Nat Turner.

[Andy *enters and, as he speaks, continues crossing the stage to the other side.*]

ANDY [*chuckles to himself*]: I remember Nat Turner. [*sings*] "Unforgettable . . ." [*exits*]

JOJO: Fellas way down the corridor, but nobody this corner but me, nine years I been monasteryin'. 'Til now. Welcome to the neighborhood.

SCENE 2

[*The sound of a clock ticking, second by second. Crazy Horse has removed his shirt, socks and shoes. He stands bare-chested, barefoot. Jojo rubs his forearms, cold. Nat does calisthenics to keep warm.*]

JOJO: Stud!

[Andy *enters.*]

ANDY: I ain't gettin' in the game. In Vegas, dealer's the one in charge. [*chuckles*]

JOJO: "How the hell you play poker on death row?" you're thinkin'. "The excitement's in the bettin', what we got to bet?" Minutes. One hour every twenty-four we let outa our cells, outside. These sixty minutes is now up for grabs, for every minute you lose you stay inside, tell the C.O., "Sorry, needta crap, gotta stay in my cell 'til I'm done. C.O. say, "Your time, your loss." That you already knew.

ANDY: Hey, Jojo, ain't this a thrill? Other hands beside mine and yours? [*chuckles*]

NAT: Card playing not on my mind, late November chill out. When they turn on the heat?

JOJO: Card playin' somethin' keep your brain off the chill. [*No reply.* Jojo *shrugs.*] Kills time.

NAT: Kill that clock! When'd it start?

JOJO: Somethin' in the mechanism went outa whack years ago, dead, who cares? Clock watchin' hardly a popular death row sport. But every few months, no rhyme or reason, suddenly it resurrect: Tick. Tick. Tick. Tick.

ANDY [*deals to* Nat *first*]: Crazy got the button. One with the button's the imaginary dealer.

NAT: What's the point? Never be granted more than your daily sixty, so what? you win. Where's the booty?

JOJO: Winnin' the right to do your sixty, the knowledge you get to keep what's yours. If you don't find that precious and rare, you ain't been in long. [*beat*] You ain't been in long?

NAT [*shakes his head no*]: And won't be here much longer.

[Andy *has dealt two facedown cards to each and laid one apiece faceup outside of the cells.* Jojo *and* Crazy Horse *have picked up their cards;* Andy *and* Nat *are staring at each other. Then* Nat *picks up his cards.*]

ANDY: Here's what shows: Nat—queen a hearts, Jojo—tray a diamonds, Crazy—ace a spades. Nat first.

[*Now* Andy *sits outside the cells, staring in.*]

JOJO: How soon? Your date.

NAT: Soon. But someone else I know's going down sooner. Five minutes.

ANDY [*staring at* Nat]: And the openin' bet's been placed well I notice a little twitch to his right eye. No, left. And just a moment a clutchin' his cards tighter.

NAT: The cell next to me, this boy, twenty-eight, going to die tomorrow. Gordon.

JOJO: I remember Gordon! Decade ago, when they first bring him here put him right down the hall. Eighteen. Talker!

NAT: When the C.O. throws his dinner at him, Gordon smiles, "Thank you, Mr. Reece." He cleans his plate and is proud of it, tells me. Armed robbery, murder, the two boys he did the deed with usually call him dummy but this day let him play. When the shop owner came running in, screaming, somebody pulled the trigger. Other boys fled. When the police came, Gordon still kneeling, trying to wake the shop owner from his nap.

JOJO: Raise. Ten minutes.

ANDY: Whew! Pushin' the stakes. [*staring at* Jojo] Eyelids lifted ever so slightly. The lashes give 'em away. [*chuckles*]

NAT: Police ask Gordon if he did it, they've already decided he did. "Yes, sir," he says. I ask Gordon if he did it, I don't believe he did. "No, sir," he says. Gordon's a good boy. Gordon just aims to please.

JOJO: I remember this about Gordon—one belongin': *One Fish Two Fish Red Fish Blue Fish* by Dr. Seuss, which he read every single day like it was the first time.

NAT: In our block I started the loud chanting. "Injustice," "racism," "ABA Resolution 2," which is related to mental incapacity. None of these terms did Gordon understand, he didn't understand we were chanting for him. But he joined in. COs knew I was the fire starter, moved me out. A hundred times, this way and that he's been told his date's tomorrow, going to die tomorrow. In case he's got anything left to do, think about, that information he has a right to. He says "I know" but doesn't. When they take me away, he says he's going to practice, by the time I get back he'll count clear up to twenty, no mistakes.

ANDY [*to* Crazy Horse]: Mr. Horse! The game's waitin' for you. Hey! [*the interjection because he just took a good look at* Crazy Horse]

CRAZY HORSE: Call.

ANDY: Aintchu cóld? [Crazy Horse *doesn't answer.*] Hey! He ain't got no shirt on he ain't got no shoes, aintcher nose and toes ice cubed like ours?

NAT: Let him alone.

ANDY: This mornin' in the shower you complainin' cuza the lukewarm quality, you beggin' for steam, now look like you beggin' for pneumonia.

JOJO: Ain't eatin' nothin' neither. Starvin', freezin'. Like he tryn to get the fever.

NAT: Fasting. Which is a universe apart from starving, and the shower complaint wasn't about comfort. He's trying to find higher ground. He's looking for a vision, longs to see. Showers aren't a sweat lodge but through sultrier temps he was hoping for a facsimile. Lukewarm didn't cut it. [*to* Andy] Hit the deck.

ANDY: Fourth Street. [*deals another card to each of them*]

JOJO: Rape-murder I'm in for, that tend to be a arbitrary thing. But mass killin' usually got some kinda motive.

ANDY: Seven a diamonds to Nat, Jojo got the club deuce, four a spades to Crazy.

NAT: I was the sharp one. Preacher. I could read but that just made me their book-smart nigger, a novelty showpiece, twelve years old they turn me into the fields like everyone else. When I'm twenty-one, country hits a depression so they have a choice: sell us or work us harder, and already we work sunup to sundown. Guess which choice Master Turner makes? Hires a new overseer, new whip, I escape. Fifteen.

ANDY: Cool movin', not even a break in the inflection.

NAT: Month later I return. God gave me the sign: I wasn't yet finished serving my earthly master. Weren't the black people bitter: "You the one s'posed to be so smart?" It wasn't time. But time came.

JOJO: Call.

CRAZY HORSE: Twenty.

ANDY [*staring at* Crazy Horse]: Straight face, I catch nothin'. Wait. Twitch a the pinkie?

NAT: Funny thing about Virginia.

ANDY: Fifth Street. [*deals cards*]

NAT: North South, considered themselves the benevolent slavers. "We're the good masters," said they. "Look at Alabama, Mississippi." Compared to them, we were treated well, they thought. Not well enough. Thirty.

CRAZY HORSE: Freezing! The whites gave them blankets. Old days, before Indians learned Never Trust 'Em. Thanked them for their generosity, they didn't know the blankets had been infected with smallpox. Whole camps disappeared, *their* disease. [*pause*] She was five. [*pause*] My only child.

JOJO: Call.

CRAZY HORSE: We called her They Are Afraid Of Her. [*beat*] Call.

ANDY: Six Street. [*deals*]

JOJO: I got a daughter. Charmaine. She was a baby. Now she's thirty-two, her age is always how long I been inside plus one. Newlyweds with a baby, I married cuz she was pregnant. Lucy and me livin' in the trailer park, a little grass to each house. Lucy was rockin' my screamin' baby when I go out to pull the weeds crowdin' out the back door. Then Isaiah drives by. "Jojo! Let's go on a adventure ride."

NAT: Pass.

JOJO: Her name was Katie. I forget the other girl's name, the one Isaiah done it to. Their little light blue car stalled, a basketball sits in the back winda. All through the court proceedin's they's mentioned, how come I can't remember that other gal's name? Maybe I Freud-blocked it.

ANDY [*to* Nat *and* Jojo]: He'll die tonight. Your friend. Gordon. His official date's tomorra so they watchin' the clock now. They like to get it done with, they waitin' for the minute hand to turn midnight. At twelve o' one, it happens.

NAT: Fold. [Nat *drops his cards, folding.*]

ANDY: You can't fold, you just passed, it ain't your turn!

[Nat *doesn't pick up the cards.*]

JOJO: Forty.

CRAZY HORSE: Call.

ANDY: Whew! we ain't never flown this high before. Seventh Street: The Wire. [Andy *deals.*]

NAT [*more to himself*]: My mother was a teenager kidnapped from Africa. When I was born a slave on American soil she tried to kill me. The whites saved me. [*laughing*] The whites saved me!

ANDY: Thirty-one years together, Jojo, thirty-one years you here, and I started workin' just weeks after you come. All that time, just you and me and the cards. How you know I never cheat? [*chuckles*]

JOJO: When I first hear you shufflin', Poker you say, I think Why? I got nothin' to lose. You got one hour to lose you point out to me, and I ponder that. *Cheat* me? You *gave* me, Andy, plenty! Now I see: I got stuff a value, worth. Hear it?

[*silence except for the ticking of the clock*]

SCENE 3

[Jojo *closes his eyes.*]

JOJO: Come on.

[*A bloodcurdling scream off.* Jojo, *eyes open now, slaps his hands together; the sound implies he is slapping someone else.*]

JOJO: Scream again, I'll kill ya. [*sound of fast, loud breathing, off*] Be quiet!

KATIE [*off*]: I can't help my breathin'!

JOJO: I said Shut up, bitch! [Katie *enters, carrying a basketball.*] Katie!

KATIE: Didn't think you be callin', look like you got new people to kill time with.

JOJO [*guilty*]: Almost didn't but . . . I gotta see you.

KATIE: Almost didn't. Ain't you fickle. Tease, the haunted house, your ol' deserted next-door residences been filled, now guess your social calendar's too jam-packed for your previous acquaintances.

JoJo: No! you always with me. Just . . . you never come 'less you make me remember it first. My bad day, bad hour when I lose my morality you won't come see me without me livin' it again, I'm all alone 'less I put it back fresh in my mind: that time, hour I become a beast. That hour I make you fear and that's the worst: havin' to hear you fear again hear you tremble, and I done it.

KATIE: Didn't seem to bother you at the time.

JoJo: I know! I know! ·

KATIE: Think I'm gonna let you forget? You're a losin' son of a bitch and you're gonna burn for it. The chair: how many bodies caught fire in what was s'posed to be a smooth-sailin' go?

JoJo: Here we go again.

KATIE: The gas chamber: you know what death by asphyxiation feels like? I do.

JoJo: I'm sorry!

KATIE: *Hey!*

JoJo: I take it back!

KATIE: You better. Death by asphyxiation is a long ass death cuz breathin's a habit you been hooked on too long it's a hard one to kick. Just be easier to close your eyes and die but ya can't help it: ya keep tryn and tryn to gasp air, it just keep gettin' harder, harder.

JoJo: I remember it once. Gettin' caught the undertow I accidentally swam beyond the lifeguard recommended boundaries. Alone. Fourteen and dumb, every time I tried to choke the water out, more flowed in. My body tight, it wanna explode and crushin', I feel my face turnin' blue like that water, I know what you're sayin'. I been at that place.

KATIE: Fourteen and dumb? Shit, twenty-two you weren't no smarter. Most rape is separate but equal: white men rape white women, black men rape black women. But you had to go find a white girl, stupid! Nobody goes to jail for rapin' black girls.

JOJO: I wake up, somebody mouth-to-mouthin' me, I see white people, bikinis. Leisure sailboat, if it hadn't happened by I never woulda lived to . . . [*trails off*]

KATIE: Remember the old days when you'da hung? And sometimes it went like this: rope snap your neck, your head go flyin' right off your shoulders.

JOJO: The needle.

KATIE: Hah! Hope your veins are easy to find, otherwise they'll poke you like a pincushion. They'll bring in paramedics. Paramedics to kill ya! Whole thing'll seem so sweet and sanitary and they got your best care in mind to the outside world. Before they inject ya they'll alcohol your skin to prevent infection. [*rolls on the floor laughing*]

JOJO: Isaiah was twenty-one, year younger'n me, he got thirty years, I got death. Thirty years was last year, he's out free. They found Isaiah first, he ratted me out. They pronounce us equally guilty, but I die, he serves time and leaves. I ain't resentful. Why should I. He lost everything, family. And how he gonna live? only knows prison, and what they teach him thirty years? Nobody gonna hire someone fifty-two no skills, I ain't bitter, his punishment was severe enough. And continues.

KATIE [*dribbles*]: If I was fifteen now, I mighta had a chance for a b-ball scholarship. Not s'much around then for girls, thirty years back, but things was changin', and they saw my potential, who knows? I was fifth, baby a my family, all boys before me. My brothers taught me the game. Think they'd have me shoot like a girl? [*gets into shooting position*]

JOJO: Isaiah's the one done in your friend. What was her name?

KATIE [*stops aiming*]: I had potential but someone aborted it, fifteen my life all ahead but someone stopped time.

JOJO: I'm s—! [*stops himself; pause*]

KATIE: Soon?

JOJO: The appeal might come through. [*She stares at him.*] If it don't . . . soon.

KATIE: So, you think you might die, but there's a slight chance maybe not. This person you never met before suddenly holdin' your whole future in his hands, some stranger got the control whether you live whether you die, you go through all the torture but you think Please God just don't let him kill me. And he does anyway. See how it feels. [*pause*] How come you always callin' on me? you know I ain't never got nothin' nice to say.

JOJO: Company.

KATIE: You got neighbors now.

JOJO: Not for long. [*pause*]

KATIE: Hey! You think me bein' mean to you means I get my little revenges you don't got to feel so bad!

JOJO: No!

KATIE: Good! Cuz you stole everything from me, don't think you takin' my smart-assness is comparable repay!

JOJO: I know!

KATIE: It hurts.

[*long pause*]

JOJO: Maybe I think you bend the rules once. Let me say it, what I feel. [*pause*] Apology.

KATIE: My way. My friend Darla—

JOJO: Darla! She was the other one? Isaiah's?

KATIE: No! I ain't tellin' ya her name, Darla was somebody else, my best friend since second grade 'cept no matter what couldn't say "I'm sorry." She broke the brown crayon, never admit it. She flirt away the guy I told her I liked, she just say, "Well he wasn't your boyfriend." Her stupidity. "I'm sorry" coulda changed her outlook, but 'til you can say it, you never know how good it feels. Relief. That relief I ain't offerin' you. [*pause*] You want forgiveness?

JOJO: Thought you wasn't offerin'.

KATIE: I ain't. But wish I could. The best killin' is killin' with kindness, if I acted all sweet and angelic and smiled sad and spoke of divine absolution you'd keel over and die, the guilt. Wish I was cruel enough to be so kind.

JOJO: It ain't forgiveness I want nohow. Not the main thing. Just want you to hear it, hear me say it. I think I owe you that.

KATIE: I can't hear "I'm sorry." "I'm sorry" I'm deaf to. Sorry. [*starts to exit*]

JOJO: Not premeditated! [Katie *turns around.*] Me and him didn't say Let's take these white girls and kill 'em. Not even Let's take 'em and do 'em. I don't know how it became that, rape, it grew into somethin' not planned. And the killin' . . . fear. When we let you go, you took off screamin' and cryin', it hits us: you'll tell. [*She stares at him.*] I ain't sayin' this cuz it makes it okay. Just figured it's information you might be innerested in.

KATIE: Like junior high innermurals, to save time we did all the foul shots the enda the game. But, 43–42, us ahead, Blue team, it's up to Tammy Feldman from the Reds to make her foul basket. She never misses. 'Til to-day. The pressure on, the nervousness, she had that. Like you. That what you mean?

JOJO: No! not like junior high innermurals. [*pause*] *I am bad.*

[*pause*]

KATIE: You were.

SCENE 4

[Nat *stoops, head bowed, face concealed.* Crazy Horse *stands tense, in thought.*]

JOJO: We heard it again. The scufflin'. Then holdin' you down, forcin' the medicine down your throat. Feel better?

[*No answer.* Andy *enters with a tray, sees* Crazy Horse's *face.* Andy *is confused, looks from the tray to* Crazy Horse.]

ANDY: This ain't what you ordered? [*shows tray*]

CRAZY HORSE: Newly killed game, bear. Or deer. Corn. Sweet potatoes. Ground coffee. Fruit. If they could find it fresh.

[Andy *opens* Crazy Horse's *cell door, hands him the tray: burger and fries.*]

ANDY: Least they charcoaled the burger, I always like that. The dark stripes acrost.

JOJO: Hey Crazy, you get your vision? The fever?

[Crazy Horse *sits on the floor cross-legged, the tray on his knees. Pours hot water from a small pot into a mug, picks up his spoon and starts dipping out instant coffee. One at a time, he takes out many, many spoonsful, then stops. Now his head is bowed, face concealed. A long stillness before he speaks.*]

CRAZY HORSE: Hungry, Jojo?

JOJO: No! I ain't takin' a man's last meal from him.

CRAZY HORSE: Nat?

NAT [*who hasn't moved from his position*]: Fasting.

CRAZY HORSE: Andy?

[Andy *nervously shakes his head no.* Crazy Horse *can't see him but senses the answer.*]

CRAZY HORSE: I DON'T WANT FOOD WASTED! [*silence*] For my last request, I'd like to see this food eaten. I'd like to hear someone enjoy it. [*beat*] In my vision someone enjoyed it.

JOJO: Okay.

[Andy *passes the tray from* Crazy Horse *to* Jojo. Jojo
stares at the food in front of him. Crazy Horse *begins
holding his stomach as if he is in great pain. The others aren't aware of this.*]

CRAZY HORSE: JOJO!

[Jojo *begins to clink the plate with his fork, making
sounds as if he is eating.*]

JOJO: Not bad. I like my fries this way. Crispy.

SCENE 5

[Andy *stares at his wristwatch.*]

ANDY: 11:59.

NAT: The rate for imprisonment of black men in
America was determined to be five times the rate for
imprisonment of black men in South Africa. This was
during apartheid. All U.S. nuclear testing occurs on
Western Shoshone land because there still is Indian land
to take and the government is still taking. In 1985 the
Philadelphia police department dropped a bomb on a
house in a black neighborhood, letting the fire spread to
destroy sixty surrounding houses. When the children
tried to come out, the police shot them down or sent
them running back into the flames. Cain killed Abel,
then God put a mark on Cain to protect him from the
death penalty—Genesis 4. The Brazilian rainforests are
destroyed at the rate of a football field every hour. A
popular sport with European colonists in Australia was
Lobbing the Distance: burying black children live up to
their necks and competing as to how far a white man
could kick the child's head off his shoulders, don't forget history, history made today!

ANDY: Midnight.

NAT [*faster*]: Holocaust: One hundred million captured black people died on the slave ships from Africa to America! The only places where children can be sentenced to death today are Saudi Arabia, the Congo, Iran, Pakistan, Yemen, Nigeria and the U.S.! In 1973, after an Indian stole a white's cowboy boots, the FBI declared war on Pine Ridge Reservation, fireworksed the night sky with thousands of bullets, then got surprised when a bullet or two fired back! Then gave one Indian two life sentences! In 1995 Texas a man was proven innocent, then executed anyway! But killing the innocent comes with the territory. Ask Christ on the cross about that!

ANDY: Twelve o' one.

NAT [*cowers*]: WHAT'S HAPPENING?

ANDY: They puttin' him up on the gurney. [*pause*] Now they strappin' him down, six belts. [*pause*] Now they stickin' in the saltwater i.v. [*pause*] Now they stickin' in the three needles: one to put him to sleep, one to stop his heart, one to stop his breath. [*pause*] Now maybe he's gettin' in a little movement, last word. [*pause*] Now he's dead. Takes less than a minute, assumin' all went accordin' to schedule. [*chuckles*] But you know how that goes 'round here. [*chuckles*]

[*a silence*]

JOJO: Dr. Baith. Ol' lush, just before he get malpractice-lawsuited the outside they residence him here, three years ago he diagnose a sore throat, too late man find out it's cancer. But execution a different story, preexecution they always seek out a physician in good standin' so Crazy be healthy and clear-headed for his needle. They got the witnesses comin'.

NAT: A Texas man was involved in a crime but not the trigger puller. He took the rap for his sister. After he was proven innocent, they executed him anyway. 1995. A journalist asked people what they thought about that and the people said this: "Better a few innocent die than a few guilty go free."

SCENE 6

[Andy *stares down at his wristwatch.* Nat Turner's *cell is empty.* Jojo *is screaming while kicking and pounding all sides of the cell. Finally, exhausted,* Jojo *falls down, panting heavily.*]

ANDY: Twelve o' two.

SCENE 7

[Jojo *has a worn blanket wrapped around him. Shivers.* Andy *enters.*]

ANDY: Merry Christmas. [*pulls from his pocket a little wrapped gift*]

JOJO [*stares at it*]: Guess best thing 'bout my date's the Twentieth is I get my Christmas early.

ANDY: Open it, Jojo.

[Jojo *does. It is a brightly colored child's plastic top.*]

JOJO: Thank ya!

[Jojo *starts spinning the top on the floor. Smiles.*]

ANDY: They set up the phone call with Lucy. Ten a.m. tomorra.

JOJO [*looks up from the top*]: Lucy comin'?

ANDY: Not tomorra. You wanna talk to her before she come, that's what you tol' me to tell her, right?

JOJO: Yeah, I gotta ast her bring me a coupla things. But she's comin'?

ANDY: Said she was.

JOJO: Day after tomorra?

ANDY: Thursday.

JOJO [*taken aback*]: Thursday? [Andy *nods.*] But . . . that's the day.

ANDY: Yeah.

JOJO: Friday's the date but that means minute after Thursday midnight.

ANDY: Yeah. She'll come earlier in the day.

JOJO: Oh. [*beat; suddenly*] Charmaine be with her?

ANDY [*beat*]: Think she couldn't get off work.

JOJO: Oh.

ANDY: My shift ain't 'til three tomorra but don't worry. I'll be in early, make sure the powers that be don't mess you up, make you miss that call.

JOJO: Thank you. [*pause*]

ANDY: Jojo. I told Lucy about Charmaine's picture. Not a ol' one, right? You wanted it recent?

JOJO: I wanna see what she look like now.

ANDY: That's what I said to Lucy. She said don't getcher hopes up. Charmaine don't like gettin' her picture took, Lucy said she ain't got but one recent snapshot herself, she wanna hold on to that.

JOJO: Charmaine ain't got one to spare? My daughter got a lotta years ahead a her, get more pictures took. I ain't got but days.

ANDY: That's what I said. Lucy said she ast Charmaine, Charmaine said Yeah, but mailin' it, it might not get here on time.

JOJO: What about that overnight mail company? They dependable, quick.

ANDY: That's what I said. Lucy said Charmaine said overnight mail's kinda steep. Ten dollars.

JOJO: Then regular mail. Usually it ain't a disaster, right? We could try—

ANDY: Lucy said Charmaine said no.

[*Pause. Then* Jojo *goes back to playing with the top.*]

ANDY: You put in your order for your meal? [Jojo *nods.*] Don't let the recent bureaucratic slipups intimidate ya, mosta the time that room service ain't so shabby.

JOJO: Your family doin' the traditional? Dinner at Ellen's sister's? the holiday?

ANDY: Sure.

JOJO: Ellen make them peanut butter cookies again, the chocolate kiss in the center?

ANDY: First batch already made, I'll bring ya a couple, 'course. [*pause*] Cold rain last night. Heard it?

JOJO: Hm. The poundin' wet, and thunder, lightnin': wa'n't that a show.

ANDY: Last night I have to eat my vegetables in shifts. First the mash potatas, then she cleans the pot. Then the corn. She cleans the pot. Then the string beans. Cleans the pot.

JOJO: *The* pot? When yaw become Bob Cratchit?

ANDY: All the others is use, leaky roof, we got so many damn leaks now . . . [*pause*] Fix it when we can afford it.

JOJO: Aintchu up for a end-a-year raise?

ANDY: Freeze on raises. Again. [*pause*] While back, I put in a request. Told 'em they need any more strappers, I be willin'. [*Pause. Jojo stops the top, doesn't look up.*] I wouldn't be administerin' the needles. I ain't qualified for that. Just bucklin' the straps. [*pause*] Three hundred dollars! They said if a space opens, they keep me in mind. I didn't think you . . . [Jojo *starts spinning the top again.*] They know I could use the money, they think they doin' me a favor. If I turn 'em down, they peg me ungrateful, no tellin' when . . .

[Jojo *lets the top spin to a stop. Pause.*]

JOJO: Might not be so bad. Have a friend with me.

ANDY: I can't, never mind. Don't know why I brought it up forget it, please forget I said it.

JOJO [*pause*]: Three hundred's good money but one fifty ain't bad neither. Split the pot. Send my half to my daughter, her daddy ain't no cheap-o, you write out the check, and a letter. At the top—

To Charmaine Warren
From Joseph Warren
Re: Inheritance.

SCENE 8

[Jojo *deep in thought*. Katie *enters, stares at him*. Jojo *looks up*.]

JOJO: Who ast for you?

KATIE: Maybe I ain't always at your beck 'n' call summons. [*pause*] I need you to tell me somethin'. I wanna know everything you accomplished the last thirty-one years.

[Jojo *turns to her.*]

JOJO: That's just mean, Katie, plain out. Mostly I live with your shenanigans and smart aleckin' fine, but this . . . [*trails off*]

KATIE: Tell me.

[*pause*]

JOJO: My place is six foot by ten, and that includes my toilet that includes my cot, six by ten no windas and they let me have nothin' else in here. They don't let me out but one hour a day, now what you think I accomplished? [Katie *stares at him.*] NOTHIN'! Okay? It been a waste! life a waste! Fifteen years ago was a mirror in here, I smash it with my bare hand so I don't got to look at my ugly face WASTE!

[*pause*]

KATIE: We're tied.

JOJO [*beat*]: What?

KATIE: What you took from me, what they took from you: We're even.

[*beat*]

JOJO: Ya mean it?

KATIE: I been thinkin' it awhile now. Years. Time to say it.

JOJO: Thank you.

KATIE: Sorry my family won't settle for that though. Not their fault, they can't see it, never happened to them. Murder. Cuz once you been through it, you never wish it on nobody else.

[*pause*]

JOJO: Talkin' to Lucy tomorra mornin', she's comin' day after. Ain't visited so often, last time was eighteen years ago, but I ast, she said okay. Now I'm makin' a list, what I want to take with me. Underground. My weddin' band, gave that to her 'fore I left. My football trophy, it ain't too big. And high school diploma, accomplished that! Snapshot: Fourtha July at my family's, ten people in the Polaroid, me and Lucy off to the side. And Charmaine, newborn, Lucy hold her in her baby blanket, can't even see her face, but she's there! [*pause*] I think I have everything. Think they let me take all that?

KATIE: Your coffin. Long's it all fits.

JOJO: That red and black hanky my mama make for me! God, how'm I gonna remember all this, tell Lucy?

KATIE: Wait. You want your trophy, diploma, family picture and hanky, right?

JOJO: *And* weddin' band.

KATIE: Ring—R. Diploma—D. Trophy—T. Picture—P. Hanky—H. [*thinks*] I got it! First change the high school diploma from diploma—D—to school—S. Then . . . Ain't Charmaine the centerpiece a the picture? why you wannit?

JOJO: Yeah.

KATIE: So change picture—P—to Charmaine—C. Get it? Charmaine—C. Hanky—H. Ring—R. School—S. Trophy—T. "Christ!" How could you forget that? you'll be callin' on him anyway. "Christ" except for the "I" but you're takin' yourself so the "I" is you.

JOJO: What if I thinka somethin' else?

KATIE: Jojo, you can't take everything—

JOJO: What if I thinka somethin' small?!

KATIE: Then we'll just have to change "Christ" to a new one. Don't worry. I'm good at memory devices. [*She sits cross-legged in his cell.*] Go on. I'll help ya pack.

SCENE 9

[*A table, two chairs.* Lucy *sits. Waits. Then, sound of the door unlocking.* Lucy *stands.* Jojo *enters, wrists handcuffed in front.* Andy *follows, gently holding* Jojo's *arm.* Andy *shuts the door and steps away from* Jojo. Jojo *and* Lucy *stare at each other from opposite sides of the room. Finally:*]

LUCY: Hi, Jojo.

JOJO: Hi, Lucy.

[*More staring. Then* Jojo *sits.* Lucy *sits.* Andy *tries not to look at them.*]

LUCY: You took up all the tape on my machine.

JOJO: Sorry, everything's a mess around here, we got no competent people around here, I complained. Believe me, I said Hey! I got this appointment, ten a.m. These screwups done scheduled two calls for ten, not Andy! Andy done his best to straighten out the situation but the damage been done and unfortunately the other ten beats me to the phone. Then all the trouble he has gettin' his line through, I don't know what the problem is, I keep starin' at the clock: ten o' seven, ten ten, ten thirteen, please cantcha get through faster? Please wontcha let me do my business, my call scheduled for ten a.m., my wife gotta go to work. Andy tol' me her boss expectin' her at nine well she got someone to cover the phones 'til eleven but ten thirty she gotta go, lemme talk! They look at me like I'm from outer space, go back to their business. Finally ten thirty-four I'm on the line, one ring. Two rings please God let her still be there. Three, I move the receiver away from my face, shakin' so hard receiver bang bang my chin receiver gimme a uppercut, four, click: machine! I got a lotta stuff, Lucy, a list, I pray tape don't run out I don't wanna forget nothin'! [*Pause. They stare at each other.*] Things. To take with me.

LUCY: I couldn't find nunna them things, Jojo, them things is ol' things.

[*pause*]

JOJO: *Nothin'?* [*They stare at each other.*] Where you live, aintchu got a place? dusty trunk for ol' stuff? You search under the cobwebs?

LUCY: More 'n thirty years, I don't know where that stuff is! I don't know what picture you talkin' about. The five years after you left I moved three times, how I keep up?

JOJO: Weddin' band? [Lucy *glances away. Quiet:*] How much you get? Hockin'.

LUCY: Sixty yours. Seventy-five mine. [*pause*] You was here a long time 'fore I done that, twenty years, and blizzard comin', if again I'da put nothin' toward that overdue heat they'da cut us off.

[*pause*]

JOJO: Last time I seen you Charmaine was fourteen. Now she thirty-two. What she been up to?

LUCY: Fourteen she had a singular solitary issue, all her energy absorbed in the solution to the acne problem. Fifteen she know she the only girl on earth don't got a boyfriend. Eighteen she get the graduation award: science.

JOJO: Science!

LUCY: Eighteen and a half she in Chester Community.

JOJO: College?

LUCY: Twenty she transfer to Canton State, zoology.

JOJO: *Vet'rinarian?*

LUCY: Headed toward it, she love them animals. But she graduate, say she work awhile, year, save up for vet school. So she work in this bank. Ain't never left. Ten years.

JOJO: She like it? Fingerin' that green all day.

LUCY: Calls it her life sentence. The chain gang, calls her boss Massa Rollins and know that don't even make sense for *Miz* Rollins. Give her a nice apartment though, if ya don't count the dog stink, cat hair. Loves them damn animals. [*beat*] She gets the blues. "I hate my job, hate my life," broken record, I ignore it. But once I call three days, no answer, worried to death I march over. She just sittin' in the dark, starin' at the TV. Ain't switched the channel, ain't moved from the couch *three days*. [*shrugs*] Life.

[*pause*]

JOJO: How she wear her hair? She like it wavy?

LUCY: Cut it all off recently, like a boy. So she don't gotta fool with it—

JOJO: She ain't really that, low, she don't spend her days wishin' she weren't born, SHE OUT THERE! Nothin' to be blue, she got the WORLD!

[*silence*]

JOJO: Short hair. That's practical. [*chuckles*]

LUCY: I gotta go, Jojo. I don't mean to rush I'm havin' a nice time I just . . . I gotta go.

JoJo: That nail polish color. What you call it?

Lucy [*shrugs*]: Peach. Somethin'.

JoJo: It match you. Your skin or . . . eyes.

[Lucy *nods. Pause.*]

Lucy: See ya, Jojo. [*stands and turns to leave*]

JoJo [*quiet*]: Search her. [Lucy *is now at the door.*] Search her!

Andy: Huh?

JoJo: 'At's your job she coulda took anything offa me!

Andy: That ain't my job—

JoJo: *Is!*

Andy: My job's to search *you*—

JoJo: *Search her!*

Lucy: I ain't took nothin' off you, Jojo—

JoJo: I don't know that!

Lucy: *Do* know that! We had a nice time—

JoJo: Search her.

Lucy: Why you gotta end our nice time rotten?

JoJo: SEARCH HER!

[Lucy, *keeping her eyes on* Jojo, *raises her arms, outstretched to the sides.* Andy *reluctantly begins gently patting her down.*]

ANDY [*quiet*]: Turn around.

[Lucy *does, facing the door now, her back to* Jojo.
Andy *pats again.*]

JOJO: She could walk away with a gran' piana the way
you doin', *feel her!*

[Andy *rubs* Lucy *a little harder and more rapidly,
then abruptly stops.*]

ANDY: She's clean, Jojo.

[Lucy *rushes out without turning back around. The
door closes.*]

JOJO [*eyes on the door*]: Just a caution. Can't be too
careful with my valuables.

[Jojo *chuckles.* Andy *does not chuckle.*]

JOJO: Hey, Andy. Can I smell your hands?

[Andy *holds his hands out.* Jojo *comes to him, takes*
Andy's *hands. Inhales deeply.*]

JOJO: I remember this! Fall on my pilla every night,
journeyin' to dreams but first I have this. And this I take
with me.

SCENE 10

[Andy *enters, looks at* Jojo *for several seconds.* Jojo
doesn't notice.]

ANDY: Okay, Jojo.

JOJO [*a hesitation*]: Hey. Hey, they owe me my last meal! They ain't cheatin' me!

ANDY: Pork chops and bake beans, you cleaned the plate. Remember?

JOJO [*hesitation*]: That preacher! Somethin' I forgot to tell him!

ANDY: He hung with ya a hour, Jojo, he said you didn't have nothin' to say.

JOJO: *I just thought of it!* [Andy *looks away. Silence.*] We have time to practice the breathin' exercises first?

ANDY: Sure.

JOJO: Wait! What I got to take with me? Someone dig me up, think I was some worthless bum, whole life no possessions.

ANDY: Take your Christmas present.

JOJO: Okay. [*beat*] Okay.

[Jojo *picks up the top.* Andy *opens the cell. They start to walk.*]

ANDY: Breathe in deep. [Andy *does.* Jojo *follows.*] Now let it out, short and fast.

[Andy *expels the air many times quickly.* Jojo *takes his lead.*]

ANDY: In deep. [Andy *does, then* Jojo.] Out fast. [Andy, *then* Jojo] In deep. [Andy *does;* Jojo *doesn't.*] In deep.

JOJO: I done it, Andy.

ANDY: Thought you wanted to practice.

JOJO: I got the hang of it, I know how to die faster. Hey. What if I wanna linger on? Breathe in fast and hard and out slow?

ANDY: Don't say that, Jojo, you confuse yourself. [*pause*] You don't wanna linger on.

JOJO [*beat*]: In deep.

[*He does. Then expels the air properly. Now the gurney is visible.* Jojo *stops deep breathing. Silence.*]

ANDY: Ready?

[Jojo *nods.* Andy *leads him to the gurney and starts strapping him down.* Jojo *begins nervously heavy breathing. His rhythm is fast and incorrect. When* Andy *has completed his task—*Jojo *is immobile—* Andy *speaks.*]

ANDY: In deep.

[Andy *demonstrates.* Jojo *attempts this but, in the midst of the inhale, begins gagging.* Andy *quickly searches for something for* Jojo *to vomit in: nothing.* Andy *offers his cupped hand; it touches* Jojo's *cheek.* Jojo *recovers.* Andy *looks at his wristwatch.*]

ANDY: Well. I better go.

[Andy *stares at* Jojo *in silence for several seconds.* Jojo, *looking straight up at the ceiling, now seems unaware of* Andy. *Finally* Andy *quietly turns to leave. Just before he is gone,* Jojo *suddenly speaks.*]

JOJO: I'm by myself. [*pause*] I'M BY MYSELF! WHERE'S THE PARAMEDICS? WHERE'S THE PARAMEDICS?

[Andy *quickly moves over to stand next to* Jojo.]

ANDY: It's midnight, Jojo. They'll be here in a minute.

JOJO [*still stares at the ceiling*]: I DON'T WANNA BE ALONE FOR A MINUTE! NOT A SECOND!

ANDY: Okay! Okay.

[*Another lengthy silence. Then:*]

JOJO [*big smile*]: Andy, you always lied about your age, said between us you was the younger. Come on. How old are ya? Really?

ANDY: Fif—

[*Before* Andy *can utter it,* Jojo *laughs hard, drowning out* Andy's *reply.*]

JOJO: I knew it!

[*The* Paramedic *enters, pushing* Andy *out of the way.*]

PARAMEDIC [*to* Andy]: Okay.

[Andy *exits. The* Paramedic *does his job quickly. As he does,* Katie *enters with her basketball. The* Paramedic *does not see her.*]

JOJO [*calm, but pleasantly surprised*]: Katie.

KATIE: I heardja say you didn't wanna be alone for a second. You got a few a those left. [*The* Paramedic *exits.*] I know you're tired. Go ahead, you can close your eyes. I won't be insulted. [Jojo *does.* Katie *dribbles, fake shoots.*] The bonus long shot disappeared with the American Basketball League, 1930s. The notion a bringin' it back was still a few years away the time you done me, but I had the vision. I saw it comin'. I'm a long shooter, you know how many times I shoulda had three points but they only counted two?

JOJO: Hey, Katie, what was the name a that other girl? Your buddy. All the time they mention her name in court, you think I remember. [*He dies.*]

KATIE: The game against Frederick we lost 52–47. But I always keep mental tabs a my would-be three-pointers to calculate later, seven of 'em. Seven extra points! woulda put us over the top. 'Course we'd already been eliminated from the finals, this was just the consolation game. Still, dontcha hate that, Jojo? Scoreboard says ya lost. When, this time, you shoulda won.

FARLEY AND BETSY

———— ᴥᴥ ————

by Daisy Foote

To my husband, Tim Guinee

CHARACTERS

FARLEY COOK, early
    forties
BETSY COOK, mid-forties,
    his sister

*Lights come up to the kitchen-living area of the Cook
House located in Tremont, New Hampshire. Typical of
an older New England house. It is low-ceilinged and
dark. The room is filled with old furniture including a
long trestle dining table, straight back chairs, and two
wing chairs. The kitchen half of the room is equipped
with outdated kitchen equipment and in one corner of
the room is a wood stove. Also are piles and piles of
books—paperbacks and hardbacks, all written on the
subject of the Civil War. Also, many collectibles from
the Civil War era displayed around the room. The
jacket of a union officer hangs on one wall. The cap of
an enlisted man on another wall. Knives and sabers
are in abundance and an original musket used in the
battle of Gettysburg hangs above the wood stove.*

    Farley Cook, *late forties, sits in front of the tele-
vision. It is late in a fall day, and the room is starting to
get dark. It should be noted that he breathes, raspy,
shallow breaths—the breathing of an asthmatic. He is
surrounded by medicines for his condition. He is a
rather sour-looking man. He is watching soap operas,
which is evident by the type of dialogue and marked
music coming out of the box. As he watches, fascinated,
he shakes his head and clucks his tongue against his
teeth. He then sighs, coughs, and leans back.*

FARLEY: Takes all kinds. All kinds of people. That's
for sure. All kinds.

[*A book drops to the ground. A large thud. Farley jumps. He looks around.*]

FARLEY: Who's there?

[*He hears nothing. He leans back to enjoy the television again. Watches for a few more moments and then just as suddenly turns his head.*]

FARLEY: Is someone there?

[*He reaches over to the television. It is an old-fashioned set with no remote control and a knob that controls the volume and turns the television on and off. Farley goes to turn the television off. But instead of doing this he turns it up, way up. It blasts through the house. He is frantic. He reaches over and turns the knob the other way, finally turning off the power. He stands up again, looking suspiciously around the room. He hears someone's footsteps outside the front door. He quickly picks up a book. Opens it to the middle and settles back into his chair.*
His sister, Betsy Cook, *walks through the door. She is four years older than* Farley. *She is a strong woman with a resolute air. She carries several ledger books. She puts them on the table. She indicates the television.*]

BETSY: Take that into your room if you want to watch it.

[Farley *looks as if he doesn't understand.*]

BETSY: The television. Go ahead and watch it. Just watch it in your room. I'll call you when lunch is ready.

[*She begins to clean up her brother's mess. She throws away used tissues, puts dirty dishes into the sink, and so on. She does everything in a quick, efficient manner.*]

BETSY: Farley . . . Farley . . . Farley . . . what you can do in one day.

FARLEY: I wasn't watching anything.

[Betsy *continues to clean. She heaves a big sigh.*]

FARLEY: I wasn't.

[*She looks him straight in the eye.*]

BETSY: It's all right. I know you like your soap operas.

FARLEY: I do not.

BETSY: Yes, you do.

FARLEY: I would never watch one of those things. [*a beat*][*disgusted*] Soap operas . . . smope operas . . .

[Betsy *goes over to the kitchen area. She opens up a cupboard and takes out soup and crackers for lunch.*]

BETSY: It will have to be soup from a can today. I don't have time for anything else.

FARLEY: Fine with me. Don't need to fuss on my account.

[*She starts to prepare the soup—opening cans and heating them in pan.*]
[Farley *starts to pace around the room. As he talks his voice gets more raspy and labored.*]

FARLEY: Soap operas! For the housewives and the old people. I'm a working man. Working men don't have time for that kind of nonsense. No they do not.

[Betsy *starts to stir the soup on the stove.*]

BETSY [*laughing*]: Well Mr. Working Man, let's not forget those several days every month you're home with an attack.

FARLEY: Not that much . . .

BETSY: At least several days every month when you're home for the bad breathing. Just like when you were in school there. All those days off from school with your bad breathing. Uncle Edward feeling sorry for you. Bringing that thing . . . [*indicates television*] home from the dump for you.

FARLEY: Gave it to all of us.

BETSY: Father and I didn't want it. Fine without it. Perfectly fine. You were the one. Something to keep you occupied. Father and I could have cared less.

[*As she talks* Farley *takes one of the small Civil War knives off the wall. He picks it up. His sister's back to him he simulates a stabbing attack. Lifting the knife high up and viciously tearing at the air.*]

BETSY: Well . . . there you are. Got me off on the ancient history.

[*She starts to turn to face him. He quickly puts the knife back.*]

BETSY: Point is, Farley, when I'm here, I want you keeping it in your room. Keep it there so I don't have to hear it. All that silliness.

[*The soup splatters. She turns back and starts to furiously wipe the stove as if attacking the enemy. She is as neat as her brother is messy.*]
[*She then starts to set the table with bowls and spoons. She also puts out crackers.*]

BETSY: Important we start being open and honest about our habits as we'll be spending a lot of time in the house together. Open and honest. Only way to go. [*She looks up at her brother and smiles. He merely ducks his head.*] Would you mind serving the milk?

[Farley *goes to do this as* Betsy *serves the soup. She then takes a seat. She starts to eat her soup.* Farley *gets the milk out of the refrigerator and two glasses out of the cupboard.*]

BETSY: Pardon me for starting without you. Don't have a lot of time. [*She looks around the room.*] Rush. Rush. Rush. I'm so tired of rushing. [*points to her favorite chair*] Sit in that chair there. My chair. All kinds of things about the Civil War still to learn.

FARLEY: Mother's chair . . .

BETSY: What's that?

FARLEY: That was Mother's chair. [*He indicates the other wing chair.*] And that was Father's. [*indicating* Betsy's *chair again*] Mother died in that chair. She was holding me in her arms there, and she just died.

BETSY: Yes, Farley, I know all about it. I was on the other side of the room watching her. Just a baby you were. Last thing Mother says to me . . . a small girl of just four years old. She said, "Take care of your brother and father. Take care of them, Betsy. [*sighs*] And then that blood clot exploded in her brain. She was gone. [*repeating*] Take care of your father and brother, Betsy girl. Take care of them.

FARLEY [*barely*]: I know. I was there.

BETSY: But you were barely a year. It's my memory . . . not yours. [*As she talks,* Farley *slowly pours the milk into the glasses.*] How's that milk coming? [*He takes the two filled glasses over to the table.*] Thank you. [*He takes a seat and starts to eat.*] How are you feeling?

FARLEY: Okay.

BETSY: Breathing better?

[*He nods and continues to eat. He glares at his sister.*]

FARLEY: I don't watch soap operas.

[*His sister grabs for some crackers. She crumbles them in her soup.*]

BETSY: All right. Have it your way. You don't watch soap operas. [*a beat*] But keep it in your room when I'm here. That's my point.

[*They eat in silence.* Farley *indicates the books.*]

FARLEY: Catching up on your bookkeeping?

[Betsy *looks over to where he is pointing.*]

BETSY [*sounds annoyed*]: Don't be sarcastic, Farley.

FARLEY: Just wondering.

BETSY: The first Monday of every month. That's when we do the bookkeeping. The first Monday. [*a beat*] What day is today?

[Farley *says nothing. Sullen.*]

BETSY: Farley, what day is today?

FARLEY [*barely*]: Wednesday.

BETSY: Wednesday. Not Monday. [*a beat*] Told you, Farley. Told you on Sunday that Doug Granger had requested to see the store books. Paid his five hundred dollars. And that gets him a look at the store figures. I told you. He wanted to see them today. Wednesday. I told you, Farley. [*a beat*] I have a good feeling about this. [*a beat*] I think he might even give us our full asking price.

FARLEY: I don't want to sell the store.

BETSY [*ignoring him*]: Might even give it to us in one payment. One hundred percent. $500,000. Ours. In the bank. No payments. No installments. Just sign the dotted line and hand the money over.

[Farley *eats his soup.*]

FARLEY: I've been thinking further about my ideas for expansion. We need to think about selling the wine and cheese. You know . . . the gourmet sorta stuff. [*a beat*] Like the general store over in Francestown there. Move out of the dark ages. Get chic!

[*He reaches for his milk. His sister grabs it before he can do this.*]

BETSY: Maybe you shouldn't have that . . .

FARLEY: Why?

BETSY: The dairy, Farley. You know all about it. When you have an attack . . . it's best to stay away from the dairy for a few days. Keep your pipes from clogging up. [*She picks up the glass of milk. She carries it over to the sink. As she pours it down the drain in the sink:*] If Doug likes what he sees and I think he will, I bet he'll want to tie things up right away. No messing around. [*She turns back to the table and takes her seat again.*]

FARLEY: I believe the time is right for expanding. Develop the larger vision. A lunch room. On the second floor. Course . . . we'll have to bring it up to code first. But that shouldn't be a problem. A new floor. Some rewiring. Shouldn't be a problem. We'll serve the soups, sandwiches, salads. The homemade fare. Simple but good. [*a beat*] And then once we've got a leg up, we'll bring it even farther. [*a beat*] An idea I have to bring in the special sort of customer. [*pauses dramatically*] Tea. You know. How they do it over to England there. Crumpets, scones, cucumber sandwiches. Serve it around four o'clock. You could do that raspberry layer cake of yours and your trifle.

[Betsy *leans back. She sighs.*]

BETSY: Someone's been watching too much television.

FARLEY: *Yankee Magazine!* I read about it in *Yankee Magazine*! All the really nice places are doing it.

BETSY: *Yankee Magazine.* How I hate *Yankee Magazine*. Everyone's quaint idea about New England living. Well, times have changed. And they will continue to change.

FARLEY [*barely*]: Voted us the number one General Store in New Hampshire.

BETSY: Don't start with that, Farley. Don't remind me of that disaster. After Father asked you not to send in that entry blank. But you did it anyway. And every tourist this side of the Connecticut and the Mississippi started coming in to the store. Wanted to have their picture taken. Didn't want to buy anything. Just a picture. [*a beat*] Don't tell me about *Yankee Magazine*. Have no use for it.

FARLEY: Well, I think it's a good idea. Opening a restaurant. Keeping up with the times.

BETSY: And just where may I ask will you get the money to pay for these great schemes of yours?

FARLEY: Get a loan.

BETSY: Uh huh. And just who is going to give us this loan?

FARLEY: Yes . . . Betsy . . . I believe that would be the bank.

BETSY: I see. Which bank would this be?

FARLEY: Yes . . . Betsy . . . I think you also know the answer to that one. Our bank. The Amoskeag.

BETSY: The Amoskeag?

FARLEY: That's right. The Amoskeag.

BETSY: You think they'll loan you the money?

FARLEY: Soon as they hear my idea. They'll give me more than enough.

BETSY: More than enough?

FARLEY: That's right.

BETSY: I see. The Amoskeag Bank will give you more than enough.

FARLEY: Oh sure. Pick up the phone tomorrow. Set the whole thing up with Parker Owen.

BETSY: Mmm . . . well then I guess I can forget all about that conversation I had with Parker last week.

FARLEY: Which one is that?

BETSY: The one where he told me that there is no future in the general store business. It's all SUPER SAVERS AND PRICECOS. The one where he told me to take the money and run. [*a beat*] Now I wonder why he would tell me that, Farley, when you're so sure he'll just hand the bank's money over? I wonder why? [*With that,* Betsy *stands up. She takes her empty soup bowl.*] Just finish up here and then it's off to see Doug with my books.

[*As she starts to wash the dishes,* Farley *takes his soup bowl from the table. He brings it over to his sister at the sink.*]

BETSY: Don't know whether I should leave the books with Doug overnight . . .

[*Her brother is behind her now. As she talks and does dishes he puts his hands above her neck and pretends to strangle her. He continues to make the strangling motions as his sister continues with the dishes. She then shakes out her hands and turns.* Farley *quickly drops his hands to the side.*]

BETSY: What do you think?

[Farley *looks vague.*]

BETSY: You have no opinion.

FARLEY: I don't want to sell, so why should I have an opinion?

[*His sister lets out a large sigh. She turns and starts to wipe off the counter areas. She does this for a few minutes before speaking.*]

BETSY: Let's see . . . what would Father do? [*a beat*] [*as if listening*] Stay with the books. That's right. Stay with them. Watch out for any funny business. [*She gives*

one last wipe with a flourish. She turns to her brother.]
So I may be a while. Supper will probably be late tonight.

FARLEY: Who's watching the store?

BETSY: Why Darcy of course. Do you think I would have left the store if Darcy wasn't there?

FARLEY: No.

BETSY: I see. You just wanted to hear yourself talk. [Betsy *turns back to her cleaning and busy making. Farley's breathing becomes shorter and more labored.*] Just like Father always says . . . Farley's got to hear himself talk. Asking a lot of questions. Because . . . Farley's trying to make himself seem important.

[*His breathing gets worse.*]

FARLEY [*with difficulty*]: Father says . . . Father says . . .

[Betsy *suddenly whips around to face her brother.*]

BETSY: What?!

[Farley *pulls back. He is clearly afraid of his sister.*]

FARLEY: Would be Father *said* not says.

[*She reaches for her brother's pills. Puts them in his face.*]

BETSY: Time for your medicine.

[*Her brother's hands shake as he opens his pill bottle. As he takes his pills with a glass of water . . .*]

BETSY: That fat Nazi . . . Deidre Gunter was in the store today. [*doing a bad German accent*] "Oh Betsy, I think I might have a buyer for the store. And willing to pay much more than Doug Granger." [*a beat*][*back to her own voice*] More than Doug is paying, Deidre? And how would you know about what Doug is paying?

[*She turns to her brother, whose breathing is worse again.*]

BETSY [*back to German*]: "Because Betsy, sweetheart, Farley told me."

FARLEY: No.

BETSY: Don't play innocent with me, Farley Cook. Father told me. He warned me to be careful of you. "You know Farley. You know how he likes to flap his lips in the wind. Always willing to bend someone's ear. Flap. Flap. Flap." [*a beat*] I'll tell you I won't miss it. Flap. Flap. Flap. Talk. Talk. Talk. Like it were part of the job. We buy our milk at your store when we could be buying it for a cheaper price at Shop and Save. So we expect . . . we demand conversation. Chit chat. Flap. Flap. Flap. All for the price of a goddamn quart of milk.

FARLEY: I like talking to people.

BETSY: Sure you do. Getting us all into trouble. And this time you've really done it. Fat Deidre Gunter driving me crazy with her real estate lies. What she'll do for us if we sign her broker's agreement. No thank you, Deidre. I don't think so. [*a beat*] Father says . . . whatever you do, Betsy, don't let the real estate scavengers get a hold of the store.

[Farley *looks worried.*]

FARLEY: He said that to you? When did he say that?

BETSY: You know how he felt about real estate people, Farley. You know how he hated all of them.

[Farley *nods weakly.* Betsy *picks up the ledger books. She goes to the door.*]

BETSY: Wish me luck . . . [*her hand on the doorknob*] If you're feeling up to it, would you please light a fire in the stove later. Our fuel bill was through the roof last month. Can't have that again. We'll soon be living on a *fixed* income.

[*She exits. As soon as the door closes behind her* Farley *runs for the old rifle/musket hanging on the wall. He pulls it down. He pretends to cock it and shoot it at the door.*]

FARLEY: Listen up, you silly bitch, and listen good. I'm the man of the house now. You better believe it.

[*He lifts the gun as though he is pointing it at her head.*]

FARLEY: Father's dead. I was there. I tossed the dirt on his coffin. He's dead. And Farley here is number one. [*a beat*] There will be no more talk of the Civil War. "Pull up a chair, Farley. Time to hear the latest biography of Grant." Ulysses S. Grant! You know what I say, Father? You know what I say, Betsy? I say he wasn't half the man Robert E. Lee was. No sir. Abe Lincoln offered the job to him first, didn't he? Not that idiot Grant. He was second string. Drunken idiot. Almost lost the war.

[*He jumps as if he's heard something. Raises his gun higher.*]

FARLEY: I'll say it if I want to. I'll say anything I want because I'm the man of the house now. I'm number one. [*a beat*] And we won't sell the store. We won't. Will not!

[*The door to the kitchen suddenly opens.* Betsy *walks in.* Farley *drops the gun. It tumbles to the floor. A loud crash.*]

BETSY: Farley, what on earth are you doing?

FARLEY: What are *you* doing?

[*She goes over to wear a hardback sits next to her chair. She picks it up.*]

BETSY: I wanted to bring something to read in case I was there a while.

FARLEY: A new biography of Grant?

BETSY: Yes, as a matter of fact it is. How he really was a better general than Lee. Much better. Lincoln only offered the job to Lee first for political reasons. Thought it might win him some converts. And Mary, of course, was putting pressure on him.

FARLEY: Mary?

BETSY: Mary Todd Lincoln, Farley. She was enamored with Lee. Her Kentucky roots and everything. She thought he hung the moon. Bit of a southern snob. Got her into all sorts of trouble. [*looks down at the gun*] What are you doing with Father's musket? That's not a toy, you know.

[Farley *picks it up.*]

FARLEY: I was cleaning it. It needs to be cleaned.

[*She reaches over and takes the gun. She puts it back on display.*]

BETSY: Better leave that to the experts. [*She opens the door. A small smile on her face. She looks beyond her brother.*] Yes, I know. And he's to pay all the closing costs too. Don't worry. It's all under control.

FARLEY [*panicked*]: Who are you talking to?

BETSY: See you later . . .

FARLEY: Betsy . . .

[*She goes through the door and closes it behind her. Farley runs to the door. Opens it. Yells after her.*]

FARLEY [*screaming*]: Betsy . . . who are you talking to? Betsy?!

[*Lights come down. Black.*]
[*The lights come up.*]
[*Early evening of the same day. Farley sits in front of the television. He watches one of the more sordid news programs like* Hard Copy *or* Inside Edition. *As he sits in front of the television he keeps leaning over to turn the volume up. Again and again. Each time he does this he looks around the room as if someone might say something. One final turn on the volume. The television blasts through the house. He sits back to watch. A few minutes go by.*]
[*The door to the house opens. His sister comes in. She carries ledger books, some official-looking papers, and her biography of Grant. Farley ignores her.*]

BETSY [*annoyed*]: Farley . . .

[*He doesn't turn to look at her. He continues to watch the television. She comes over to him.*]

BETSY: Farley . . . I could hear it in the driveway.

[Farley *still won't acknowledge her.*]

BETSY: Farley!

[*She leans over and snaps off the television. Farley then leans over and turns it on again. He faces his sister and gives her a taunting smile. She goes and turns it off again.*]

BETSY: Take it to your room.

[Farley *looks at his sister. She stands between him and the television. He doesn't feel quite so brave.*]

FARLEY: I wasn't watching soap operas.

BETSY: Television, Farley. I can't stand the television. Any of it.

[*She leans over and unplugs it. She picks it up.* Farley *stands.*]

FARLEY: Hey.

BETSY: I'll just do it for you.

[*She walks offstage carrying the television.* Farley *sits back down in his chair, defeated.*]
[*As* Betsy *walks back into the room she is talking . . .*]

BETSY: You were right. Stand firm from the start, and they know you won't be pushed around.

[Farley *jumps up.*]

FARLEY: Who's that?

[Betsy *turns to her brother smiling.*]

BETSY: Doug Granger has agreed to everything. To the letter. Five hundred thousand dollars, not a penny less. [*laughs*] A pizza shop. That's what he'll do with it. Pizzas and subs. Call it . . . A LITTLE BIT OF ITALY. Not that Doug Granger would know Italy if he fell over it . . . [*a beat*] Now . . . how about a celebration . . . cook a few steaks? [*She pats* Farley *condescendingly on the head.*] Well done, sister dear. Thank you for looking out for me. Bringing me comfort and security in my old age.

FARLEY: A few meaning three?

[Betsy *gives him an odd look.*]

BETSY: Excuse me?

FARLEY: You said you were gonna cook a few steaks. A few means three. Only two of us here. You and me.

BETSY: A thank you, Farley, that's all I'm asking for. A thank you . . . if you don't mind.

FARLEY: Father wouldn't like this. Not one bit. His store. The oldest General Store in the state of New Hampshire. Started by his grandfather. A pizza parlor. I don't think so.

BETSY: Oh Farley, you know so little. So very, very little about anything.

FARLEY: Father . . .

BETSY: Don't tell me about Father. Don't tell me anything. Because you don't *know* anything.

FARLEY: I know I like the store. Don't ever want to sell it.

BETSY: I see. You like getting up at 4:30 every morning?

FARLEY: I don't mind.

BETSY: And you like working every night until nine?

FARLEY: I don't mind.

BETSY: And you like worrying and scraping every month? Wondering if Mrs. Barss will pay her monthly balance or if Mr. Orbit will make up his bad check.

FARLEY [*sighs*]: I don't mind.

BETSY: Yes, well, I do mind, Farley. I mind very much. [*a beat*] And since I'm the one who does most of the work, and I'm the one who takes on most of the responsibility, then I suppose I should be the one who decides when and if we sell.

FARLEY: We can open a tea room on the second floor.

BETSY: Yes, Farley, I know all about it. And I'm not interested. Really I'm not. Not interested in taking on more responsibility. More headaches. Not at all interested.

[*She moves in closer to her brother. Challenging. She indicates the official-looking papers on the table.*]

BETSY: Doug Granger doesn't want to draw this out. After he was finished with the books, we went by the bank. Saw Parker Owen. He drew up the papers for you and me to sign.

FARLEY: No!

[Betsy *takes her brother's arm.*]

BETSY: Farley . . .

FARLEY: No . . .

[Betsy *lets go of his arm. She goes over to the freezer. She takes out three steaks. Tosses them on the counter.*]

FARLEY: Three steaks. You have three steaks.

BETSY: So . . .

FARLEY [*excited*]: So there's only two of us.

BETSY: They're small steaks.

[*She takes the steaks and starts to pound them with a meat hammer. Salt and pepper. She leans over to turn on the oven.*]

FARLEY: I'm all you have, Betsy. You're forty-six years old, and I'm all you have. Doesn't that bother you? [*a beat*] Doesn't it bother you that you've never had a boyfriend? Never been married. Had children of your own? Doesn't that bother you? Make you feel like some sort of freak?

BETSY: I don't think I like this conversation. I think we'll end this conversation. Right now. We'll end it.

FARLEY: That's what we are, Betsy. You and me. We're a couple of freaks. People in town say things about us. Wonder about the two of us. Never going anywhere. Staying tied to our father. Never striking out on our own. [*a beat*] And now that he's dead . . . now that it's just the two of us . . .

BETSY: Flap, flap, flap, Farley. Flap, flap, flap. Good riddance to all of them. To all their nasty talk. I'll stay in this house now. I will. I'll stay in it. And I'll read my books on the Civil War. So much to learn. Why we haven't even scratched the surface . . .

[*She turns away from him. He jumps in front of her.*]

FARLEY: No! [*a beat*] I won't sell! I won't! I like seeing other people. Hearing other voices.

BETSY: You like hearing gossip? You like knowing that people are talking about you? Saying nasty things behind your back? You like that, Farley? You like that?

[*He takes his sister's arms.*]

FARLEY: I'll take my money. I'll take it, and I'll leave here. I will. I'll go far away and never see you again.

BETSY: Whatever you say, Farley. Whatever you say . . .

FARLEY: You'll be all alone. You'll have nobody. No one!

BETSY [*small smile*]: So then you will sign . . .

[Farley *hesitates. Realizes he has been tricked.*]

FARLEY: No!

[*He goes over and starts screaming at her.*]

FARLEY: I won't sign. I won't! I won't!

[*She turns away from him. She starts preparing the rest of the meal for the evening. Making a salad. Boiling water for rice. Measuring out the rice.*]

BETSY: It's just like Father says. Always doing your little dance. Have to show you're important. All right, Farley. We know you're important. It's been acknowledged.

FARLEY: Are you saying that Father wants us to sell the store?

[Betsy *lets out a long frustrated sigh.*]

BETSY: I'm talking about family loyalty, Farley. Because in the end your family is all you have. One hundred percent all that you can trust.

FARLEY: What are you trying to say?

BETSY: It's a family decision, Farley. The Cook family has decided to sell the store. And you're a Cook through and through. And your Cook heart is telling you . . . I know it is . . . it is telling you that selling the store is the right thing to do. It's the right decision. In your heart you know that, Farley. You know that.

FARLEY: I'm lonely, Betsy.

[*She looks away from him and smiles.*]

BETSY: Isn't that right?

FARLEY: Who are you talking to?

BETSY: I think so. I think it's time.

[*She turns back to* Farley.]

BETSY: Time to sign the papers, Farley.

FARLEY: No.

BETSY: Yes, Farley.

[*He explodes.*]

FARLEY: No!!!

[*He lunges at his sister. He grabs her by the throat and starts to choke her. She screams and tries to pull away.*]

BETSY: Farley . . . stop . . . Farley . . .

[*But he keeps strangling her. She gets weaker and weaker.*]

BETSY [*barely*]: Farley . . .

[*She finally falls to the floor. He looks over at her "dead" on the floor. Triumphant. He walks out of the room. He comes back into the room carrying the television. He plugs it in. He turns it up. He sits down and*

*starts to watch. He doesn't see his sister get up off the
floor. She goes over and gets the papers and pen. She
walks over to him.*]

BETSY: Farley . . .

       [*He looks up. Startled.*]

BETSY: Sign them now . . .

[*He looks devastated. Defeated. He takes the papers
from his sister. Signs them as she reaches over and
turns off the television. Lights go black.*]
[*Lights come up to* Farley *sitting in a chair.* Betsy *is in
another chair. She reads out loud from* The Biography
of Ulysses S. Grant. Farley *looks over to his right to
see his father come into the living room from stage
right. A slight pause in the reading as the father takes
a seat.* Betsy *then resumes her reading.*]

       [*The lights fade to black.*]

BLIND DATE

by Horton Foote

CHARACTERS

ROBERT HENRY   DOLORES HENRY
SARAH NANCY   FELIX ROBERTSON

TIME—1928. PLACE—Harrison, Texas.

The living room of Robert *and* Dolores Henry. *It is empty.* Robert *comes in. He is a lawyer and has a briefcase, several newspapers, a package of purchases from the drugstore. He drops all these on the sofa and takes his coat off, throwing it over a chair. He calls:* "Dolores." *There is no answer. He kicks his shoes off and calls:* "Children." *Again no answer. He goes to the radio and turns it on. He gets one of the newspapers and spreads it around the room as he looks through it. He calls again:* "Dolores, I am home." *A voice calls back:* "She's not here."

ROBERT [*calling*]: Where is she?

SARAH NANCY [*the voice—calling*]: Yes.

ROBERT: Where?

SARAH NANCY: She took the children to a friend's to spend the night.

ROBERT: Where are you?

SARAH NANCY: In my room.

ROBERT: Did your aunt say when we were having supper?

SARAH NANCY: We've had supper. We ate with the children.

ROBERT: What did you have?

SARAH NANCY: Peanut butter and jelly sandwiches.

[*He is depressed by that. He goes to the window and looks out. He goes to the radio and turns it off. He sees two college yearbooks on a table. He goes and picks them up to look at them when his wife* Dolores *comes in.*]

ROBERT: Where is my supper?

DOLORES: What?

ROBERT: Where is my supper? Do you know what time it is? I'm starved. I have been here at least half an hour.

DOLORES: Have you forgotten our conversation at breakfast?

ROBERT: What conversation?

DOLORES: Oh, Robert. I told you to eat uptown tonight.

ROBERT: I don't remember that.

DOLORES: I told you I was not going to fix supper tonight.

ROBERT: I don't remember a single word of that.

DOLORES: You were looking right at me when I told you. I said I was giving the children peanut butter and jelly sandwiches at five-thirty, and at six-thirty after their baths I was taking them over to Hannah's to spend

the night so they would not be running in and out of here
while Sarah Nancy was entertaining her date.

ROBERT: Does Sarah Nancy have another date?

DOLORES: Yes. Thank God. I told you that too this
morning.

ROBERT: If you did I don't remember.

DOLORES: Of course not. You never listen to a word I
say. Oh, if I live through this I'll live through anything.
[*whispering*] Don't you remember my telling you this
morning that at last I had arranged another date for her?
After trying desperately for three days?

ROBERT: No.

DOLORES: Well, I did. And I hope this one turns out
better than the last time. I talked to Sister late this afternoon. She is just beside herself. "You know suppose,"
she said, "she takes it into her head to insult this date
too." "Sister," I said, "I refuse to get discouraged. I did
not get on the beauty pages of the University of Texas
and the Texas A&M yearbooks on my looks alone. It was
on my personality. And that can be acquired." Don't you
agree?

ROBERT: I guess.

DOLORES: I wasn't born a conversationalist, you
know. I can remember being as shy as the next one, but I
gritted my teeth and forced myself to converse, and so
can Sarah Nancy. Don't you agree?

ROBERT: I guess. Who did you get her a date with?

DOLORES: Felix.

ROBERT: Felix who?

DOLORES: Felix Robertson.

ROBERT: Is that the best you could do? My God.

DOLORES: My God, yourself. I have been calling all over town all week trying to arrange dates for the poor little thing, and you know very well I had absolutely no luck. Not a one wanted to come over here until I called Felix Robertson. I finally called Sister two days ago I was so depressed and had a frank talk with her. I explained the situation to her and she said it was nothing new. She said every time a boy has come around they don't stay long, because Sarah Nancy either won't talk or is very sarcastic. She wants me to have a frank talk with her before Felix gets here and try and help her improve her disposition and I said I would. But it's not so easy to do, you know. I have been worrying over how to talk to her about all this all afternoon. And I almost have a sick headache.

ROBERT: What about supper?

DOLORES: What about your supper? What about it?

ROBERT: I forgot about eating uptown and I'm tired and I don't want to go back out. Is there anything to eat in the kitchen?

DOLORES: My God, Robert. I don't know what's in the kitchen. I feel this is a crisis in my niece's life and I really haven't had time to worry about what is in the kitchen. [*a pause*] And don't start pouting, Robert.

ROBERT: I'm not pouting.

DOLORES: Yes, you are. I know you very well.

ROBERT: Well, my God, how much longer is this going on? Ever since your niece has been here all you've done is worry about her.

DOLORES: I tried to explain to you. [*She looks at the room.*] Oh, look at this room. I spent all afternoon cleaning it. [*She starts to pick up his shoes, his coat, etc.*]

ROBERT: I'll do that.

DOLORES: Just take them all out. I need to be alone now with Sarah Nancy.

[*He goes. She fixes pillows on the couch and re-arranges a few chairs about the room, all the while singing in a bright, happy manner. After a moment she calls:* "Sarah Nancy." *She gets no answer and she calls again:* "Sarah Nancy, Sarah Nancy, I don't want to hurry you, but it's almost time for your date to be here." *Again, no response from* Sarah Nancy *and she is about to leave the room when* Sarah Nancy *appears. She is as doleful looking as* Dolores Henry *is cheerful.* Dolores *gives her a bright, determined smile, which* Sarah Nancy *does not return.*]

DOLORES: Well, you do look sweet. Is that a new dress?

SARAH NANCY: Oh, no.

DOLORES: Well, it's new to me. It's very becoming. It has a lot of style. That's what I always look for first in my clothes, style. [Sarah Nancy *gives no reaction.*] Now, precious lamb, let me tell you a little about the young man who is coming to see you tonight. I don't know whether you remember meeting him or not, but he says he met you at Louise Davis's swim party as you were the only one that didn't want to swim. He is Felix Robertson. [Sarah Nancy *groans.*] What's the matter, dear? Do you remember him?

SARAH NANCY: I remember him.

DOLORES: That's nice. He felt sure you would. Why do you remember him?

SARAH NANCY: Because he kept slapping me on the back and asking me how I was.

DOLORES: He is a very sensitive boy. He was just trying to make you feel at home. And he is, as I'm sure you could tell, from a lovely family. His mother and your dear mother were girlhood friends. Now, difficult as it is for me to do, I feel I have to discuss a few things with you, Sarah Nancy, before Felix arrives. I think, dear, you have to learn to be a little more gracious to the young men that come to see you. Now I am extremely puzzled why my phone hasn't been rung off the wall since you've been my guest, but I think last night I was given a clue. Sam and Ned, those two boys that called last week, told their mother you were extremely hard to converse with. Boys, you know, need someone peppy to talk to. [Sarah Nancy *rolls her eyes.*] Now don't roll your eyes, darling. You know I have your best interest at heart. I want you to be just as popular as any girl here. But to accomplish that you have to learn to converse.

SARAH NANCY: I don't know what to talk about.

DOLORES: I know. I know. I called up your mother this very morning and told her all this, and she said that always seemed to be your trouble. When boys come around, you can't think of things to say. [*She goes to desk and opens a drawer and takes out a list.*] So I sat down and made a list of topics to talk about. And I thought before Felix got here, you and I could go over it, and you could memorize them and then you would always be sure of making conversation. All right, dear?

[Sarah Nancy *doesn't answer. Robert enters.*]

ROBERT: Excuse me.

DOLORES: Robert?

ROBERT: How much longer are you going to be?

DOLORES: Why?

ROBERT: Because I am starving, that's why.

DOLORES: Did you look in the icebox?

ROBERT: I looked in the icebox.

DOLORES: Well . . .

ROBERT: The ice has all melted.

DOLORES: Well, maybe you had better ride over to the icehouse and get a block of ice.

ROBERT: I will after I've eaten. I'm hungry.

DOLORES: All right. Just be patient. I won't be long with Sarah Nancy.

ROBERT: Honey, I'm starved.

DOLORES: I know you are starved. You have told us that a thousand times. Honestly, I'm not deaf. And I'll be out there as soon as I can, but Felix will be here any minute and Sarah Nancy and I have to go over some things first. Now excuse us, please. [*He goes.*] Now where were we? Oh, yes. I was going over my list of things to talk about. [Dolores *picks up her list and begins reading.*] One: Who is going to win the football game next Friday? Two: Do you think we have had enough rain for the cotton yet? Three: I hear you were a football player in high school. What position did you play? Do you miss football? Four: I hear you are an insurance salesman. What kind of insurance do you sell? Five: What is the best car on the market today do you

think? Six: What church do you belong to? Seven: Do
you enjoy dancing? Eight: Do you enjoy bridge? [*She
puts the list down.*] All right, that will do for a start. Now
let's practice. I'll be Felix. Now. Hello, Sarah Nancy. [*A
pause.* Sarah Nancy *looks at her like she thinks she's
crazy.*] Now what do you say, Sarah Nancy?

SARAH NANCY: About what?

DOLORES: About what? About what you say when
someone says hello to you, Sarah Nancy. Now let's start
again. Hello, Sarah Nancy.

SARAH NANCY: Hello.

DOLORES: Honey, don't just say hello and above all
don't scowl and say hello. Smile. Hello, how very nice to
see you. Let me feel your warmth. Now will you remember that? Of course you will. All right, let's start on our
questions. Begin with your first question. [*a pause*] I'm
waiting, honey.

SARAH NANCY: I forget.

DOLORES: Well, don't be discouraged. I'll go over the
list carefully and slowly again. One: Who is going to
win the football game next Friday? Two: Do you think
we have had enough rain for the cotton yet? Three: I hear
you were a football player in high school. What position
did you play? Do you miss football? Four: I hear you are
an insurance salesman. What kind of insurance do you
sell? Five: What is the best car out on the market today
do you think? Six: What church do you belong to?
Seven: Do you enjoy dancing? Eight: Do you enjoy
bridge? Now we won't be rigid about the questions, of
course. You can ask the last question first if you want to.

SARAH NANCY: What's the last question again?

DOLORES: Do you enjoy bridge?

SARAH NANCY: I hate bridge.

DOLORES: Well then, sweetness, just substitute another question. Say, do you enjoy dancing?

SARAH NANCY: I hate dancing.

DOLORES: Now you don't hate dancing. You couldn't hate dancing. It is in your blood. Your mother and daddy are both beautiful dancers. You just need to practice is all. Now . . .

SARAH NANCY: Why didn't you get me a date with Arch Leon? I think he's the cute one.

DOLORES: He's going steady, honey, I explained that.

SARAH NANCY: Who is he going steady with?

DOLORES: Alberta Jackson.

SARAH NANCY: Is she cute?

DOLORES: I think she's right cute, a little common looking and acting for my taste.

SARAH NANCY: He sure is cute.

DOLORES: Well, Felix Robertson is a lovely boy.

SARAH NANCY: I think he's about as cute as a warthog.

DOLORES: Sarah Nancy.

SARAH NANCY: I think he looks just like a warthog.

DOLORES: Sarah Nancy, precious . . .

SARAH NANCY: That's the question I'd like to ask him. How is the hogpen, warthog?

DOLORES: Precious, precious.

SARAH NANCY: Anyway, they are all stupid.

DOLORES: Who, honey?

SARAH NANCY: Boys.

DOLORES: Precious, darling.

SARAH NANCY: Dumb and stupid. [*She starts away.*]

DOLORES: Sarah Nancy, where in the world are you going?

SARAH NANCY: I'm going to bed.

DOLORES: Sarah Nancy, what is possessing you to say a thing like that? You're just trying to tease me.

SARAH NANCY: Oh no I'm not. [*She starts away.*]

DOLORES: Sarah Nancy, you can't go to bed. You have a young man coming to call on you at any moment. You have to be gracious. . . .

SARAH NANCY: I don't feel like being gracious. I'm sleepy. I'm going to bed.

DOLORES: Sarah Nancy, you can't. Do you want to put me in my grave? The son of one of your mother's dearest friends will be here at any moment to call on you, and you cannot be so rude as to go to bed and refuse to receive him. Sarah Nancy, I beg you. I implore you.

SARAH NANCY: Oh, all right. [*She sits down.*] Ask me some questions.

DOLORES: No, dear. You ask me some questions.

SARAH NANCY: What church do you attend?

DOLORES: That's lovely. That's a lovely question to begin with. Now I'll answer as Felix will. Methodist.

SARAH NANCY: That's a dumb church.

DOLORES: Sarah Nancy.

SARAH NANCY: I think it's a dumb church. It's got no style. We used to be Methodist but we left for the Episcopal. They don't rant and rave in the Episcopal church.

DOLORES: And they don't rant and rave in the Methodist church either, honey. Not here. Not in Harrison.

SARAH NANCY: Last time I was there they did.

DOLORES: Well, things have changed. Anyway, you're not supposed to comment when he answers the questions, you're just supposed to sit back and listen to the answers as if you're fascinated and find it all very interesting.

SARAH NANCY: Why?

DOLORES: Because that's how you entertain young men, graciously. You make them feel you are interested in whatever they have to say.

SARAH NANCY: Suppose I'm not?

DOLORES: Well, it is not important if you are or not, you are supposed to make them think you are.

[Robert *enters*.]

ROBERT: Dolores.

DOLORES: What?

ROBERT: The children are on the phone.

DOLORES: What do they want?

ROBERT: They want to talk to you.

DOLORES: Ask them what they want. Tell them I can't talk now.

[Sarah Nancy *is looking at the yearbook.*]

SARAH NANCY: How did you make the beauty page at two colleges?

DOLORES: Personality. I always knew how to keep a conversation going.

ROBERT: Dolores.

DOLORES: Yes.

ROBERT: They say they won't tell me what they want. They'll only tell you.

DOLORES: All right. [*She goes.*]

SARAH NANCY: Did you go to college with Aunt Dolores?

ROBERT: We met the year she graduated.

SARAH NANCY: She was beautiful.

ROBERT: I guess she was.

[Dolores *comes in.*]

DOLORES: They forgot their teddy bears. I said you would bring them over.

ROBERT: They're nine and ten years old. What do they want with teddy bears?

DOLORES: They still sleep with them. You know that.

ROBERT: Well, I'm not driving anywhere with two teddy bears for two half-grown children.

DOLORES: Why are you being so difficult?

ROBERT: I am not difficult. I am hungry and tired. I worked hard all day.

DOLORES: Well, I didn't exactly have a ball today myself, mister. If I find you something to eat will you take those teddy bears over to the children?

ROBERT: All right. I'll be the laughingstock of the town, but I'll do it.

[*She goes.*]

SARAH NANCY: How do you get on a beauty page?

ROBERT: Well, you have to be pretty to start with I guess. I think a committee of some kind looks the girls on campus over and makes recommendations and I guess they have judges. But I really don't know. You'll have to ask your aunt that.

SARAH NANCY: How did you meet Aunt Dolores?

ROBERT: At a dance. I think. Yes, I think it was at a dance the first time I met her. And I asked her for a date and six weeks later I popped the question.

SARAH NANCY: What does that mean?

ROBERT: What?

SARAH NANCY: Popping the question.

ROBERT: You know. I asked her to marry me. [Sarah Nancy *makes a face*.] What are you making a face about?

SARAH NANCY: I don't know. I sure hope nobody pops a question to me.

ROBERT: Well, they will someday.

SARAH NANCY: Who?

ROBERT: Some boy or other.

SARAH NANCY: I don't know any boys.

ROBERT: Of course you know some boys.

SARAH NANCY: Not any I'd want to pop the question to me.

[Dolores *comes in*.]

DOLORES: I opened a can of chile and a can of tamales and sliced some tomatoes. Will that do you?

ROBERT: Thanks. [*He goes*.]

SARAH NANCY: Any of the dumb boys I know try popping a question to me, I'll kick them in the stomach.

DOLORES: What in the world are you talking about, honey? [*The doorbell rings*.] There he is. Now quickly, let me see how you look. [*She forces* Sarah Nancy *to stand up*.] Oh, pretty. [Sarah Nancy *sticks out her tongue*.] Oh, Sarah Nancy. [Dolores *goes to the door and opens it*.] Come in, Felix. [Felix *comes in*.] How handsome you look. I believe you two have met?

FELIX: Yes.

SARAH NANCY: What church do you attend?

FELIX: What?

SARAH NANCY: What church do you attend?

FELIX: Methodist.

DOLORES [*jumping in nervously*]: Sarah Nancy is an Episcopalian. She is very devout. Felix is very devout too, you know.

SARAH NANCY: Who is going to win the football game on Friday?

FELIX: We are.

SARAH NANCY: Why?

FELIX: Because we are the best team.

SARAH NANCY: Who says so?

FELIX: Everybody knows that. Do you like football?

SARAH NANCY: No.

FELIX: No?

SARAH NANCY: No.

FELIX: Do you like . . . ?

SARAH NANCY: I hate sports. I like to read. Do you like to read?

FELIX: No.

DOLORES: Well, you know what they say, opposites at-tract. [*She laughs merrily.* Felix *laughs.* Sarah Nancy *scowls.*] Well, I'll stay and visit just a few minutes longer and then I'll leave you two young people alone. How is your sweet mother, Felix?

FELIX: Okay.

DOLORES: Your mother and Sarah Nancy's mother and I were all girls together. Did your mother tell you that? My, the good times we used to have together.

FELIX: Do you have a radio?

DOLORES: Yes, over there.

[*He goes to the radio and turns it on.*]

FELIX: Do you want to dance?

SARAH NANCY: No, I hate dancing. What church do you belong to?

DOLORES: You asked him that before, Sarah Nancy honey, remember? He said he was a Methodist and I said you were an Episcopalian.

SARAH NANCY: Oh. [Dolores *finds a way to get be-hind* Felix *and she begins mouthing a question for* Sarah Nancy *to ask.*] What do you do?

FELIX: What do you mean?

SARAH NANCY: For a living.

FELIX: Right now I'm in insurance. But I'm leaving that. Not enough money in it. I'm going to be a mortician.

SARAH NANCY: What's that?

DOLORES: An undertaker, honey.

SARAH NANCY: How do you get to do that?

FELIX: You go to school.

SARAH NANCY: What kind of school?

FELIX: A mortician school.

SARAH NANCY: Oh, who teaches you?

FELIX: Other morticians.

[Dolores *begins to subtly mouth another question to her;* Sarah Nancy *continues to ignore her, so* Dolores *finally gives up.*]

DOLORES: I'm going now and leave you two young people alone to enjoy yourselves. [*She goes. He goes to the radio and moves the dial from one program to another.*]

FELIX: There is nothing on I want to hear. [*He turns the radio off. He sits down and, smiling, looks at* Sarah Nancy.] Having a good time on your visit here?

SARAH NANCY: It's okay.

FELIX: Let's play some games. What games do you like to play?

SARAH NANCY: I never played any.

FELIX: Never played any games?

SARAH NANCY: No.

FELIX: All right, I'll teach you one. How about ghosts?

SARAH NANCY: Ghosts?

FELIX: It's the name of the game. You start a word to
be spelled and the one that spells a word is a third of a
ghost. Get it?

SARAH NANCY: No.

FELIX: Well, maybe it isn't too much fun with just two
playing. I know, let's see who can name the most books
of the Bible. I'll go first. [*He doesn't wait for her to comment and he begins to rattle off the books of the Bible.*]
Genesis, Exodus, Leviticus . . . [*He closes his eyes as he
thinks of them and he takes it all very seriously. Sarah
Nancy stares at him as if he is insane. When he gets to
Daniel she slips quietly out of the room and is gone by
the time he begins the New Testament. He is not aware
she is gone.* Robert *comes in.* Felix *is so concentrated he
doesn't see him.* Robert *looks at him as if he is crazy,
shakes his head in disbelief and leaves the room.* Felix *is
unaware of any of it. He says the names very fast as if
speed were part of the game, so fast in fact that the
names should not always be distinct. When he finishes,
he opens his eyes.*] How did I do? I think I got every one.
[*He looks at his watch.*] I did it in pretty fair amount of
time too. Now let's see what you can do. [*He suddenly
becomes aware she is not in the room. Calling.*] Sarah
Nancy. [*He is puzzled by her disappearance and is about
to go to the door leading into the rest of the house to call
her when* Robert *comes in with two teddy bears.*]

ROBERT: Hello, Felix. [*They shake hands.*] What's new?

FELIX: Not a whole lot.

ROBERT: You're looking well.

FELIX: Thank you, sir. [Robert *starts out the front
door.*] Excuse me. Do you know where Sarah Nancy is?

ROBERT: No, I don't, son.

FELIX: She was here a minute ago. We were having a contest to see who could name the most books of the Bible.

ROBERT: Who won?

FELIX: I don't know. She was here when I started, but when I finished and opened my eyes she was gone.

ROBERT: Just sit down and relax. She'll be back.

FELIX: Yes, sir.

[Robert *goes out.* Felix *sits down.* Dolores *comes in looking stricken.*]

DOLORES: Felix, Sarah Nancy has sent me out to apologize to you and beg your forgiveness. She has been stricken, suddenly, with a very bad sick headache. She's suffered from them, she says, since childhood, and the worst of it is the poor darling never, never knows when they will strike. She says she was sitting here listening to you rattle off all the books of the Bible and having one of the liveliest times of her life, when her attack began. She is just heartbroken, the poor little thing. She slipped out not wanting to disturb you, to take an aspirin, hoping to find relief for her headache, so she could resume the lovely time she was having with you, but she got no relief from the aspirin, and she says now the only relief are cold packs on her head and total, total silence. She is quite stricken, poor sweet thing. Too stricken to even come and say good night. "Whatever will Felix think of me?" she said. "Why, precious darling," I reassured her, "he will most certainly understand." I know you do. Don't you?

FELIX: Oh, yes, ma'm.

DOLORES: How is your sweet mother?

FELIX: Just fine, thank you, ma'm.

DOLORES: And your daddy's well?

FELIX: Oh, yes, ma'm.

DOLORES: Tell your mother and daddy hello for me.

FELIX: I will. [*a pause*] They said when I came over here to say hello for them.

DOLORES: Thank you. [*a pause*]

FELIX: Well, I guess I'll be going on home.

DOLORES: All right, Felix.

FELIX: Tell Nancy Sarah . . .

DOLORES: Sarah Nancy.

FELIX: Oh, yes. Sarah Nancy. Tell her I hope she feels better.

DOLORES: I will.

FELIX: Tell her I said all the books in the Bible in under ten minutes, and if she thinks she can beat that to call me up and I'll come over and time her.

DOLORES: I'll tell her that.

FELIX: Well, good night again.

DOLORES: Good night to you, Felix dear. [*He goes. Dolores sighs. She begins to turn the lights off when* Sarah Nancy *comes out.*] What are you doing out here, Sarah Nancy?

SARAH NANCY: I want to listen to the radio.

DOLORES: You cannot listen to the radio. You can be seen from the street if you sit in this room listening to the radio. I told that boy that you were mortally ill with a sick headache and you cannot appear five minutes later perfectly well and sit in the living room and listen to the radio.

SARAH NANCY: I want to hear Rudy Vallee.

DOLORES: You will not hear Rudy Vallee and run the risk of someone seeing you and telling Felix about it. What possesses you? I ask two lovely young men over last week and you refuse to speak to either of them all evening. I ask this sweet, charming boy over tonight and you walk out of the room while he is saying the books of the Bible. Well, I tell you one thing, I will not ask another single boy over here again until you decide to be gracious. And I know you can be gracious, as gracious as any girl here. Anyone with the lovely mother you have can certainly be gracious. [Robert *enters*.] Oh, you gave me such a start. I thought you were Felix. How were the children?

ROBERT: All right.

DOLORES: Did you tell them to behave themselves and to mind Hannah and to get to bed when she told them to?

ROBERT: No.

DOLORES: Why not?

ROBERT: Because it would have done no good. They were all running around like a bunch of wild Indians. They weren't any more interested in those teddy bears than I am. Did Felix pop the question to you, Sarah Nancy?

SARAH NANCY: No. And if he had I'd have knocked his head off.

DOLORES: What's all this about popping questions?

ROBERT: I was telling Sarah Nancy how we met and after six weeks I asked you to marry me.

DOLORES: Six weeks? It was three months.

ROBERT: Six weeks.

DOLORES: I only went out twice with you in the first six weeks. We didn't start going steady until our third date. You took me to a tea dance at your frat house and you asked me to wear your fraternity pin and I said I had to think about it, as I wasn't in the habit of just casually accepting fraternity pins like some girls I knew.

[*The door opens and* Felix *enters.*]

FELIX: Excuse me. I left my hat.

DOLORES: Oh, Felix. Isn't this remarkable? I was just about to go to the phone and call you and tell you that Sarah Nancy had completely recovered from her headache. You hadn't gone five minutes when she came out and said the aspirin worked after all and where is Felix and she was so distressed that you had gone that she insisted I go to the phone and see if you wouldn't come back which I was about to do. Isn't that so, Sarah Nancy?

[Sarah Nancy *doesn't answer.*]

FELIX: Did Mrs. Henry tell you I said all the books of the Bible in under ten minutes?

DOLORES: Yes, I did. Didn't I, Sarah Nancy? [Sarah Nancy *doesn't answer.*] And she was so impressed.

Weren't you, Sarah Nancy? [*again no answer from Sarah Nancy*]

FELIX: Want to hear me do it again? You can time me this time.

SARAH NANCY: No.

FELIX: Want to play another game then? How about movie stars?

DOLORES: That sounds like fun. Doesn't it, Robert? How do you play that?

FELIX: Well, you think of initials like R. V., and you all try to guess who I'm thinking of.

SARAH NANCY: Rudy Vallee.

FELIX: No, you give up?

DOLORES: I do. I never can think of anything. Can you think of who it is, Robert?

ROBERT: No.

FELIX: Do you give up, Sarah Nancy?

SARAH NANCY: No. [*A pause. There is silence.*]

FELIX: Now do you give up?

SARAH NANCY: I'll die before I give up. [*again silence*]

DOLORES: Honey, you can't take all night. It won't be any fun then. I think there should be a time limit, Felix, and if we don't guess it . . .

FELIX [*interrupting*]: Give up?

SARAH NANCY: No.

DOLORES: Let's have a five-minute time limit. [*She looks at her watch.*] Five minutes is almost up.

FELIX: Give up?

SARAH NANCY: No.

DOLORES: Time is up. Who is it?

FELIX: Rudolph Valentino.

DOLORES: Rudolph Valentino. Imagine. Now why couldn't I have thought of that? Isn't that a fun game, Sarah Nancy honey? Why don't you pick some initials?

SARAH NANCY: O. B.

DOLORES: O. B. My. O. B. Can you think of an O. B., Felix?

FELIX: Not yet.

DOLORES: Can you, Robert?

ROBERT: No.

DOLORES: My, you picked a hard one, Sarah honey. O. B. Can she give us a clue?

FELIX: Yes. You can ask things like is it a man or a woman.

DOLORES: Is it a man or a woman?

SARAH NANCY: A woman.

DOLORES: A woman. My goodness.

SARAH NANCY: Give up?

DOLORES: I do. Do you, Felix?

FELIX: Yes. Who is it?

SARAH NANCY: Olive Blue.

FELIX: Olive Blue. Who is she?

SARAH NANCY: A girl back home.

FELIX: She's not a movie star.

SARAH NANCY: Who said she was?

FELIX: Well, goose. They're supposed to be movie stars.

SARAH NANCY: You're a goose yourself.

DOLORES: Sarah Nancy.

SARAH NANCY: It's a dumb game anyway.

FELIX: Well, let's play popular songs.

DOLORES: That sounds like fun. How do you do that?

FELIX: Well, you hum or whistle part of a song and the others have to guess what it is.

DOLORES: Oh, grand. Doesn't that sound like fun, Sarah Nancy? [*again no answer from* Sarah Nancy] Why don't you whistle something, Sarah Nancy?

SARAH NANCY: I can't whistle.

DOLORES: Well, then hum something.

SARAH NANCY: I can't hum either.

FELIX: I'll hum and you all guess. [*He hums.*] Can you guess?

DOLORES: I can't. Can you, Robert?

ROBERT: No.

DOLORES: Can you, Sarah Nancy?

SARAH NANCY: No, but I never will be able to guess what he hums, because he can't carry a tune.

DOLORES: Well, I don't agree at all. I think Felix has a very sweet voice.

ROBERT: Then how come you can't tell what he's humming?

DOLORES: Because I didn't know the song, I suppose.

ROBERT: What was the song, Felix?

FELIX: "Missouri Waltz."

ROBERT: Don't you know the "Missouri Waltz" when you hear it?

DOLORES: Yes, I know the "Missouri Waltz" when I hear it. Hum something else, Felix. [*He hums another tune. Again very flat.*] Now what's the name of that, honey?

FELIX: "Home Sweet Home."

ROBERT: "Home Sweet Home." My God!

[Dolores *glares at* Robert.]

DOLORES: Oh, of course. It was on the tip of my tongue. All right, Sarah Nancy honey, it's your turn.

FELIX: No, it's still my turn. I keep on until you guess what I'm singing.

SARAH NANCY: How are we going to guess what you're singing when you can't sing?

FELIX: I certainly can sing. I'm in the choir at the Methodist Church. I'm in a quartet that sings twice a year at the Lions Club.

SARAH NANCY: If you can sing, a screech owl can sing.

DOLORES: Sarah Nancy, honey.

SARAH NANCY: I'd rather listen to a jackass bray than you sing. You look like a warthog and you bray like a jackass.

FELIX: Who looks like a warthog?

SARAH NANCY: You do.

FELIX: I'm rubber and you're glue, everything you say bounces off of me and sticks on you.

SARAH NANCY: Warthog. You are a stinking warthog and I wish you would go on home so I could listen to Rudy Vallee in peace.

FELIX: Don't worry. I'm going home. I didn't want to come over here in the first place but my mama bribed me to come over here. Well, a million dollars couldn't make me stay here now and two million couldn't ever get me here again if you were here. [*He leaves.*]

DOLORES: Oh, my God. I have never seen such carrying on in my life. Sarah Nancy, what am I going to tell

Sister? She will take to her bed when I report this. Absolutely have a breakdown.

SARAH NANCY: I'm sorry. I'm not going to lie and tell some old fool jackass they can sing when they can't.

ROBERT: I agree with Sarah Nancy. He can't carry a tune at all.

DOLORES: Nobody asked your opinion.

ROBERT: Well, I'm giving it to you whether you asked for it or not.

DOLORES: And I don't want to hear it. How can you expect Sarah Nancy to learn to be gracious if we don't set an example?

ROBERT: I didn't tell her not to be gracious. I just told her that I agreed with what she said about his singing. I'm being honest. If that's ungracious, all right. I'd rather be honest than gracious.

DOLORES: That's all right for you. You're a man. But let me tell you right now I didn't get on two beauty pages by being honest, but by being gracious to people. But I'm whipped now and worn out. I've done all I can do. I can do no more. [*She leaves.*]

ROBERT: I guess your aunt's a little upset.

SARAH NANCY: I guess so. Do you mind if I listen to Rudy Vallee on the radio?

ROBERT: No.

[*She turns on the radio. She turns the dial.*]

SARAH NANCY: What time is it?

ROBERT: Almost ten.

SARAH NANCY: Shoot. I missed Rudy Vallee.

ROBERT: Well, you can hear him next week.

SARAH NANCY: I'll be home next week.

ROBERT: I'm going to go see to your aunt. Will you be all right?

SARAH NANCY: Sure.

[*He goes. She gets the yearbooks. She looks at one and then at the other.* Felix *comes in.*]

FELIX: Where's Mrs. Henry?

SARAH NANCY: I don't know.

FELIX: I told my mama what happened and she said I owed Mrs. Henry an apology for speaking like I did. I told her what you said to me and she said it didn't matter how other people acted, I had to remember that I was a gentleman and that I was always to act in a gentlemanly fashion. So tell Mrs. Henry I'm here and I want to apologize. [*She goes. He sees the yearbooks. He looks at them.* Sarah Nancy *comes in.*] Did you tell her?

SARAH NANCY: No. I couldn't. She's gone to bed. She has a sick headache.

FELIX [*He points to the book.*]: She was pretty, wasn't she?

SARAH NANCY: Yes, she was.

FELIX: You don't sing any better than I do.

SARAH NANCY: I didn't say I did.

FELIX: And you're never going to be on any beauty pages, I bet.

SARAH NANCY: I didn't say I would.

FELIX: Don't you care?

SARAH NANCY: No.

[*There is silence. An uncomfortable silence. He closes the yearbook.*]

FELIX: I can't think of a whole lot to talk about. Can you?

SARAH NANCY: No.

FELIX: Your aunt is quite a conversationalist. It's easy to talk when she's around.

SARAH NANCY: I guess. [*A pause. Silence.*]

FELIX: Do you mind if I stay on here for a while?

SARAH NANCY: No.

FELIX: I told my mother I'd stay at least another hour. If you get sleepy, you just go on to bed. I'll just sit here and look at these yearbooks.

SARAH NANCY: I'm not sleepy.

FELIX: You want one of the yearbooks?

SARAH NANCY: Thank you.

[*He hands her one. She opens it. He takes one and opens it. After a beat they are both completely absorbed in looking at the yearbooks. They continue looking at them as the light fades.*]

Suppressed Desires

A COMEDY

—◦◦◦—

by Susan Glaspell

in collaboration with
George Cram Cook

CHARACTERS

HENRIETTA BREWSTER   STEPHEN BREWSTER
MABEL

SCENE 1

A studio apartment in an upper story, Washington Square South. Through an immense north window in the back wall appear tree tops and the upper part of the Washington Arch. Beyond it you look up Fifth Avenue. Near the window is a big table, loaded at one end with serious-looking books and austere scientific periodicals. At the other end are architect's drawings, blue prints, dividing compasses, square, ruler, etc. At the left is a door leading to the rest of the apartment; at the right the outer door. A breakfast table is set for three, but only two are seated at it—Henrietta and Stephen Brewster. As the curtains withdraw Steve pushes back his coffee cup and sits dejected.

HENRIETTA: It isn't the coffee, Steve dear. There's nothing the matter with the coffee. There's something the matter with *you*.

STEVE [*doggedly*]: There may be something the matter with my stomach.

HENRIETTA [*scornfully*]: Your stomach! The trouble is not with your stomach but in your subconscious mind.

STEVE: Subconscious piffle! [*takes morning paper and tries to read*]

95

HENRIETTA: Steve, you never used to be so disagreeable. You certainly have got some sort of a complex. You're all inhibited. You're no longer open to new ideas. You won't listen to a word about psychoanalysis.

STEVE: A word! I've listened to volumes!

HENRIETTA: You've ceased to be creative in architecture—your work isn't going well. You're not sleeping well—

STEVE: How can I sleep, Henrietta, when you're always waking me up to find out what I'm dreaming?

HENRIETTA: But dreams are so important, Steve. If you'd tell yours to Dr. Russell he'd find out exactly what's wrong with you.

STEVE: There's nothing wrong with me.

HENRIETTA: You don't even talk as well as you used to.

STEVE: Talk? I can't say a thing without you looking at me in that dark fashion you have when you're on the trail of a complex.

HENRIETTA: This very irritability indicates that you're suffering from some suppressed desire.

STEVE: I'm suffering from a suppressed desire for a little peace.

HENRIETTA: Dr. Russell is doing simply wonderful things with nervous cases. Won't you go to him, Steve?

STEVE [*slamming down his newspaper*]: No, Henrietta, I won't!

HENRIETTA: But Stephen—!

STEVE: Tst! I hear Mabel coming. Let's not be at each other's throats the first day of her visit.

[*He takes out cigarettes. Mabel comes in from door left, the side opposite Steve, so that he is facing her. She is wearing a rather fussy negligee in contrast to Henrietta, who wears "radical" clothes. Mabel is what is called plump.*]

MABEL: Good morning.

HENRIETTA: Oh, here you are, little sister.

STEVE: Good morning, Mabel.

[Mabel *nods to him and turns, her face lighting up, to Henrietta.*]

HENRIETTA [*giving Mabel a hug as she leans against her*]: It's so good to have you here. I was going to let you sleep, thinking you'd be tired after the long trip. Sit down. There'll be fresh toast in a minute and [*rising*] will you have—

MABEL: Oh, I ought to have told you, Henrietta. Don't get anything for me. I'm not eating breakfast.

HENRIETTA [*at first in mere surprise*]: Not eating breakfast? [*She sits down, then leans toward Mabel who is seated now, and scrutinizes her.*]

STEVE [*half to himself*]: The psychoanalytical look!

HENRIETTA: Mabel, why are you not eating breakfast?

MABEL [*a little startled*]: Why, no particular reason. I just don't care much for breakfast, and they say it keeps down— [*a hand on her hip—the gesture of one who is reducing*] that is, it's a good thing to go without it.

HENRIETTA: Don't you sleep well? Did you sleep well last night?

MABEL: Oh, yes, I slept all right. Yes, I slept fine last night, only [*laughing*] I did have the funniest dream!

STEVE: S-h! S-t!

HENRIETTA [*moving closer*]: And what did you dream, Mabel?

STEVE: Look-a-here, Mabel, I feel it's my duty to put you on. Don't tell Henrietta your dreams. If you do she'll find out that you have an underground desire to kill your father and marry your mother—

HENRIETTA: Don't be absurd, Stephen Brewster. [*sweetly to* Mabel] What was your dream, dear?

MABEL [*laughing*]: Well, I dreamed I was a hen.

HENRIETTA: A hen?

MABEL: Yes; and I was pushing along through a crowd as fast as I could, but being a hen I couldn't walk very fast—it was like having a tight skirt, you know; and there was some sort of creature in a blue cap—you know how mixed up dreams are—and it kept shouting after me, "Step, Hen! Step, Hen!" until I got all excited and just couldn't move at all.

HENRIETTA [*resting chin in palm and peering*]: You say you became much excited?

MABEL [*laughing*]: Oh, yes; I was in a terrible state.

HENRIETTA [*leaning back, murmurs*]: This is significant.

STEVE: She dreams she's a hen. She is told to step lively. She becomes violently agitated. What can it mean?

HENRIETTA [*turning impatiently from him*]: Mabel, do you know anything about psychoanalysis?

MABEL [*feebly*]: Oh—not much. No—I— [*brightening*] It's something about the war, isn't it?

STEVE: Not that kind of war.

MABEL [*abashed*]: I thought it might be the name of a new explosive.

STEVE: It *is*.

MABEL [*apologetically to* Henrietta, *who is frowning*]: You see, Henrietta, I—we do not live in touch with intellectual things, as you do. Bob being a dentist—somehow our friends—

STEVE [*softly*]: Oh, to be a dentist! [*goes to window and stands looking out*]

HENRIETTA: Don't you see anything more of that editorial writer—what was his name?

MABEL: Lyman Eggleston?

HENRIETTA: Yes, Eggleston. He was in touch with things. Don't you see him?

MABEL: Yes, I see him once in a while. Bob doesn't like him very well.

HENRIETTA: Your husband does not like Lyman Eggleston? [*mysteriously*] Mabel, are you perfectly happy with your husband?

STEVE [*sharply*]: Oh, come now, Henrietta—that's going a little strong!

HENRIETTA: Are you perfectly happy with him, Mabel?

[Steve *goes to work-table.*]

MABEL: Why—yes—I guess so. Why—of course I am!

HENRIETTA: Are you happy? Or do you only think you are? Or do you only think you *ought* to be?

MABEL: Why, Henrietta, I don't know what you mean!

STEVE [*seizes stack of books and magazines and dumps them on the breakfast table*]: This is what she means, Mabel. Psychoanalysis. My work-table groans with it. Books by Freud, the new Messiah; books by Jung, the new St. Paul; the *Psychoanalytical Review*— back numbers two-fifty per.

MABEL: But what's it all about?

STEVE: All about your sub-un-non-conscious mind and desires you know not of. They may be doing you a great deal of harm. You may go crazy with them. Oh, yes! People are doing it right and left. Your dreaming you're a hen— [*shakes his head darkly*]

HENRIETTA: Any fool can ridicule anything.

MABEL [*hastily, to avert a quarrel*]: But what do you say it is, Henrietta?

STEVE [*looking at his watch*]: Oh, if Henrietta's going to start that! [*during* Henrietta's *next speech settles himself at work-table and sharpens a lead pencil*]

HENRIETTA: It's like this, Mabel. You want something. You think you can't have it. You think it's wrong. So you try to think you don't want it. Your mind protects you—avoids pain—by refusing to think the forbidden thing. But it's there just the same. It stays there shut up in your unconscious mind, and it festers.

STEVE: Sort of an ingrowing mental toenail.

HENRIETTA: Precisely. The forbidden impulse is there full of energy which has simply got to do something. It breaks into your consciousness in disguise, masks itself in dreams, makes all sorts of trouble. In extreme cases it drives you insane.

MABEL [*with a gesture of horror*]: Oh!

HENRIETTA [*reassuring*]: But psychoanalysis has found out how to save us from that. It brings into consciousness the suppressed desire that was making all the trouble. Psychoanalysis is simply the latest scientific method of preventing and curing insanity.

STEVE [*from his table*]: It is also the latest scientific method of separating families.

HENRIETTA [*mildly*]: Families that ought to be separated.

STEVE: The Dwights, for instance. You must have met them, Mabel, when you were here before. Helen was living, apparently, in peace and happiness with good old Joe. Well—she went to this psychoanalyzer—she was "psyched," and biff!—bang!—home she comes with an unsuppressed desire to leave her husband. [*He starts work, drawing lines on a drawing board with a T-square.*]

MABEL: How terrible! Yes, I remember Helen Dwight. But—but did she have such a desire?

STEVE: First she'd known of it.

MABEL: And she *left* him?

HENRIETTA [*coolly*]: Yes, she did.

MABEL: Wasn't he good to her?

HENRIETTA: Why, yes, good enough.

MABEL: Wasn't he kind to her?

HENRIETTA: Oh, yes—kind to her.

MABEL: And she left her good, kind husband—!

HENRIETTA: Oh, Mabel! "Left her good, kind husband!" How naïve—forgive me, dear, but how bourgeois you are! She came to know herself. And she had the courage!

MABEL: I may be very naïve and—bourgeois—but I don't see the good of a new science that breaks up homes.

[Steve *applauds.*]

STEVE: In enlightening Mabel, we mustn't neglect to mention the case of Art Holden's private secretary, Mary Snow, who has just been informed of her suppressed desire for her employer.

MABEL: Why, I think it is terrible, Henrietta! It would be better if we didn't know such things about ourselves.

HENRIETTA: No, Mabel, that is the old way.

MABEL: But—but her employer? Is he married?

STEVE [*grunts*]: Wife and four children.

MABEL: Well, then, what good does it do the girl to be told she has a desire for him? There's nothing can be done about it.

HENRIETTA: Old institutions will have to be reshaped so that something can be done in such cases. It happens, Mabel, that this suppressed desire was on the point of landing Mary Snow in the insane asylum. Are you so tight-minded that you'd rather have her in the insane asylum than break the conventions?

MABEL: But—but have people always had these awful suppressed desires?

HENRIETTA: Always.

STEVE: But they've just been discovered.

HENRIETTA: The harm they do has just been discovered. And free, sane people must face the fact that they have to be dealt with.

MABEL [*stoutly*]: I don't believe they have them in Chicago.

HENRIETTA [*business of giving* Mabel *up*]: People "have them" wherever the living Libido—the center of the soul's energy—is in conflict with petrified moral codes. That means everywhere in civilization. Psychoanalysis—

STEVE: Good God! I've got the roof in the cellar!

HENRIETTA: The roof in the cellar!

STEVE [*holding plan at arm's length*]: That's what psychoanalysis does!

HENRIETTA: That's what psychoanalysis could *un*-do. Is it any wonder I'm concerned about Steve? He dreamed the other night that the walls of his room melted away and he found himself alone in a forest. Don't you see how significant it is for an architect to have *walls* slip away from him? It symbolizes his loss of grip in his work. There's some suppressed desire—

STEVE [*hurling his ruined plan viciously to the floor*]: Suppressed hell!

HENRIETTA: You speak more truly than you know. It is through suppressions that hells are formed in us.

MABEL [*looking at* Steve, *who is tearing his hair*]: Don't you think it would be a good thing, Henrietta, if we went somewhere else?

[*They rise and begin to pick up the dishes.* Mabel *drops a plate, which breaks.* Henrietta *draws up short and looks at her—the psychoanalytic look.*]

I'm sorry, Henrietta. One of the Spode plates, too. [*surprised and resentful as* Henrietta *continues to peer at her*] Don't take it so to heart, Henrietta.

HENRIETTA: I can't help taking it to heart.

MABEL: I'll get you another. [*pause; more sharply as* Henrietta *does not answer:*] I said I'll get you another plate, Henrietta.

HENRIETTA: It's not the plate.

MABEL: For heaven's sake, what is it then?

HENRIETTA: It's the significant little false movement that made you drop it.

MABEL: Well, I suppose everyone makes a false movement once in a while.

HENRIETTA: Yes, Mabel, but these false movements all mean something.

MABEL [*about to cry*]: I don't think that's very nice! It was just because I happened to think of that Mabel Snow you were talking about—

HENRIETTA: *Mabel* Snow!

MABEL: Snow—Snow—well, what was her name, then?

HENRIETTA: Her name is Mary. You substituted *your own* name for hers.

MABEL: Well, *Mary* Snow, then; *Mary* Snow. I never heard her name but once. I don't see anything to make such a fuss about.

HENRIETTA [*gently*]: Mabel dear—mistakes like that in names—

MABEL [*desperately*]: They don't mean something, too, do they?

HENRIETTA [*gently*]: I am sorry, dear, but they do.

MABEL: But I'm always doing that!

HENRIETTA [*after a start of horror*]: My poor little sister, tell me about it.

MABEL: About what?

HENRIETTA: About your not being happy. About your longing for another sort of life.

MABEL: But I *don't*.

HENRIETTA: Ah, I understand these things, dear. You feel Bob is limiting you to a life in which you do not feel free—

MABEL: Henrietta! When did I ever say such a thing?

HENRIETTA: You said you are not in touch with things intellectual. You showed your feeling that it is Bob's profession—that has engendered a resentment which has colored your whole life with him.

MABEL: Why—Henrietta!

HENRIETTA: Don't be afraid of me, little sister. There's nothing can shock me or turn me from you. I am not like that. I wanted you to come for this visit because I had a feeling that you needed more from life than you were getting. No one of these things I have seen would excite my suspicion. It's the combination. You don't eat breakfast. [*enumerating on her fingers*] You make false moves; you substitute your own name for the name of another *whose love is misdirected*. You're nervous; you *look* queer; in your eyes there's a frightened look that is most unlike you. And this dream. A *hen*. Come with me this afternoon to Dr. Russell! Your whole life may be at stake, Mabel.

MABEL [*gasping*]: Henrietta, I—you—you always were the smartest in the family, and all that, but—this is terrible! I don't think we *ought* to think such things. [*brightening*] Why, I'll tell you why I dreamed I was a hen. It was because last night, telling about that time in Chicago, you said I was as mad as a wet hen.

HENRIETTA [*superior*]: Did you dream you were a *wet* hen?

MABEL [*forced to admit it*]: No.

HENRIETTA: No. You dreamed you were a *dry* hen. And why, being a hen, were you urged to step?

MABEL: Maybe it's because when I am getting on a street car it always irritates me to have them call "Step lively."

HENRIETTA: No, Mabel, that is only a child's view of it—if you will forgive me. You see merely the elements used in the dream. You do not see into the dream; you do not see its meaning. This dream of the hen—

STEVE: Hen—hen—wet hen—dry hen—mad hen! [*jumps up in a rage*] Let me out of this!

HENRIETTA [*hastily picking up dishes, speaks soothingly*]: Just a minute, dear, and we'll have things so you can work in quiet. Mabel and I are going to sit in my room. [*She goes out left, carrying dishes.*]

STEVE [*seizing hat and coat from an alcove near the outside door*]: I'm going to be psychoanalyzed. I'm going now! I'm going straight to that infallible doctor of hers—that priest of this new religion. If he's got honesty enough to tell Henrietta there's nothing the matter with my unconscious mind, perhaps I can be let alone about it, and then I *will* be all right. [*from the door in a loud voice*] Don't tell Henrietta I'm going. It might take weeks, and I couldn't stand all the talk. [*He hurries out.*]

HENRIETTA [*returning*]: Where's Steve? Gone? [*with a hopeless gesture*] You see how impatient he is—how unlike himself! I tell you, Mabel, I'm nearly distracted about Steve.

MABEL: I think he's a little distracted, too.

HENRIETTA: Well, if he's gone—you might as well stay here. I have a committee meeting at the bookshop, and will have to leave you to yourself for an hour or two. [*As she puts her hat on, taking it from the alcove where* Steve *found his, her eye, lighting up almost carnivorously, falls on an enormous volume on the floor beside the work-table. The book has been half hidden by the wastebasket. She picks it up and carries it around the table toward* Mabel.] Here, dear, is one of the simplest

statements of psychoanalysis. You just read this and
then we can talk more intelligently.

[Mabel *takes volume and staggers back under its
weight to chair rear center.* Henrietta *goes to outer
door, stops and asks abruptly.*]

How old is Lyman Eggleston?

MABEL [*promptly*]: He isn't forty yet. Why, what
made you ask that, Henrietta? [*As she turns her head to
look at* Henrietta *her hands move toward the upper cor-
ners of the book balanced on her knees.*]

HENRIETTA: Oh, nothing. Au revoir.

[*She goes out.* Mabel *stares at the ceiling. The book
slides to the floor. She starts; looks at the book, then
at the broken plate on the table.*]

MABEL: The plate! The book! [*She lifts her eyes, leans
forward, elbow on knee, chin on knuckles and plain-
tively queries.*] Am I unhappy?

SCENE 2

*Two weeks later. The stage is as in Scene 1, except that
the breakfast table has been removed. During the first
few minutes the dusk of a winter afternoon deepens.
Out of the darkness spring rows of double street-
lights almost meeting in the distance.* Henrietta *is at
the psychoanalytical end of* Steve's *work-table, surrounded by open books and periodicals, writing.*
Steve *enters briskly.*

STEVE: What are you doing, my dear?

HENRIETTA: My paper for the Liberal Club.

STEVE: Your paper on—?

HENRIETTA: On a subject which does not have your sympathy.

STEVE: Oh, I'm not sure I'm wholly out of sympathy with psychoanalysis, Henrietta. You worked it so hard, I couldn't even take a bath without its meaning something.

HENRIETTA [*loftily*]: I talked it because I knew you needed it.

STEVE: You haven't said much about it these last two weeks. Uh—your faith in it hasn't weakened any?

HENRIETTA: Weakened? It's grown stronger with each new thing I've come to know. And Mabel. She is with Dr. Russell now. Dr. Russell is wonderful! From what Mabel tells me I believe his analysis is going to prove that I was right. Today I discovered a remarkable confirmation of my theory in the hen-dream.

STEVE: What is your theory?

HENRIETTA: Well, you know about Lyman Eggleston. I've wondered about him. I've never seen him, but I know he's less bourgeois than Mabel's other friends— more intellectual—and [*significantly*] she doesn't see much of him because Bob doesn't like him.

STEVE: But what's the confirmation?

HENRIETTA: Today I noticed the first syllable of his name.

STEVE: Ly?

HENRIETTA: No—egg.

STEVE: Egg?

HENRIETTA [*patiently*]: Mabel dreamed she was a *hen*. [Steve *laughs*.] You wouldn't laugh if you knew how important names are in interpreting dreams. Freud is full of just such cases in which a whole hidden complex is revealed by a single significant syllable—like this egg.

STEVE: Doesn't the traditional relation of hen and egg suggest rather a maternal feeling?

HENRIETTA: There is something maternal in Mabel's love, of course, but that's only one element.

STEVE: Well, suppose Mabel hasn't a suppressed desire to be this gentleman's mother, but his beloved. What's to be done about it? What about Bob? Don't you think it's going to be a little rough on him?

HENRIETTA: That can't be helped. Bob, like everyone else, must face the facts of life. If Dr. Russell should arrive independently at this same interpretation I shall not hesitate to advise Mabel to leave her present husband.

STEVE: Um—hum! [*The lights go up on Fifth Avenue. Steve goes to the window and looks out.*] How long is it we've lived here, Henrietta?

HENRIETTA: Why, this is the third year, Steve.

STEVE: I—we—one would miss this view if one went away, wouldn't one?

HENRIETTA: How strangely you speak! Oh, Stephen, I *wish* you'd go to Dr. Russell. Don't think my fears have abated because I've been able to restrain myself. I had to on account of Mabel. But now, dear—won't you go?

STEVE: I— [*He breaks off, turns on the light, then comes and sits beside* Henrietta.] How long have we been married, Henrietta?

HENRIETTA: Stephen, I don't understand you! You *must* go to Dr. Russell.

STEVE: I have gone.

HENRIETTA: You—what?

STEVE [*jauntily*]: Yes, Henrietta, I've been psyched.

HENRIETTA: You went to Dr. Russell?

STEVE: The same.

HENRIETTA: And what did he say?

STEVE: He said—I—I was a little surprised by what he said, Henrietta.

HENRIETTA [*breathlessly*]: Of course—one can so seldom anticipate. But tell me—your dream, Stephen? It means—?

STEVE: It means—I was considerably surprised by what it means.

HENRIETTA: *Don't* be so exasperating!

STEVE: It means—you really want to know, Henrietta?

HENRIETTA: Stephen, you'll drive me mad!

STEVE: He said—of course he may be wrong in what he said.

HENRIETTA: He *isn't* wrong. *Tell* me!

STEVE: He said my dream of the walls receding and leaving me alone in a forest indicates a suppressed desire—

HENRIETTA: Yes—yes!

STEVE: To be freed from—

HENRIETTA: Yes—freed from—?

STEVE: Marriage.

HENRIETTA [*crumples, stares*]: Marriage!

STEVE: He—he may be mistaken, you know.

HENRIETTA: *May* be mistaken?

STEVE: I—well, of course, I hadn't taken any stock in it myself. It was only your great confidence—

HENRIETTA: Stephen, are you telling me that Dr. Russell—Dr. A. E. Russell—told you this?

[Steve *nods.*]

Told you you have a suppressed desire to separate from *me*?

STEVE: That's what he said.

HENRIETTA: Did he know who you were?

STEVE: Yes.

HENRIETTA: That you were married to me?

STEVE: Yes, he knew that.

HENRIETTA: And he told you to leave me?

STEVE: It seems he must be wrong, Henrietta.

HENRIETTA [*rising*]: And I've sent him more patients—! [*catches herself and resumes coldly*] What reason did he give for this analysis?

STEVE: He says the confining walls are a symbol of my feeling about marriage and that their fading away is a wish-fulfillment.

HENRIETTA [*gulping*]: Well, is it? Do you want our marriage to end?

STEVE: It was a great surprise to me that I did. You see I hadn't known what was in my unconscious mind.

HENRIETTA [*flaming*]: What did you tell Dr. Russell about me to make him think you weren't happy?

STEVE: I never told him a thing, Henrietta. He got it all from his confounded clever inferences. I—I tried to refute them, but he said that was only part of my self-protective lying.

HENRIETTA: And that's why you were so—happy—when you came in just now!

STEVE: Why, Henrietta, how can you say such a thing? I was *sad*. Didn't I speak sadly of—of the view? Didn't I ask how long we had been married?

HENRIETTA [*rising*]: Stephen Brewster, have you no sense of the seriousness of this? Dr. Russell doesn't know what our marriage has been. You do. You should have laughed him down! Confined—in life with me? Did you tell him that I *believe* in freedom?

STEVE: I very emphatically told him that his results were a great surprise to me.

HENRIETTA: But you accepted them.

STEVE: Oh, not at all. I merely couldn't refute his arguments. I'm not a psychologist. I came home to talk it over with you. You being a disciple of psychoanalysis—

HENRIETTA: If you are going, I wish you would go tonight!

STEVE: Oh, my dear! I—surely I couldn't do that! Think of my feelings. And my laundry hasn't come home.

HENRIETTA: I ask you to go tonight. Some women would falter at this, Steve, but I am not such a woman. I leave you free. I do not repudiate psychoanalysis; I say again that it has done great things. It has also made mistakes, of course. But since you accept this analysis— [*She sits down and pretends to begin work.*] I have to finish this paper. I wish you would leave me.

STEVE [*scratches his head, goes to the inner door*]: I'm sorry, Henrietta, about my unconscious mind.

[*Alone,* Henrietta's *face betrays her outraged state of mind—disconcerted, resentful, trying to pull herself together. She attains an air of bravely bearing an outrageous thing. The outer door opens and* Mabel *enters in great excitement.*]

MABEL [*breathless*]: Henrietta, I'm so glad you're here. And alone? [*looks toward the inner door*] Are you alone, Henrietta?

HENRIETTA [*with reproving dignity*]: Very much so.

MABEL [*rushing to her*]: Henrietta, he's found it!

HENRIETTA [*aloof*]: Who has found what?

MABEL: Who has found what? Dr. Russell has found my suppressed desire!

HENRIETTA: That is interesting.

MABEL: He finished with me today—he got hold of my complex—in the most amazing way! But, oh, Henrietta—it is so terrible!

HENRIETTA: Do calm yourself, Mabel. Surely there's no occasion for all this agitation.

MABEL: But there is! And when you think of the lives that are affected—the readjustments that must be made in order to bring the suppressed hell out of me and save me from the insane asylum—!

HENRIETTA: The insane asylum!

MABEL: You said that's where these complexes brought people!

HENRIETTA: What did the doctor tell you, Mabel?

MABEL: Oh, I don't know how I can tell you—it is so awful—so unbelievable.

HENRIETTA: I rather have my hand in at hearing the unbelievable.

MABEL: Henrietta, who would ever have thought it? How can it be true? But the doctor is perfectly certain that I have a suppressed desire for— [looks at Henrietta, is unable to continue]

HENRIETTA: Oh, go on, Mabel. I'm not unprepared for what you have to say.

MABEL: Not unprepared? You mean you have suspected it?

HENRIETTA: From the first. It's been my theory all along.

MABEL: But, Henrietta, I didn't know myself that I had this secret desire for Stephen.

HENRIETTA [*jumps up*]: Stephen!

MABEL: My brother-in-law! My own sister's husband!

HENRIETTA: *You* have a suppressed desire for *Stephen*!

MABEL: Oh, Henrietta, aren't these unconscious selves terrible? They seem so unlike *us*!

HENRIETTA: What insane thing are you driving at?

MABEL [*blubbering*]: Henrietta, don't you use that word to me. I don't *want* to go to the insane asylum.

HENRIETTA: What did Dr. Russell say?

MABEL: Well, you see—oh, it's the strangest thing! But you know the voice in my dream that called "Step, Hen!" Dr. Russell found out today that when I was a little girl I had a story-book in words of one syllable and I read the name Stephen wrong. I used to read it S-t-e-p, step, h-e-n, hen. [*dramatically*] Step Hen is Stephen.

[*Enter* Stephen, *his head bent over a time-table.*]

Stephen is Step Hen!

STEVE: I? Step Hen?

MABEL [*triumphantly*]: S-t-e-p, step, H-e-n, hen, Stephen!

HENRIETTA [*exploding*]: Well, what if Stephen is Step Hen? [*scornfully*] Step Hen! Step Hen! For that ridiculous coincidence—

MABEL: Coincidence! But it's childish to look at the mere elements of a dream. You have to look *into* it—you have to see what it *means*!

HENRIETTA: On account of that trivial, meaningless play on syllables—on that flimsy basis—you are ready—[*wails*] O-h!

STEVE: What on earth's the matter? What has happened? Suppose I *am* Step Hen? What about it? What does it mean?

MABEL [*crying*]: It means—that I—have a suppressed desire for *you*!

STEVE: For me! The deuce you have! [*feebly*] What—er—makes you think so?

MABEL: Dr. Russell has worked it out scientifically.

HENRIETTA: Yes. Through the amazing discovery that Step Hen equals Stephen!

MABEL [*tearfully*]: Oh, that isn't all—that isn't near all. Henrietta won't give me a chance to tell it. She'd rather I'd go to the insane asylum than be unconventional.

HENRIETTA: We'll all go there if you can't control yourself. We are still waiting for some rational report.

MABEL [*drying her eyes*]: Oh, there's such a lot about names. [*with some pride*] I don't see how I ever did it. It all works in together. I dreamed I was a hen because that's the first syllable of *Henrietta's* name, and when I dreamed I was a hen, I was putting myself in Henrietta's place.

HENRIETTA: With Stephen?

MABEL: With Stephen.

HENRIETTA [*outraged*]: Oh!

[*turns in rage upon* Stephen, *who is fanning himself with the time-table*]

What are you doing with that time-table?

STEVE: Why—I thought—you were so keen to have me go tonight—I thought I'd just take a run up to Canada, and join Billy—a little shooting—but—

MABEL: But there's more about the names.

HENRIETTA: Mabel, have you thought of Bob—dear old Bob—your good, kind husband?

MABEL: Oh, Henrietta, "my good, kind husband!"

HENRIETTA: Think of him, Mabel, out there alone in Chicago, working his head off, fixing people's *teeth*—for you!

MABEL: Yes, but think of the living Libido—in conflict with petrified moral codes! And think of the perfectly wonderful way the names all prove it. Dr. Russell said he's never seen anything more convincing. Just look at Stephen's last name—Brewster. I dream I'm a hen, and the name Brewster—you have to say its first letter by itself—and then the hen, that's me, she says to him: "Stephen, Be Rooster!"

[Henrietta *and* Stephen *collapse into the nearest chairs.*]

MABEL: I think it's perfectly wonderful! Why, if it wasn't for psychoanalysis you'd never find out how wonderful your own mind is!

STEVE [*begins to chuckle*]: Be Rooster! Stephen, Be Rooster!

HENRIETTA: You think it's funny, do you?

STEVE: Well, what's to be done about it? Does Mabel have to go away with me?

HENRIETTA: Do you want Mabel to go away with you?

STEVE: Well, but Mabel herself—her complex, her suppressed desire—!

HENRIETTA [*going to her*]: Mabel, are you going to insist on going away with Stephen?

MABEL: I'd rather go with Stephen than go to the insane asylum!

HENRIETTA: For heaven's sake, Mabel, drop that insane asylum! If you *did* have a suppressed desire for Stephen hidden away in you—God knows it isn't hidden now. Dr. Russell has brought it into your consciousness—with a vengeance. That's all that's necessary to break up a complex. Psychoanalysis doesn't say you have to *gratify* every suppressed desire.

STEVE [*softly*]: Unless it's for Lyman Eggleston.

HENRIETTA [*turning on him*]: Well, if it comes to that, Stephen Brewster, I'd like to know why that interpretation of mine isn't as good as this one? Step, Hen!

STEVE: But Be Rooster! [*He pauses, chuckling to himself.*] Step-Hen Be rooster. And *Hen*rietta. Pshaw, my dear, Doc Russell's got you beat a mile! [*He turns away and chuckles.*] Be rooster!

MABEL: What has Lyman Eggleston got to do with it?

STEVE: According to Henrietta, you, the hen, have a suppressed desire for *Egg*leston, the egg.

MABEL: Henrietta, I think that's indecent of you! He is bald as an egg and little and fat—the idea of you thinking such a thing of me!

HENRIETTA: Well, Bob isn't little and bald and fat! Why don't you stick to your own husband? [*to* Stephen] What if Dr. Russell's interpretation has got mine "beat a mile"? [*resentful look at him*] It would only mean that Mabel doesn't want Eggleston and does want you. Does that mean she has to have you?

MABEL: But you said Mabel Snow—

HENRIETTA: *Mary* Snow! You're not as much like her as you think—substituting your name for hers! The cases are entirely different. Oh, I wouldn't have *believed* this of you, Mabel. [*beginning to cry*] I brought you here for a pleasant visit—thought you needed brightening *up*—wanted to be *nice* to you—and now you—my husband—you insist— [*In fumbling her way to her chair she brushes to the floor some sheets from the psychoanalytical table.*]

STEVE [*with solicitude*]: Careful, dear. Your paper on psychoanalysis! [*gathers up sheets and offers them to her*]

HENRIETTA: I don't want my paper on psychoanalysis! I'm sick of psychoanalysis!

STEVE [*eagerly*]: Do you mean that, Henrietta?

HENRIETTA: Why shouldn't I mean it? Look at all I've done for psychoanalysis—and— [*raising a tearstained face*] What has psychoanalysis done for me?

STEVE: Do you mean, Henrietta, that you're going to stop *talking* psychoanalysis?

HENRIETTA: Why shouldn't I stop talking it? Haven't I seen what it does to people? Mabel has gone crazy about psychoanalysis!

[*At the word "crazy" with a moan* Mabel *sinks to chair and buries her face in her hands.*]

STEVE [*solemnly*]: Do you swear never to wake me up in the night to find out what I'm dreaming?

HENRIETTA: Dream what you please—I don't care what you're dreaming.

STEVE: Will you clear off my work-table so the *Journal of Morbid Psychology* doesn't stare me in the face when I'm trying to plan a house?

HENRIETTA [*pushing a stack of periodicals off the table*]: I'll *burn* the *Journal of Morbid Psychology*!

STEVE: My dear Henrietta, if you're going to separate from psychoanalysis, there's no reason why I should separate from *you*.

[*They embrace ardently.* Mabel *lifts her head and looks at them woefully.*]

MABEL [*jumping up and going toward them*]: But what about me? What am I to do with my suppressed desire?

STEVE [*with one arm still around* Henrietta, *gives* Mabel *a brotherly hug*]: Mabel, you just keep right on suppressing it!

LILY'S CROSSING

—⁓—

A one-act play based on the book by Patricia Reilly Giff

**Adapted by
Greg Gunning**

CHARACTERS

ALBERT   MARGARET
IMMIGRATION OFFICER   EDDIE DILLON
LILY   BULLY
GRAM   NUN
MR. JERRY MOLLAHAN
   (DAD)

TIME—Summer 1944. PLACE—Rockaway Beach,
New York.

PROLOGUE

Onstage, there are bits and pieces of the Mollahan summer beach house (the living room) on Rockaway Beach—summer 1944.

The dominant piece of furniture is a large free-standing old (1930s) radio—center stage. There is also an old overstuffed chair with floor lamp next to it, a piano stool, a hat rack, a window upstage. To the side are other artifacts—a small wooden pier—some crates— a church kneeler.

The set has a feeling of openness. All the different elements of the set can be moved around easily by the actors during the play to keep the action moving quickly. Also some World War II posters hang in back: "Buy War Bonds! Remember December Seventh!"

(Note: there are two types of music for Lily's Crossing— original music written just for the show to underscore scenes—and music taken directly from the time of the 1940s as heard on the radio back then.)

Opening music (original) transitions into the prologue. The prologue to the show is done with no dialogue, only the sounds and the music of the 1940s world at war.

SOUND FX: Boat whistle blast

We hear the sound of a loud whistle blast from a large ocean liner—followed by the sound of a large crowd of people. Announcements are heard over a bad public address system—first in French, then in English: "Attention . . . attention—all passengers must report to the immigration office with their passports before boarding the ship." *We seem to be at the docks in France. Entering into all this is* Albert.

Albert *is a young man—carrying an old beat-up suitcase, wearing a rather worn winter coat and eastern European hat. He looks a bit lost and alone—not sure where he is supposed to be.*

A rather severe Immigration Officer *enters with clipboard and an abrupt, harsh attitude. He seems harried, annoyed, overworked.* Albert *crosses to him—hands* Officer *his papers.* Officer *looks at papers, checks them, stamps them, starts to hand them back to* Albert. *At this point, the announcement over the public address system changes into . . .*

SOUND CUE: A speech of Adolph Hitler—growing intense—an ominous chord grows . . . both men are looking straight out—listening—worried. Segues into . . .

SOUND FX: *Large crowd ominously chanting* "Sieg Heil"—*wildly, threateningly.*

Immigration Officer *nervously exits.* Albert *remains—stands center stage—listening to crowd—scared/ worried.*

SOUND CUE: Boat whistle blast

Albert *decides to exit. He picks up suitcase. As he crosses to exit stage, he passes a young girl coming from the opposite direction also carrying a suitcase.* Albert *exits.*

Sound Cue: Radio

Lily Mollahan *is the young girl who has entered carrying her small suitcase and a book. She crosses to radio up center—puts down her suitcase—quickly turns to the radio, starts to turn the dial—listening a few seconds to different stations until she can find something that she is satisfied with.*

Lily *is young, energetic, positive, intelligent, and right now—glad to be here at her family's summer house. She is dressed for the summer—filled with enthusiasm for whatever the summer and life may have in store.*

She turns the dial on the radio. Selections are not only songs, but also actual radio shows of World War II America in June 1944. We hear only short segments— like someone is turning the dial of a radio—with some static in between.

(*Note: Short radio selections will be used throughout the play—for example: during scene changes. The radio will then become another character in the play— setting the place and time of 1944 America. Short radio selections we hear now are:*

- *Andrews Sisters: "Don't Sit under the Apple Tree"*
- *General Eisenhower's D-day speech:* ". . . a landing was made yesterday on the shores of France . . ."
- *Kate Smith: "God Bless America"*
- *FDR's D-day speech:* ". . . our sons, pride of our nation, this day have set upon a mighty endeavor . . ."
- The Amos and Andy Show
- *Benny Goodman's "Let's Dance!"*)

Lily *has been turning stations—now seems satisfied with this big band swing—she listens—*

SCENE 1

*The Rockaway beach house. The living room. The first
Friday of the summer of 1944.*

As Lily *fiddles with the radio dial,* Gram *enters
down left. She calls straight out to* Lily. Gram *is not
angry, just a bit exasperated by* Lily. Gram *loves*
Lily *very much; while* Lily (*like some girls her age*)
sometimes sees Gram *as the enemy—constantly telling her what to do.* Gram *is really quite warm and
loving. Fate has cast her in the role of* Lily's *discipli-
narian.*

GRAM [*calling*][*facing the audience*][*not angry*][*instructions*]: LI-LY! . . . No radio! . . . Finish unpacking
first!

LILY [*calls back*][*her excuse*][*not unpleasant*]: I was
just checking to see if it worked!

GRAM [*calls*]: We've got work to do! And the Orbans
expect us at six o'clock!

LILY [*calls back*]: Okay!

[Lily *switches off the radio.* Gram *exits.* Lily *turns to
the audience—she speaks to us.*]

LILY [*to the audience*][*referring to the radio*]: Not
that much to listen to anyways . . . [*derogatory*] . . .
mostly war news. [*changes subject*][*happily excited*]
[*takes deep breath—joyously taking in her surroundings*]
Well, we made it! School's out! No more St. Albans! No
more homework! [*gesturing to her surroundings*] Rockaway Beach! The Atlantic Ocean! All summer long! I
love it! As Poppy would say—nothing ever changes
around here! [*enthusiastically explains*] We've been
coming out here ever since I can remember—Dad,
Gram, me and . . . [*stops herself*] . . . well . . . [*quickly*

crosses to her suitcase which has her book on it] Before Mom died, she pasted all these little stars above my bed back home in the city. So now, each summer, I always bring one star out here to the beach. [*has picked up her book—the book has a bookmark in it—the bookmark has one of her mother's stars pasted to it*] See? This year I pasted it onto my bookmark—for my summer reading. [*puts bookmark back into book—puts book down on chair*]

[*Upstage, unknown to Lily, Lily's father Mr. Jerry Mollahan (Dad) enters. He is carrying into the house more suitcases and his fishing pole. Lily's father is warm, kind, intelligent, caring and loving of his daughter, and has a strong sense of responsibility toward his daughter—particularly since his wife is dead. He is energetic, positive, and very likable. He and Lily are very close.*][*Dad is in shirtsleeves with a tie, suspenders, wire-rim glasses, and a summer fedora hat—like he may have just come from his office work.*][*Dad sees Lily—smiles, then puts down his load and quietly crosses over to the radio as Lily continues talking to the audience—unaware Dad has entered.*]

LILY [*continued*][*to the audience*]: Dad only gets to be here weekends. He works—civil engineer for the city of New York. . . . Imagine! Stuck all summer back on Two hundredth Street! [*enthusiastically explaining*] I mean—this house is right on the water!—right *over* the water—on stilts!—last one on the canal where the ocean fights with the bay!

[*With that, Dad has turned on the radio—loud—searches for a station he wants—quickly finds a big band swing sound he likes—happily/playfully turns to his daughter—laughing. Sound cue: Tommy Dorsey's "Opus One"*]

DAD [*turning the radio dial*][*to* Lily][*happily/playfully*]: Hey Lady, wanta dance?!

[Lily *spins around—sees her dad—laughs.* Dad *crosses downstage and grabs* Lily *to swing dance with her.* Lily *protests, but loves to dance with her father.*]

LILY [*protests, but really loves it*]: Dad . . .

DAD [*crossing downstage to her—grabbing her*][*having a great time*]: C'mon! Here we go!

LILY [*still protests, but loving every second of this*]: Dad . . . wait . . . we're supposed to be unpacking!

[*Radio blares loudly—they swing dance—both laugh. Finally,* Gram *again appears down left—calls again straight out.*]

GRAM [*facing audience—calling*][*again calling straight out, trying to be firm, but not really*]: Elizabeth Mary Mollahan! . . . I thought I told you—no radio!

[Dad *and* Lily *look at each other—can't help but laugh—knowing that they are in trouble—playing the mischievous children together. They stop dancing.*]

DAD [*stops dancing*][*calling straight out to his mom*][*laughing and apologizing*]: Sorry, Mom, that was me!

[Dad *and* Lily *look at each other—mischievous laughing*]

GRAM [*calling*][*reminding them*][*shaking her head—acting stern, but really amused by them*]: We are all supposed to be unpacking. Remember?

DAD [*calls to* Gram][*his excuse*][*crossing up to radio*][*trying not to laugh*]: Just wanted to see if there was any more news!

GRAM [*has to smile*]: Jerry Mollahan, you're as bad as your daughter.

[Gram *exits*. Dad *and* Lily *laugh*. Lily *happily falls back into the chair to rest*. Dad *has crossed up to the radio—turns it off*. Dad *hangs up his fedora hat on the hat rack*.]

DAD [*to* Lily][*enthusiastic*][*excited*][*energetic*]: Hey, what do you think, LilyBilly? Maybe our boys have finally made it off the beach at Normandy!

LILY [*bit unenthusiastic, but tries to hide it*]: Yeah, maybe.

DAD [*hearing his daughter's less than enthusiastic response*][*trying to get her as enthusiastic as he is*]: Hey, this is it! The big push!

LILY: I know.

DAD [*enthusiastic*]: Our army's landed in France! D-day! Now it's on to Paris—Berlin—and kick Hitler!

LILY: After three whole years, will this finally be the end of the war?

DAD [*admits*][*excited*]: Well, could be another year. But it's the beginning of the end!

[Dad *has picked up his fishing pole and sits on piano stool—casts. Meanwhile,* Gram *has entered—carrying her suitcase from the car—crossing the stage from left to right—not stopping*.]

GRAM [*to both of them—chiding them both a bit to get to work*]: And we'll all listen to what President Roosevelt has to tell us after dinner . . . [*pointedly reminding them so they get to work*] . . . at the Orbans'—at six! Remember?!

[Gram *exits down right with her suitcase.*]

DAD [*happily remembering*][*excited*][*not picking up* Gram*'s hint to get to work*]: Hey, that's right! Friday night! Dinner at the Orbans'! [*mimes casting his fishing pole*] [*excited*][*to* Lily] ... And all day tomorrow—fishing! [*laughs*][*joyful*] ... See? What did I tell you, LilyBilly?— nothing ever changes around here!

LILY [*laughs*]: You always say that.

DAD [*laughs*]: It's true!

LILY [*emphatic*]: Good! I don't want the war changing stuff!

DAD [*happily thinks*][*his list of proof*] : Fishing every Saturday.

LILY [*excited*]: And swimming!

DAD: And summer reading!

LILY [*happily remembering*]: Hey, I've got to get over to the library!

DAD: We'll make a summer reading list!

LILY [*enthusiastic*]: I love to read out on the pier!

DAD [*laughs*][*his point proven*]: See?! World can go crazy everywhere else. But here—nothing ever changes around here!

LILY [*laughs*]: Promise?

DAD [*laughs*]: Promise.

LILY: And promise you'll be here every weekend?

DAD: Fast as that train can get me here.

LILY: Wish you could be here all the time.

DAD [*teasing her*]: Hey, someone's got to do some work around here!

[Gram *has reentered—crosses to retrieve* Lily's *suitcase— picks it up*.]

GRAM [*picking up suitcase—dropping a broad hint for the two of them to help her by getting back to work*]: My sentiments exactly.

[*But neither* Dad *nor* Lily *pick up on* Gram's *hint*. Dad *is fiddling with his fishing rod and reel*. Lily's *imagination is running away*. Gram *puts down suitcase*.]

LILY [*thinking*]: Hey, Poppy?

DAD: Yeah?

LILY [*asks, bit nervous but also excited*]: Think there are any Nazi spies out here at the beach?

GRAM [*rolling her eyes*][*She's heard this before*.]: Lily . . .

DAD [*has to admit the possibility*]: Well, the Brooklyn Navy Yard is right across the way.

LILY [*to prove her point*][*in her defense*][*to* Gram]: With all the ships coming and going.

DAD [*repeating the warning on the posters*]: "Loose lips sink ships."

LILY [*her point proven*][*to* Gram]: See? I'm going to have to be on spy patrol all summer.

GRAM [*stern*][*instructions*]: *You* are going to practice your piano.

LILY [*protesting*]: Gram!

GRAM [*in charge*][*points at piano*]: Don't "Gram" me. Your father spent good money to have this piano shipped out here.

DAD [*asks*]: You like the piano, don't you, Lily?

LILY [*trapped, unenthusiastic*][*sits on stool*]: Yeah, I guess.

DAD [*remembering*][*smiles*]: You should have heard your mother. She played beautifully.

[Lily, *sitting on piano stool, idly runs her right hand up the piano—playing a C major scale.*]

[*Note: piano is mimed—Sound FX for scale. The piano is mimed downstage—Lily faces audience to play.*]

[*Sound FX: C,D,E,F,G,A,B,C*]

GRAM [*further instructions to* Lily]: Which takes practice—everyday—half hour, at least.

LILY [*protesting*]: Half hour?

GRAM: You heard me.

LILY [*being funny*][*sarcastic*][*à la headlines*][*her protest*]: "Brooklyn Navy Yard blows up; but Lily Mollahan plays perfect C major scale"!

DAD [*laughs*][*leans his fishing pole against the hat rack*]: Well, as Roosevelt says—find what you do best, and do your fair share.

GRAM [*picking up that sentiment*][*sarcastic*][*to get them both to help her get back to work*]: So why am I the only one still bringing in stuff from the car? [Gram *wearily exits left.*][Dad *laughs—realizing their mistake.*]

DAD [*to* Lily][*playfully getting* Lily *to join him at the car*]: C'mon "Sad-sack," you and me got "K. P."

LILY [*stands*][*complaining*][*being funny*]: When did I enlist?

[*Both start to exit stage left after* Gram.]

DAD [*changing the subject*][*asks* Lily]: So what have you and Margaret got planned for the summer?

LILY [*suddenly stops—remembering*]: Oh my gosh—Margaret!

DAD [*confused*]: Huh?

LILY [*quickly*]: I promised Margaret we'd go down to the beach—first thing!

DAD [*quickly asks*]: What about unpacking?

LILY [*quickly thinking*]: Cover for me! [*quickly kissing him goodbye*]

DAD: But . . .

LILY [*quickly*][*running out the door*]: Thanks! Bye!

[Lily *runs out.*]

DAD [*trying to call after her*]: Wait! What will I tell your . . . [*gives up*][*has to smile*][*then calls after her again*] Okay! But don't blame me if you get court-martialed and sentenced to the piano all summer! [*He laughs—watching her run off.*]

[*Music. Scene change. Crossover. As the set is being changed by the others,* Lily *crosses downstage and talks to the audience.*]

LILY [*to the audience*][*enthusiastic*]: Summer is a time to do a ton of fun stuff! So I'm not going to let Gram or the war change that. [*thinks, smiles*] That's why I like to go over to my friend Margaret's house. She lives just a couple of doors down—with two cats, her folks, and her older brother Eddie. [*thinks of* Eddie, *has to laugh*] Eddie is always so funny! I mean, every summer he . . . [*stops herself*] [*thinks*][*disappointed*] . . . well . . . this summer—Eddie's away—in the Navy. [*annoyed*] See? This war again! [*back to business*][*getting her enthusiasm back up*] Well, at least Margaret's still here—even if she does have this weird thing about getting too much sun. She always has to wear lots of "protection."

[*She laughs, crosses stage.*]
[*Segues into . . .*]

SCENE 2

Margaret's *house. The living room. Similar to* Lily's *house—but the dominant piece of furniture in the room is a large breakfront—*[*Note: reverse side of Mollahan radio*] *with drawers, doors, and a display shelf on top which has a framed photograph sitting on it. The photo is of a sailor* [Eddie's *photo*]. Margaret *is there. She is the same age as* Lily. *She is sweet and well-intentioned, but a bit flighty, gullible, and easily confused. She is all dressed for the beach—which means all covered up with beach robe, sunhat, sunglasses, and beach bag. Here—she is all excited.*

MARGARET [*to* Lily][*excited*]: Okay—before we go to the beach, I've got a ton of stuff to tell you! All secret!

LILY [*crossing into scene*]: What?

MARGARET: Promise not to tell.

LILY: I promise.

MARGARET: Swear on your aunt Celia's life.

LILY: Who?

MARGARET [*thrilled by the idea*]: You know—your aunt— the *spy*!

LILY [*remembering*][*embarrassed*][*obviously this was a lie*][*covering badly*]: Oh . . . yeah . . . right.

MARGARET [*excited by the thought*][*obviously believes Lily*][*gullible*]: That's so exciting!

LILY [*uncomfortable*]: Yeah . . . well . . . don't be telling anyone about that. It's top secret.

MARGARET [*accepting that*][*excitedly getting on with her own secrets*]: Okay—first—I want to show you something! [*She takes a small paper bag out of her large straw beach bag.*] I found this today.

LILY: What is it?

MARGARET [*holding up paper bag*][*excitedly announces*]: Candy!

LILY [*now also excited*]: A whole bag?!

MARGARET [*listing them*]: Hershey bars! . . . Milky Ways! . . . Life Savers! . . .

LILY [*grabs the bag—looks inside it*][*incredulous*]: There's a war going on. Where'd you get all this?!

MARGARET: My mom got it.

LILY [*spotting something she likes*]: Necco Wafers—
my favorite!

MARGARET [*grabbing the bag back*]: Not me! I'm
having something with chocolate!

LILY: Why did she buy all that?

MARGARET [*looking through candy in bag*]: She's sav-
ing it for Eddie.

LILY [*remembering about* Eddie]: Eddie?

MARGARET: Yeah, you know—in the Navy. He gets
everything.

LILY [*thinking of* Eddie][*obviously cares about what
happens to* Eddie]: Have you heard from Eddie lately?

MARGARET [*not concerned*]: No—overseas somewhere . . . [*But* Lily's *attention is drawn away from* Margaret, *and over to the eight-by-ten photo of* Eddie *on
the breakfront. She picks up the photo—looks at it—
remembering.* Margaret *just keeps on talking* . . .] . . .
My mom's going to send all this to him—in this heat!
Can you imagine?! One big melted mess by the time it
got there! [*finally notices* Lily *looking at photo*] Hey,
you listening to me?

LILY [*still looking at photo*][*not really listening to*
Margaret][*covers*]: Yeah . . . sure . . . sure.

MARGARET [*continues her search for the right
candy*][*excited*]: Maybe . . . maybe I'll have something
with nuts in it!

[Margaret *freezes looking into bag. Music underscores* Margaret's *freeze, entrance of* Eddie.]

LILY [*to the audience*][*still holding photo frame*]:
Margaret kept talking—as usual—but . . . well . . .
funny . . . all I could think about . . . was Eddie.

[Eddie *enters down left—stands there with duffel bag
on his shoulder—he freezes.* Eddie *is dressed in his
blue Navy uniform—seaman first class—with white
sailor hat. He is young—maybe nineteen—and extremely likable. He is fun, funny, always upbeat, and
loves to tease* Lily. *In fact, he and* Lily *have a very
close relationship: big brother—little sister. They love
to tease and poke fun at each other. No matter how
many times* Lily *may protest, you can tell she loves to
be teased by him. Now* Lily *misses him very much.
And* Eddie *misses her. Of course they would never admit it to each other—they are too busy playfully spar-
ring with each other. There is an easy, comfortable,
warm, fun feeling between them.*]

LILY [*continues, looking at photo*]: This picture was
taken last summer when he first went into the Navy.
[*thinks, has to smile*] I told my friends back at school
Margaret's brother wasn't just a sailor—he was on a secret mission—somewhere in Europe—you know, maybe
helped plan the whole invasion of France on D-day.

[Eddie *unfreezes—puts down duffel. To start, both* Eddie *and* Lily *talk to each other by looking straight out.
But very quickly, as each comes into sharper focus,
they turn and talk directly to each other—very comfortable and natural.* Eddie *even walks around the
room, at ease in his own home. Of course,* Lily *sees
and converses with him just fine. Poor* Margaret *doesn't
have a clue what's going on—she can't see* Eddie. *Eddie can't wait to tease* Lily—*just like always.*]

EDDIE [*laughs*][*teasing her*]: Lying again, huh, Mollahan?

LILY [*laughs*]: Am not!

EDDIE: Am too!

LILY: Am not!

EDDIE: Am too!

LILY [*having a wonderful time*][*playing tough*]: Take that back!

EDDIE [*having a wonderful time*][*playing tough*]: Make me!

LILY [*playing tough*]: I don't make trash, I burn it!

EDDIE [*playfully mocking her*][*challenging her*]: Ooooo! . . . Look out! She's tough! C'mon! Put 'em up! Put 'em up! [*crossing to her—starting a mock fistfight*]

LILY [*backing down*][*laughing*][*loving it*]: Hey, cut it out! Cut it out! [*Both laugh hysterically.*]

EDDIE [*to tease her*]: So, stealing my candy, huh?

LILY: Was not.

EDDIE: Was too.

LILY [*teasing him*]: You don't need it.

EDDIE: Good thing I showed up.

LILY [*sarcastic*][*laughing*]: Yeah, am I lucky!

EDDIE [*changes subject*][*to get her*]: So, what big fat lies you tellin' these days?

LILY [*acting innocent*]: Me?

EDDIE [*playfully mocking her*]: Me?

[*Suddenly* Margaret *unfreezes.*]

MARGARET [*to* Lily]: Hey, are you listening to me?

LILY [*not missing a beat*][*to* Margaret][*lying*]: Yeah,
sure . . . sure.

MARGARET [*still searching in bag*]: I definitely don't
want butterscotch. . . .

[Margaret *freezes.*]

EDDIE [*smiles at* Margaret][*rolls his eyes*][*laughs*]:
Poor Margaret, decisions, decisions.

LILY [*thinks*][*asks*][*bit more serious*]: Hey, Eddie?

EDDIE: Yeah?

LILY [*pondering*]: I wonder why you're in my thoughts
so much these days.

EDDIE [*unconcerned*][*tries to give her an honest answer*]: I don't know. Maybe it's cause you're in my house.

LILY [*accepting that answer for now*]: Yeah. I guess.
[*thinks*][*changing subject*] . . . Hey, what's it like?

EDDIE: What?

LILY: The war.

EDDIE [*teases her*]: That's restricted information,
Mollahan.

LILY [*pressing*]: C'mon. Were you at D-day? . . .
France? . . . The beach at Normandy?

EDDIE [*being a wise guy*]: Only beach I've been on is
Rockaway.

LILY [*protests*]: C'mon!

EDDIE [*laughs*][*avoiding the subject*][*asks*]: Shouldn't you be talking to Margaret?

[Margaret *unfreezes.*]

MARGARET [*taking candy bar from bag*]: So I guess I'll take this one! [*holding bag out to* Lily][*to* Lily] Okay—which kind do you want?

[Eddie *plops down into easy chair and puts his feet up.* Lily *looks at the bag of candy. Then she looks at* Eddie. Eddie *looks back at her as if to say "What are you going to do?"*]

LILY: I . . . ah . . . I guess . . . I . . . ah . . . I . . . [*decides*][*to* Margaret] You know—that's okay. I changed my mind. I don't want any.

MARGARET [*surprised*]: You don't?

LILY [*shakes head no*]: Naw.

[Lily *looks over at* Eddie. Eddie *is silently laughing at her. She knows she's been caught doing the right thing, so she playfully sneers at him.*]

MARGARET [*confused*]: Well . . . okay . . . [*looks at her own candy bar*] Guess I'll save this for later then. [Margaret *puts candy bar back into bag.*][*changing the subject*][*all excited*][*the big news*] Okay! Now it's time for the *really big secret*!

EDDIE [*playfully mocking his sister*]: Ooooo!

MARGARET [*her big moment*]: Here it is! . . . We're moving!

LILY [*shocked*]: Moving?!

EDDIE [*surprised*][*stands*]: Moving?

MARGARET [*explains*]: Till the end of the war. My dad got a job at a factory—Willow Run—building those airplanes . . .

EDDIE [*smiles*][*proud of his dad*]: All right, Dad!

MARGARET [*continues*][*explains*]: You know, B-24 bombers.

LILY [*not liking this news*]: When do you leave?

MARGARET: Tomorrow.

LILY [*dismayed*]: Tomorrow!

MARGARET: Just came to close up.

LILY [*disappointed*][*protests*]: What about our summer?

MARGARET: This is important—top secret!

LILY [*annoyed, disappointed*]: Yeah, I know, but . . .

MARGARET: I mean, it's not as good as your aunt being a spy.

EDDIE [*surprised*][*knows a lie when he hears one*]: A spy?!

MARGARET: In Berlin.

EDDIE [*to* Lily][*laughing—he's got her*]: Where?!

MARGARET: Or your cousin a general.

EDDIE [*laughing more*]: What?!

LILY [*to* Margaret *and* Eddie][*trying to lessen the lie*]: A *minor* general!

EDDIE [*chiding her—having a great time*]: Mollahan!

MARGARET: But my dad's helping.

EDDIE [*to* Lily][*playfully teasing her*]: You are such a liar!

LILY [*to* Eddie][*playfully*]: Shut up.

MARGARET [*having heard that*][*bit hurt*]: Well, thanks a lot.

LILY [*to* Margaret]: Not you.

MARGARET [*totally confused*]: Well, who are you talking to?

LILY: No one.

MARGARET: See? Knew you'd be mad. That's why I saved the best secret for last. Wait right there. [*She crosses over to breakfront, opens a drawer,* Margaret *freezes.*][Lily *crosses over to* Eddie.]

LILY [*to* Eddie][*acting annoyed*]: Will you get out of here!

EDDIE [*laughing*][*crossing over to his duffel bag*]: Don't worry. I can't listen to any more of this!

LILY: Good.

EDDIE [*laughing*]: Someday, Mollahan—your lies are gonna catch up with you.

LILY [*pretending she's not listening*]: You may still be talking, but I'm not listening.

[*Meanwhile,* Eddie *has reached into his duffel bag and taken out a second sailor cap. He quickly turns back to* Lily.]

EDDIE [*calls to her*]: Hey, kid—think fast! [*He tosses the cap to* Lily.][*She catches the cap.*] Nice catch . . . see ya!

LILY [*stopping him*][*bit worried*]: Hey, Eddie?

EDDIE: Yeah?

LILY [*honestly*][*asks*]: You'll still be coming around, won't you?

EDDIE [*laughs*][*picking up his duffel bag*]: Whenever you need me, kid.

LILY [*relieved*]: Good . . . See ya!

EDDIE [*laugh*][*waves*]: See ya!

[Eddie *exits.* Margaret *unfreezes.*]

MARGARET [*to* Lily][*confused*][*thought* Lily *was talking to her*]: What did you say?

LILY [*to* Margaret][*covering*]: Nothing.

MARGARET [*noticing sailor cap in* Lily's *hand*]: Hey, I see you've still got Eddie's hat.

LILY [*caught*][*explains it away*]: Oh . . . yeah . . . comes in handy . . . you know . . . my disguise—for spying. [*She puts on cap.*]

MARGARET [*not really listening*][*excited about her last secret surprise*][*She has taken something from drawer; now it's behind her back.*][*excited*]: Anyway, are you ready? This is the best secret!

LILY: What?

MARGARET [*holds out a key on a string to* Lily]: This is for you! The key to our back door!

LILY: Huh?

MARGARET: Even though the place will be boarded up, you can still sneak in here any time you want!

LILY [*taking key*][*taken aback*]: Really?

MARGARET: A secret place—a place to be all alone.

[Margaret *freezes.* Lily *turns to the audience, crosses down to talk to the audience.*]

LILY [*to the audience*][*unhappy*][*complains*][*bit annoyed*]: All alone. [*thinks*][*bit dismayed*] This summer's getting off to a bad start.

[Margaret *unfreezes—exits.*]

[*Scene change. Music. As scene changes behind her,* Lily *talks to the audience.* Lily *crosses down center.*]

LILY [*changing the subject*][*new energy*]: At least that first week went by pretty quick—and before you knew it, it was Friday again! That meant that Poppy would be on the six o'clock train along with the rest of the refugees from the city.

[*Unknown to* Lily, Albert *has entered—carrying his suitcase—wearing his coat and hat like at the top of the show. He has a piece of paper in his hand, glancing at it periodically—looking around him—seemingly searching for some place.*]

LILY: Sometimes he'd bring a new book. And he'd always talk about the fish we were going to catch—either

off the pier or sometimes we'd take the deep sea char-
tered fishing boat way out into the Atlantic to . . .

[Albert *has crossed to* Lily—*interrupting her*—*asking
for directions. Music out.* Albert *speaks with a slight
Hungarian accent. He seems a bit brusque, harried—
he can sometimes cover his uncertainties by acting
overconfident.*]

ALBERT [*lost—asking directions*][*in English and
Hungarian*]: Pardon . . . I . . . ah . . . [*forgets, speaks
Hungarian*] . . . meg tudna mondani hol von* . . .
[*remembers he's speaking Hungarian, changes to English*] . . . I . . . ah . . . I was looking for . . . Cross
Bay Boulevard? . . . [*pause*][Lily *just stares at him—
thinking of the possibility that he could be a Nazi
spy.*][Albert *is puzzled.*] . . . Understand? . . . [Albert
stares back at her—*waits*—*grows annoyed that she is
staring at him*—*finally, he gives up*][*impatient*][*annoyed*] Never mind . . . I'll find it myself . . . Kos-
zonum† . . . [Albert *starts to exit, mutters under his
breath*][*derogatory*] . . . Amerikai.

[Albert *exits—looking back at* Lily—*annoyed and
puzzled by her strange reaction.* Lily *has been looking
at him suspiciously—thinking—then she looks straight
out at us. Music. Scene has changed. We are at . . .*]

SCENE 3

The Rockaway Beach house. The living room. Dad *is
there, just returning from work—taking off hat, taking
off coat, putting down briefcase, etc.* Lily *has quickly*

*Can you tell me, where is . . .
†Thank you

crossed into the scene. Dad *gets his fishing pole leaning at coat rack.*

LILY [*to* Dad][*thinking of the possibility*]: . . . so maybe he was a Nazi spy—right here in Rockaway.

DAD [*has to smile at her*]: Why would you think that?

LILY: Well . . . he dressed really weird . . . asked all these questions . . . *and* he spoke a foreign language!

DAD [*not convinced*][*has to smile*]: I'm not sure that means he's a spy.

LILY [*not deterred*][*thinking*][*sits in chair*]: Yeah . . . well . . . I'm keeping my eye on him.

DAD [*with his fishing pole—plays with it—casts*] [*changing the subject*][*happily breathes the air*][*thinks, asks . . .*][*sitting on piano stool*]: Heard from Margaret yet?

LILY [*shakes head no*][*disappointed*]: No. She's probably too busy doing secret war stuff. [Lily *idly plays with her sailor hat.*]

DAD [*has to laugh*]: If it's Margaret, won't be secret long.

LILY: Wish she were still around.

DAD [*sympathetic*]: I know, Sweetheart—but . . . well . . . her dad thought it was his duty to go.

LILY [*not convinced*]: I know.

DAD: We should all do our part, you know.

LILY [*bit defensive*]: We do.

DAD [*bit evasive*][*something on his mind*]: Well . . . lately I've been thinking—maybe we could do something more.

LILY [*examples to prove they are doing their part*]: Gram and I started our victory garden—should be tons of tomatoes and stuff by August.

DAD [*not convinced*]: Well, that's good, but . . .

LILY [*cuts him off*] [*more examples*]: We always use our food rations book—no gasoline—scrap metal drives—always pull down the blackout curtains . . .

DAD [*stopping her*][*carefully*]: No, I'm talking about something *I* could do.

LILY: What? [*pause*][Dad *puts down fishing pole.*]

DAD [*seriously*]: Lily . . . [*pause*]

LILY [*apprehensive*][*fearing the worst*]: Yes? [*pause*]

DAD [*trying to be gentle—knowing she'll be upset*]: I'm going to join the army.

LILY [*her worst fear*][*scared*]: No!

DAD: I feel it's something I have to do.

LILY [*adamant*][*quickly*]: You were deferred—army said!

DAD: Lily, I *want* to go.

LILY [*adamant*]: No. Mama's gone. You have to stay here!

DAD: Gram can take care of you.

LILY [*hates the idea*]: Gram?!

DAD: Lily, listen to me . . .

LILY: But . . .

DAD: Listen. The Nazis are murdering people over there.

LILY [*petulant*]: What's that got to do with us?

DAD [*reasoning*]: Would you want them to come over here?

LILY [*petulant, whining*]: I don't care! I'm sick of the war!

DAD [*trying to reason with her*]: It'll be over soon. The Allies have landed in France and . . .

LILY [*to stop him*][*cuts him off*] [*vehement*]: Good! Then they don't need you!

DAD [*calmly explaining*]: The army needs engineers. Right behind all the destruction will be people like me—the builders. We'll put Europe back together.

LILY [*angered*][*hurt*]: But you promised nothing would ever change around here!

DAD: I'll write you every week.

LILY: But I won't even know where you are!

DAD: Sure you will.

LILY: The army censors cross everything out!

DAD: Then I'll find a way to let you know. I promise. [*From offstage, Gram calls.*]

GRAM [*calling*]: LI-LY!

DAD: I report tomorrow.

LILY: Tomorrow?!

DAD: Yes.

LILY [*grabbing another reason he can't go*]: Well, Gram won't like it!

DAD: Lily . . .

LILY. She won't let you go!

DAD: Lily . . . she knows. [*slight pause*]

LILY [*hurt*]: You told Gram first? [Gram *enters—looking for* Lily.]

GRAM [*entering*][*to* Lily][*not unpleasant*]: Lily, I thought you were going to set the table.

[*Pause.* Lily *looks at both of them—hurt.*]

LILY [*to both of them*][*accusing*][*anger, hurt*]: The two of you knew—all along—and didn't even tell me?!

GRAM [*realizing* Lily *now knows*][*to* Dad][*gently*]: Jerry, I thought we were going to tell her after dinner.

DAD [*to* Lily][*quickly*][*sincerely*]: Lily, I love you—more than Rockaway—more than anything!

LILY [*hurt, angered*]: But you promised me! You promised!

DAD [*searching for what to say*]: Lily . . . I . . .

LILY [*starting to cry*][*angry, hurt*]: Fine! Go! I don't care! I'm used to being left all alone! First Mama, now you! Well, I don't care, see? I don't care!

[Lily *runs out.* Dad *and* Gram *look at each other. Music. Scene change.*]

SCENE 4

The Pier. The next morning. Lily *enters—sits on pier—she has* Gram's *old afghan over her shoulders. She is still upset, sad, hurt—thinking.*

Dad *slowly enters. Seeing him,* Lily *purposely lies down and closes her eyes—obvious to both that she was awake.* Dad *has his coat and hat back on. Music underscores.* Dad *stands there looking at his daughter a bit, then decides to try to somehow speak to her.*

DAD [*to* Lily][*gently*][*crosses to her*][*knowing she is not asleep*]: Hey there ... you awake? [*no response*][Lily *purposely pretends to be asleep.*][Dad *decides to continue anyway.*][*searching for what to say*] I ... ah ... I just wanted to say goodbye ... Got to report to the recruiting office.... [*no response*] [*pause*][*tries again*] You awake? [*pause*][*continues*] [*slowly—lovingly explaining*] Lily, I'll be back next summer. You'll see—everything will be the same. [*no response*][*gently, lovingly*][*understandingly*] After I'm gone you might feel bad you didn't open your eyes.... Don't, okay?—I know you love me. [*pause ... then ...*] [*sadly, lovingly*] Bye ... I love you. [Dad *sadly exits.*] [Lily *opens her eyes—there are tears in them. She sits up.*]

LILY [*to audience and herself*] [*chiding herself*]
[*sad*]: I . . . I kept my eyes closed. . . . I kept my eyes
closed. . . . Why did I do that?

[*Music. Scene change.*]

SCENE 5

*The Rockaway Beach house. The living room. Bit
later that morning. Gram is there. She is hanging a
star in the front window of the house. (Blue star sewn
on small white banner with red trim.) Lily has crossed
into living room. She is carrying her book—drops
afghan onto back of chair. Lily is still upset from earlier. She watches Gram hang star.*

LILY [*still upset*][*acting annoyed, but feeling guilty*]
[*to* Gram]: Gram, does the whole world have to know
our business? Why do we have to hang that stupid star in
the window? It's dumb. The soldiers don't care. [Lily
plops down—sits in chair.]

GRAM [*calmly, gently explaining*][*to try to comfort* Lily]:
The stars aren't for the soldiers, Lily. They're for us. They
tell the world that someone we love is overseas. They tell
everyone—we wait. [*sympathetically to* Lily] Waiting can
sometimes be the hardest thing in the world to do. [Lily
sadly looks at her star on her bookmark.][*sincerely, understandingly, lovingly*] Sometimes it's good to let others know
you miss someone. It helps ease the pain. [*pause*][Lily *is
moved—wishes she could tell* Gram *her sadness, but . . .*]

LILY [*looking to get away*][*avoiding*][*sadly*][*referring
to her book*]: I . . . ah . . . I got my summer reading to catch
up on. [Lily *exits.*][Gram *watches her go—concerned.*]

[*Music. Scene change.*]

SCENE 6

The Pier. Later. Albert *is there—sitting on the pier—
no longer with same old coat. He has pencil and paper on his lap. He sits there sometimes just gazing out
over the water—thinking—lost in thoughts—seemingly kind of sad—then he writes something on his
pad of paper.* Lily *enters with her book. She spots*
Albert—*she stops—annoyed by his being there.*

LILY [*to the audience*][*annoyed*][*referring to and
looking at* Albert]: Darn! There he is again! . . . that foreign kid! . . . sitting in my favorite spot on the pier. No
fair! . . . [*She watches him a bit.*][*then notices . . .*] Hey,
wait a minute. . . . He's watching the ships . . . [*music:
chord*][*cue: spying underscore music*] . . . writing
down troop movements—to send back to Nazi head-
quarters! [*music: chord*] I knew it! He *is* a spy! [*music: chord*][*thinks*] Okay . . . maybe . . . maybe I'd better
be sure. [*gets idea—takes sailor cap—puts it on—low to
kind of cover her face—starts to slowly inch forward to
spy on* Albert. *Suddenly stops herself.*][*a new thought*]
[*concerned*][*to herself*] Hey, wait. . . . What if he has a
gun? [*music: chord*][*dismisses it*][*acts brave*][*fantasiz-
ing*] So what . . . ? "She died a hero!" . . . Then Dad will
be sorry he left . . . yeah! [*music: underscore—sneaking
up behind* Albert][Lily *inches closer behind* Albert *to
see what he is writing.*][Lily *gets closer, but* Albert *finally turns and sees her.* Lily *tries to act noncha-
lant.*][*music out*][Lily *to* Albert][*bit nervous to be
caught*] Oh . . . ah . . . hello . . . ah . . . [*trying to act non-
chalant*] . . . nice day to be sitting out on the pier, isn't
it . . . watching the ships and all. . . . [*catches herself*]
[*bit nervous*][*covers badly*] . . . oh . . . ah . . . not that
you were—watching the ships, I mean . . . I mean . . .
they're so far out there . . . ah . . . I mean . . . ah . . .

[*Meanwhile, the sound of an airplane coming over-
head has started—soft at first but growing very loud.
Cue: Sound FX: airplane motor.* Lily *looks up and*

*off left—finally notices the airplane coming closer—
flying over the beach. Grateful to be changing the
subject. Not concerned.*]

LILY: Oh . . . hey . . . gosh . . . that plane's coming in
really low, isn't it? [Albert *has now taken notice of the
airplane too, but his reaction is very different—acting
very nervous.*] . . . Man, they should be more careful,
you know—someone could get hurt.

ALBERT [*growing more and more nervous*][*He
stands—to get a better look.*]: Yeah . . . someone could.

LILY [*not understanding* Albert's *fear*]: Huh?

ALBERT [*now starting to panic, overreacts*][*builds*]:
Coming in low . . . too low . . . Take cover! . . . it's an
attack! . . . Air raid! Air raid! . . . [Albert *tries to duck
down behind a crate.*]

LILY [*simultaneously with* Albert][*trying to calm* Albert *down*][*fast*]: No! . . . No! . . . It's all right! . . . It's
not an enemy plane! . . . It' s one of ours! See?! . . . one
of the trainer planes from the naval base! . . . they do that
sometimes—fly too low, I mean. . . . but it's all right!

ALBERT [*simultaneously with* Lily][*in a panic*][*crouch-
ing down to protect himself*] : Air raid! . . . quick, take
cover! . . . get down! . . . get down! . . . you could get
killed, you fool! . . . get down! . . . it's an attack! . . . air
raid! . . . air raid! . . .

[*sound FX: airplane—fades away*]

LILY [*calming him down*][*slowing down*]: It's all right . . .
it was one of ours . . . everything's okay . . . See? . . .
it's okay.

[*Pause.* Albert *slowly stands.* Albert *looks embarrassed. Finally, he grabs his paper and pencil—exits*

by brushing past Lily—*seemingly angered, rude, scared. He is gone.* Lily *watches him go—puzzled. Music. Scene change.*]

SCENE 7

The Rockaway Beach house. The living room. Lily *is sitting at piano bench, forced to practice—playing scales.* Gram *is there—watching/listening. Sound FX: piano—scales: C,D,E,F,G,F,E,etc.*

LILY [*while mimes playing piano—scales*][*to* Gram] [*frustrated*]: I'm telling you—he's a Nazi spy.

GRAM [*calmly disagreeing*][*explaining*]: He is not. His name is Albert; and he's Mr. and Mrs. Orban's nephew, just newly arrived the other day—visiting for the summer—from Canada. [Lily *stops playing.*][*end cue*]

LILY [*not buying it*]: He wasn't speaking Canadian.

GRAM [*explaining*][*takes sailor hat off* Lily's *head— hangs it up at rack*]: Hungarian. He became a refugee from Hungary after his parents were killed. Now he lives with another aunt up in Canada. The Orbans hope the beach will help their nephew forget this terrible war. [*noticing*][*referring to piano playing*] . . . And why did you stop?

LILY [*complains*]: Been a half hour.

GRAM: It has?

LILY: More.

GRAM [*giving in*]: Oh . . . all right. [Gram *sits in over-stuffed chair, takes out sewing from her sewing basket next to the chair.*]

LILY [*referring to* Albert]: Well, I don't trust him. There's still a war on, you know.

GRAM: Even in the worst of times, something lovely can happen.

LILY: What?

GRAM [*explains*]: Margaret's gone, but you can be friends with Albert.

LILY [*derogatory*][*refusing*]: Friends with *him*?!

GRAM [*gently chiding her*]: Lily.

LILY [*gets coin purse out of* Gram's *sewing basket*] [*changing the subject*][*to escape*]: Going down to Sherman's bakery.

GRAM [*trying to stop her*]: Now don't be spending your money on . . .

LILY [*cutting her off*] [*heard this before*][*stubborn*] [*holding up her coin purse*]: My money! My Christmas, snow shoveling, allowance money.

GRAM [*reminding her*]: Supposed to last all summer.

LILY [*annoyed*]: I know.

GRAM: Don't come crying to me come August.

LILY: I won't. [Lily *starts to exit—is stopped by* Gram's *voice.*]

GRAM: And see if the mailman is on his way.

LILY: Okay.

GRAM: Maybe we'll get another letter from Poppy.

LILY: Maybe.

GRAM: Did you get those books he suggested?

LILY [*shakes head no*]: Don't know why he said *Madeline*—he read that to me when I was five.

GRAM [*more to herself*] [*worried*]: Wish we knew if he's crossed overseas yet.

LILY: I'll get *Three Musketeers* tomorrow.

GRAM: Tomorrow?

LILY: Library closed early today.

GRAM [*concerned*]: Is it that late already?

LILY: Yeah.

GRAM [*getting up—crossing to radio—turning it on*]: Well why didn't you tell me? *Portia*'s on! [Gram *fiddles with the radio, while* Lily *turns, talks to the audience.*]

LILY [*to the audience*]: Gram loved the soap opera *Portia Faces Life*.

[*cue: radio—changing channels*]

GRAM [*fiddling with the radio knob*][*to* Lily][*excited*]: Maybe Walter is rescued today!

LILY [*to audience*][*explains*]: Portia's husband was a prisoner in a Nazi camp. Now he's escaped—in a rowboat on the ocean.

GRAM [*still fiddling with radio knob*][*excited*]: Maybe some Allied ship will pick him up!

LILY [*to audience*][*bit derogatory, but has to smile*]: See? The war—gets into everything. [Lily *exits with her coin purse.*]

[*Sound FX cue: radio show:* Portia Faces Life *music . . . announcer:* "Grape Nuts Cereal *presents* Portia Faces Life . . ." *Having found her program,* Gram *happily, excitedly sits back in her chair, gets out her sewing. Then* Gram *gets an idea—looks around to see if anyone is watching, then—puts sewing back into sewing basket—takes out a Milky Way candy bar—starts to unwrap it as she leans in to listen closely to her favorite radio program. Music. Scene change. Crossover. As scene changes,* Lily *first crosses downstage, talks to audience—then* Lily *crosses over to the pier and steps up onto it.*]

LILY [*to audience*]: Poppy's been writing to us like he said he would. [*puzzled*] Lately he's been suggesting that I read all these books—like: *Madeline—The Three Musketeers—Tale of Two Cities.* [*has to smile*][*holding book with her "star" bookmark*] Guess my bookmark with Mom's star will get a real workout this summer. [*crossing up and sits on end of pier on a crate*][*She opens her book—starts to read. Segues into . . .*]

SCENE 8

The pier. Lily *is sitting there, reading. From offstage, we hear the sound of two boys shouting—fighting.*

BULLY [*offstage, then entering*][*shouting*][*meanly taunting*]: Hey . . . c'mon boy! . . . Over here! . . . What's the matter, huh? . . . C'mon! . . . C'mon, dummy!

ALBERT [*offstage, then entering*][*shouting*][*angry*]:
Hey, stop that! . . . Put her down! . . . Let her go, I said . . .
Let her go!

LILY [*to herself*] [*looking up from her reading*][*annoyed*]: Now what?

[Bully *has run on—looking back over his shoulder—egging on* Albert *to chase him. He carries a cloth sack tied together at the top with something inside the sack. He crosses toward the pier.*]

BULLY [*running—looking back*][*taunting*][*mean*]:
Hey, c'mon! . . . c'mon! . . . Over here, boy! . . . C'mon,
dummy! . . . You want it? . . . Here it is! Over here!

ALBERT [*running—following*][*angry*]: Cut it out, I
said! . . . Let her go! [Albert *stops—seeing the* Bully
standing on the pier.]

[*The* Bully *now is standing on the far end of the pier,
holding the sack up and out over the water end of pier.
He is taunting* Albert—*threatening to drop the sack
into the water.* Albert *has stopped—nervous he'll
drop it.*]

BULLY [*meanly taunting* Albert][*fast*][*holding sack
up and out over back edge of pier*]: Uh-oh . . . better
look out! . . . I think I might drop it! . . . Uh-oh . . . it's
slipping . . . it's slipping, . . . Uh-oh . . . look out . . .
look out, . . . [*He purposely drops sack into water—
behind pier.*][*meanly sarcastic*]: Oh no! . . . Right into
the water!

ALBERT [*screams*]: No!

BULLY [*taunting* Albert][*meanly laughing*]: Better go
get it, DUMMY! [Bully *meanly laughs.*][Bully *quickly
runs off—exits.*]

LILY [*annoyed*][*confused*][*to* Albert]: Hey, what is this?

[Albert *quickly runs up onto the pier, looking into water where the sack was dropped.*]

ALBERT [*running up onto the pier*][*in a panic*][*looking where sack dropped*][*fast*]: No! . . . No! . . . She's in the water!

LILY: Huh?

ALBERT: I can't swim!

LILY: What?

ALBERT [*mispronouncing*]: A cot! A cot!

LILY [*not understanding*]: A cot?

ALBERT [*frantic*]: She'll drown!

LILY [*finally understanding*]: A *cat*?!

ALBERT [*fast*][*frantic*]: Yes!

LILY [*gets an idea*][*quickly*]: Oh my gosh! Here! Maybe I can grab it before it sinks!

ALBERT: C'mon! . . . Hurry up! . . . Hurry!

[Lily *kneels on pier, reaches down over the back edge of the pier—trying to reach the sack. Lily's coin purse—which was sitting on the pier—gets knocked off the pier and down into the water. She tries to grab it, but too late.*]

LILY [*grabbing for her coin purse*][*dismayed*][*fast*]: Oh no! . . . My coin purse! . . . It fell in! . . . All my money!

ALBERT [*impatient*]: Forget it! . . . C'mon! . . . Hurry up! . . . Get the bag! Get the bag!

LILY [*fast*]: Wait! . . . I got it! . . . [Lily *is back sitting up on pier—holding up the sack.*] . . . I got it! . . . See?! . . . Told you I'd get it!

ALBERT [*fast*][*impatient*][*rude*][*demanding*]: Here! . . . Quick! . . . Give it to me! [Lily *is holding the sack.* Albert *rudely grabs it, quickly opens it, and looks inside.*] . . . She's got to be all right! She's got to be alive!

LILY [*stands*][*sarcastic*][*annoyed at* Albert's *rudeness*]: Well . . . "you're welcome"! . . . I mean, don't "thank" me or anything!

ALBERT [*fast*][*looking into sack*][*relieved but still worked up*]: She's alive! . . . She's still alive!

LILY [*quickly getting an idea*][*fast*]: Hey! We'd better take her someplace quick to get warm and dried off and stuff!

ALBERT: Where?

LILY [*fast*]: I know! A secret place! And they used to have lots of cats! C'mon!

[Lily *quickly starts to lead* Albert *off. Music. Scene change.* Albert *runs off.* Lily *stops down left, talks to the audience. Crossover. Set changes, as* Lily *crosses downstage left, talks to audience.*]

LILY [*to the audience*][*frustrated*]: Can you believe it?! . . . My money! . . . My coin purse and all my money! . . . Gone! . . . somewhere at the bottom of the ocean! . . . Great! . . . Hope Gram doesn't find out—I'll never hear the end of it. [*By now, set has changed to . . .* Margaret's *house: the living room.*] [Lily *crosses center into the scene, looks around.*] Gosh, it . . . it was kind of weird being in Margaret's house—without Margaret . . . you know . . . all alone.

[*We are at . . .*]

SCENE 9

Margaret's *house. The living room.* Eddie *is there—he sneaks up behind* Lily.

EDDIE [*playfully*][*to* Lily][*commenting on* Lily's *last remark*][*laughs*]: All alone?

LILY [*glad to see him but acts like she isn't*][*sarcastic*][*to tease him*]: Oh great . . . might have known you'd still be here.

EDDIE [*sarcastic*][*laughs*][*to tease her*]: Oh, excuse me—but you're in *my* house.

LILY: No. You're in *my* head!

EDDIE [*laughs*]: Either way—not my fault.

LILY [*frustrated*][*doesn't really mean it, but . . .*]: Go away.

[Eddie *laughs—plops down onto the stool which he has placed right in the middle of the room—to be in the way. He watches as* Albert *enters the room. Sometimes during the following scene,* Eddie *playfully tries to distract and tease* Lily. Lily *tries to ignore him.* Albert *enters the living room. Of course, he doesn't see* Eddie.]

ALBERT [*entering*][*to* Lily][*bit brusque*][*It seems like he isn't comfortable / doesn't want to make friends.*]: The cat is drinking the milk I got her.

LILY [*to* Albert]: Oh . . . ah . . . that's good.

ALBERT [*looking around*]: Hey, what is this place?

LILY: My friend Margaret lives here—but she and her family are gone.

ALBERT: Why?

LILY: Her dad got this really . . . [*stops herself*] . . . I mean . . . they're just gone.

ALBERT [*pressing*]: Why?

LILY [*bit annoyed*]: It's the war, okay?

ALBERT [*more to himself*] [*bitter*]: Like Budapest— people just disappear.

LILY: Huh?

ALBERT: Nothing.

LILY [*looks at* Eddie]: I can come here whenever I like. [*to* Albert] . . . just don't tell my grandmother. [*pause*] [*Both are a bit awkward with each other.*][*finally . . .*] . . . so . . . you're staying with the Orbans?

ALBERT [*explains*][*bit awkward*]: Just for the summer. The Orbans are my aunt and uncle. Rest of the year I live with my other aunt—up in Canada.

LILY: Oh.

[*Another pause, bit awkward. Lily and Eddie exchange looks. Finally . . .*]

ALBERT [*uncomfortable*][*wishing she would leave*]: You don't have to stay here, you know.

LILY: I don't mind.

ALBERT [*rude, brusque*]: Look. Go home. I'm going to take care of the cat myself.

LILY [*bit annoyed*]: Oh? And how do you plan on getting back in here?

ALBERT: Huh?

LILY: I have the key.

ALBERT [*bit commanding*]: Give it here.

LILY: No.

ALBERT: I'll feed the cat myself.

LILY: We'll do it together.

ALBERT: No.

LILY [*annoyed*]: My cat too! I saved her!

ALBERT [*commanding*][*rude*][*strong*]: I said *I'll* do it!

LILY [*angered*][*right back at him*]: Fine! I'll leave the key under the back steps!

ALBERT: Fine!

LILY [*annoyed*][*sarcastic*]: Don't you ever say "thank you"? Or isn't that in the Hungarian dictionary?

ALBERT [*Hungarian*][*not really meaning thank you*]: "Koszonom"—means "thank you."

LILY [*sarcastic*][*annoyed*][*not meaning it*]: "You're welcome!"

[*Pause. Both don't know what to say next . . . then . . .*]

ALBERT: I think the cat is going to be okay.

LILY: Why would anyone want to kill a defenseless kitten?

ALBERT [*hitting a sore spot for* Albert][*passionate, angered*]: Because bullies think they can rule the world!

LILY [*agreeing*]: Like the Nazis.

ALBERT: Yes.

LILY [*blurts out*]: Did the Nazis really kill your parents?

ALBERT [*surprised*]: How did you . . . ?

LILY: My grandmother told me. [*pause*]

ALBERT [*shakes head yes*][*begrudgingly*]: My parents ran a newspaper. They spoke out against the Nazis. . . . Now they are gone.

LILY: Well, my parents are too. I mean, my dad's still alive, but he left to join the army.

ALBERT [*suddenly angered again*][*bitter*]: If they loved us, our parents should still be here—to take care of us!

LILY [*trying to think*][*defensive*]: Well . . . my father didn't want to leave me, but . . . well . . . he's . . . [*got it*][*lying again*][*pushed by* Albert's *brusque attitude*] He's on this really important secret mission somewhere in Europe.

EDDIE [*surprised*][*amused*]: What?

ALBERT [*not buying it*][*rudely dismissing it*]: Is not.

[Eddie *is laughing at* Lily. *She is trying to ignore him.*]

LILY [*defensive*][*to Albert*]: Is so! In fact, he wants me to join him!

ALBERT: What?

LILY: Yep! I'm going to go to Europe too!

ALBERT [*interested*]: How? When?

LILY [*lying*]: Some night. [*explains*][*laying it on*] . . . You know how the ships from the Navy Yard form a convoy way off shore?

ALBERT: They do?

LILY [*continues*][*quickly*]: Well, I'm going to row out there—jump overboard—then swim to a ship. They'll be forced to rescue me. And they won't have time to bring me back—there's a war on, you know!

ALBERT [*wanting to believe it*]: You could really do that?

LILY [*brags*]: Of course.

ALBERT: Get all the way to Europe?

LILY: Sure.

ALBERT: Would you take me out there to see the ships?

EDDIE [*to Lily—mocking her*][*laughs*]: Uh-oh.

LILY [*surprised*]: What?

ALBERT [*insistent*]: I just want to see!

LILY [*hesitating*][*trying to get out of being caught in lie*]: Oh . . . well . . . ah . . . I don't know. It's . . . ah . . . it's kind of dangerous.

ALBERT [*challenging her*]: Or it's a *lie*.

LILY: Is not!

ALBERT [*insistent*]: So take me.

LILY [*trapped*][*finally giving in*][*annoyed*]: All right. We'll go some night I can get the rowboat.

ALBERT: Good. [*pause*][Eddie *laughs at* Lily—*she gives him a warning look.*] . . . So . . . I'll go home now. [*remembers*] . . . But leave the key under the stairs. [*getting ready to leave*] . . . so . . . see you tomorrow. . . . And we will talk more about "swimming" to Europe.

LILY [*wishing she hadn't said any of her story*]: Yeah . . . sure.

[Albert *exits.* Lily *is alone.* Eddie, *having watched all this, has to laugh—just to tease* Lily.]

EDDIE [*laughing*][*mocking her*][*to tease her*][*He applauds her.*]: Hey, way to go, Mollahan! That probably has to be the biggest lie you have ever told! [*He laughs.*]

LILY [*caught*][*annoyed*]: Oh . . . go away.

[*Frustrated,* Lily *exits.* Eddie *laughs. Music. Scene change. Crossover during scene change.* Gram *crosses downstage. She is calling to* Lily—*looking straight out over audience. She has one of Poppy's letters in her hand. She refers to letter.*]

GRAM [*straight out over audience*][*calling to* Lily] [*looking at letter in her hand*]: Lily . . . your father writes he's shipping out . . . but of course he can't say to where. [*puts letter down*][*more to herself*] I do hope that he is safe. [*back to letter*] Oh, and he asks if you've read . . . ah . . . [*reads*] *The Hunchback of Nôtre Dame—A Tale of Two Cities—*or *My Promise.* [*more to herself*] *My Promise?* . . . never heard of that book before. [*waits for a response, but gets none from* Lily][*calls*] Lily? [*still no response*][*again calls—suspicious*] Lily, did you practice your piano today? [*no response*][*calls*] LI-LY! [*Still no response—*Gram *gives up.*][Gram *exits.*]

[*Music continues. . . . Segues into . . .*]

SCENE 10

The rowboat. Late one night. Lily *and* Albert *are in the boat—*Lily *is rowing. Both are wearing life vests.* Albert *holds up a lantern.* Lily *wears her sailor cap. Both are a bit combative with each other.*

LILY [*stops rowing*][*nervous*][*annoyed*]: If Gram finds out I'm way out here in the middle of the ocean this time of night, she'd kill me.

ALBERT [*holding up lantern*][*looking into the distance*]: Is that one of the ships?

LILY [*looks*][*annoyed*]: No, that's a Coast Guard Cutter. And keep the light down, would you? We're not even supposed to be out here.

ALBERT [*impatient*][*bit demanding*]: C'mon, keep rowing.

LILY [*right back at him*][*firm*]: This is far enough.

ALBERT [*insistent*]: I want to get closer.

LILY: You can see from here.

ALBERT [*insistent*]: C'mon.

LILY [*refusing*]: You want the boat swamped by some big Navy ship?

ALBERT [*mocking her*]: So? I thought you were this great swimmer?

LILY: *You* can't swim, remember?

ALBERT [*begrudgingly admits*]: I know.

LILY [*firm*]: We'll wait right here.

ALBERT: So when do the ships come?

LILY: They'll be here.

ALBERT: When?

LILY [*the last word*]: They'll *be* here. [*pause*]

ALBERT [*pointing out into the ocean*]: Look.

LILY: What?

ALBERT: If you draw a line straight out there . . .

LILY: Yes?

ALBERT: Europe.

LILY [*laughs*]: Yeah, 'bout a million miles.

ALBERT: But it's there . . . [*thinks*][*pensive*] . . . and I have to get back.

LILY [*puzzled*]: Get back? I thought you escaped? [*pause*]

ALBERT [*finally admitting*]: My younger sister Ruth is still there.

LILY [*surprised*]: Your sister?

ALBERT: In France—near Paris.

LILY [*confused*]: But . . . how . . . ?

ALBERT [*explains*]: My Grandmamma had me and Ruth smuggled out of Hungary.

LILY: Your grandmother?

ALBERT [*sadly*]: Grandmamma wouldn't leave Budapest . . . now she may be dead.

LILY: But how did you leave your sister behind in France?

ALBERT [*upset—obviously touched upon a sore spot*] [*defensive*][*annoyed*][*overreacts*]: Ruth and I were just separated—by mistake! It was an accident, okay?!

LILY [*retreats*]: Okay. Okay.

ALBERT [*angry with himself*]: But Grandmamma told me—always stay together! As long as we were together, we were a family! [*pause*][Albert *calms down a bit.*][*finally . . .*][*asks*] . . . Lily?

LILY: Yes?

ALBERT: Teach me how to swim.

LILY [*nervous that she knows the answer*]: Why?

ALBERT [*determined*]: So I can go with you—when you swim out to the ships—so I can get back to Ruth.

LILY [*trying to think of an excuse*]: You . . . you can't swim at all?

ALBERT: There's no ocean in Budapest—only a river—the Danube.

LILY [*avoiding*]: Well . . . I . . . I don't know.

ALBERT [*insistent*]: You have to.

LILY: But . . . it would take so long.

ALBERT: How long?

LILY: Long.

ALBERT: How long?

LILY: Weeks! Months!

ALBERT [*determined*]: I'll learn fast! . . . We'll go together. . . . I won't slow you down. [*asks*] . . . What do you say? [*pause*]

LILY [*avoiding*][*starts to pick up the oars*]: It's late. We should be getting back.

ALBERT [*grabs oar*][*strong*][*stopping her*]: Please?

LILY [*avoiding*][*annoyed*]: We'll see.

ALBERT [*determined*][*strong*]: No, you'll see. We'll come out here together—jump overboard—swim to a ship—and I will get back to Ruth. . . . You'll see.

[Albert *again picks up lantern—looks out over the water.* Lily *starts to row—regretting her lies. Music. Scene change. Crossover during scene change.* Lily *crosses downstage to talk to audience.*]

LILY [*to audience*][*berating herself*] : Me and my big mouth! Eddie's right! I'm just a big fat liar! [*in disbelief*] Swim out to a convoy?! . . . What is he—crazy or something?! . . . You'd get killed! [*thinks*][*takes off life jacket*] Okay. If I stall long enough, he'll forget all about it. [*She tries to look hopeful.*] I hope. [*pause*][*changes the subject*] Anyway . . . [*takes a letter in envelope out of her pocket— holds it up*][*happily*][*crosses down right*] Today I got a letter from Margaret. [*starts to take letter out of envelope, refers to it*][*laughs*] What a mess . . . the worst handwriting . . . [*opens letter, happily reads*] "Dear Lily, please send Eddie's picture to me right away. Navy telegram says he's missing in action. . . . D-day." [*puts down letter*] [*in shock*][*getting more upset, worried, sad*] Eddie? . . . missing? . . . no . . . no, it must be some kind of mistake.

[Gram *runs in—hurried—looking for* Lily. *She seems upset. She has her hat and purse and carries her rosary. She also has* Lily's *hat and rosary.*]

GRAM [*calls from offstage*]: LI-LY! . . . [*quickly enters*][*spots* Lily][*hurried, but trying to sound calm*] [*crossing to her*] Lily . . . here . . . [*giving* Lily *hat and rosary*] . . . hurry dear, here's your hat and rosary. Come on, we're going to church.

LILY: Why?

GRAM [*worried*]: Mrs. Dillon called. Poor little Eddie Dillon is missing in action. [*resolved*][*quickly*] We're going to pray, Lily—pray very hard. [*starting to exit*] Come along—quickly now.

[Gram *exits.* Lily *looks worried—she puts on her church hat. Music. Scene change.*]

SCENE 11

The church. Gram *and* Lily *are there—kneeling—facing the audience.* Gram *is silently saying her rosary.* Lily *is also silently saying her rosary, but then decides she has to say a special prayer for* Eddie. *We hear* Lily's *prayer.*

LILY [*prays*][*out loud*][*worried*]: Dear God, I know I'm supposed to be saying my rosary—but I can't—I mean—I just wanted to say—please let Eddie be all right. Okay?

[Gram *gives* Lily *a warning look.* Lily *quickly goes back to silently praying her rosary.* Eddie *enters to the side. He looks at* Lily, *a bit puzzled, has to smile—then he crosses over and stands next to her—another chance to tease her.* Lily *is praying, but glances over—sees him. She tries to pray harder to get* Eddie *out of her mind. She stops—she looks over again at him. He is still there.*]

EDDIE [*laughs*][*to* Lily][*happily*][*casual, as always*]: Hey kid.

LILY [*quieting him*][*annoyed*][*uncomfortable*]: Shhh!!!

[Lily *looks at* Gram—*nervous.* Lily *tries again to pray—trying to ignore* Eddie. Eddie, *as always, sees this as a wonderful opportunity to have some fun and give* Lily *a hard time.*]

EDDIE [*not to be denied*][*happily*][*loves teasing her*]: Hey, Mollahan?

LILY [*stage whisper*][*gives up trying to ignore him*] [*annoyed*]: What?

EDDIE [*playing innocent—to torture her*]: What's up?

LILY [*stage whisper*][*annoyed*][*wishing he would go away*]: What are you doing here?

EDDIE [*laughs*]: You tell me.

LILY: Go away.

EDDIE: Why?

LILY [*frustrated*]: I'm trying to pray for you!

EDDIE: Me?

LILY: Yes.

EDDIE: Why?

LILY: You're missing.

EDDIE [*laughs*][*to tease her*]: I am?

LILY: Yes.

EDDIE [*laughs*]: I'm right here.

LILY [*explains*]: "Missing-in-action." D-day.

EDDIE [*laughs*][*dismissing it*]: Oh that.

LILY: Yes, that!

EDDIE [*casual*]: I wouldn't worry.

LILY: No?

EDDIE [*shakes head no*]: Naw!

LILY: Why?

EDDIE: You know the navy—probably some other Eddie.

LILY [*thinks*]: Gee, didn't think of that.

EDDIE [*laughs*]: Or I probably just decided to hang out on the beach for a while.

LILY [*relaxing*][*laughs*]: Or—you're such a dimwit—probably just got lost!

EDDIE [*laughs*]: Or went "A-wall" to see Paris!

LILY [*laughs*]: That's it! [*They both laugh.*]

GRAM [*hearing* Lily *laugh*][*annoyed—turns to her*] [*quieting her*]: Lily! . . . Shh!

[*Caught,* Lily *quickly stops laughing.* Eddie *has to smile—amused he got her into trouble. Pause.* Lily *pretends to pray—determined not to listen to* Eddie *anymore.* Eddie *accepts the challenge—gleefully.*]

EDDIE [*to tease her more*]: Hey kid.

LILY [*sharp, firm*]: Shh!

EDDIE: Hey, Mollahan . . .

LILY: Go away!

EDDIE: Question.

LILY [*annoyed*]: What?

EDDIE [*acting innocent*]: Aren't you supposed to be sending my photo to Margaret?

LILY: So?

EDDIE: How?

LILY: I'll mail it.

EDDIE: How?

LILY: The post office.

EDDIE: With what money?

[*Pause.* Lily *realizes that she has no money.*]

LILY [*deadpan*][*realizing*][*flat, deadpan*][*starts small to build*][*slowly*]: Oh . . . my . . . gosh.

EDDIE [*enjoying himself*] : All your money's at the bottom of the ocean.

LILY [*same deadpan*][*getting bit bigger*]: Oh my gosh.

EDDIE [*having a wonderful time reminding her*]: And you can't ask your Gram for the money cause then she'll know you've been breaking into my house.

LILY [*same deadpan*][*getting bit bigger*]: Oh my gosh.

EDDIE [*smiles*][*the topper*]: And the post office closes in two hours.

[*Pause.* Lily *is in a panic. She doesn't know what to do. Finally, she decides she'd better get out of here and do something. She quickly ends her prayers—loudly.*]

LILY [*loudly*][*quickly*]: Dear God—I guess that's all!—AMEN! [*quickly turns to* Gram— *giving her rosary to* Gram] . . . Bye, Gram, gotta go!

GRAM [*startled*]: What?

LILY [*already up and running out*]: See you back at the house! Bye! [Lily *runs out.*]

GRAM [*calling after her*][*annoyed*]: Elizabeth Mary Mollahan! Come back here!

[*Too late*—Lily *is gone.* Eddie *laughs. Music. Scene change. Crossover during scene change.* Lily *crosses down left.* Albert *is there.* Lily *is in a panic.*]

LILY [*to* Albert][*quickly*]: C'mon! Quick! We have to get down to the pier!

ALBERT: Why?

LILY [*quickly*]: We have to get some of my money I dropped in the water!

ALBERT: That's crazy!

LILY: Why?!

ALBERT [*fast*]: It's at the bottom of the ocean!

LILY [*never say die*][*quickly*]: So? I'll dive for it!

ALBERT [*strong*]: It's gone, Lily! Forget it!

LILY [*determined*]: I can't! I need money now! [Gram *enters to side—calls straight out.*]

GRAM [*calling*]: LI-LY! . . .

ALBERT [*quickly asks*]: This money—is it important?

LILY [*emphatic*]: Yes!

GRAM [*calling again*][*reminding* Lily]: YOU SHOULD BE PRACTICING! [Gram *exits.*]

ALBERT [*quickly*][*to* Lily][*trying to be reassuring*]: Look. Go home. I'll meet you there.

LILY: But . . .

ALBERT [*quickly*]: I have an idea about the money. Go!

[Albert *quickly exits*. Lily *crosses over to the . . . Music. Scene change.*]

SCENE 12

The Rockaway Beach house. The living room. Lily is practicing the piano—playing scales—but too fast. Gram is there watching/listening. Sound FX: piano—scales [fast].

GRAM [*to* Lily][*instructions*]: Not so fast, Lily. And try to keep the fingers curved . . . both hands . . . Good . . . [*thinks*][*takes church hat off* Lily's *head—hangs it on rack*] Lily, don't you have something else to practice besides scales? [Lily *stops playing.*]

LILY [*frustrated*]: Gram.

GRAM [*encouragingly*]: Look in your John Thompson book. I'm sure there's some piece in there. [Lily *mimes opening music book on piano, flipping through the book, looking.*] . . . Something you haven't tried before . . . new challenges . . . there's nothing you can't do.

LILY [*stops, finds something in music book she likes*]: Hey . . . hey, I know . . . how about this?

[*Hesitatingly,* Lily *starts to play "The Blue Danube Waltz." Sound FX: piano: "Blue Danube Waltz"—played badly.*]

GRAM [*approving*][*listening*]: Oh . . . that's nice . . . yes . . . "The Blue Danube Waltz." What made you pick that?

LILY [*thinking about* Albert, *but doesn't say*][*just shrugs*]: In the book.

GRAM [*approving*]: Well, it's very nice. [Lily *hits a clinker.*] Or—it will be.

[Albert *comes in. He is carrying his coat he had on when he arrived in Rockaway.* Gram *turns and greets* Albert *happily. It is obvious that* Gram *likes* Albert.]

. . . Oh . . . hello there, Albert. [*quickly to* Lily] Lily, keep practicing.

ALBERT [*happily*][*obvious he likes* Gram *too*]: Hello, Mrs. Mollahan.

GRAM [*asks*][*referring to* Albert's *coat*]: Expecting snow?

ALBERT: Huh?

GRAM: Your coat.

ALBERT [*avoiding*]: Oh . . . well . . . never know.

GRAM [*changing the subject*][*referring to* Lily]: What do you think of our virtuoso here?

ALBERT [*hearing* Lily *playing badly*][*trying to be diplomatic*]: Oh . . . ah . . . sounds . . . ah . . . sounds pretty good.

GRAM [*knowing he's being polite*][*smiling*]: Nothing that a little practice couldn't cure.

ALBERT [*smiling back at* Gram]: My sister used to play "The Blue Danube Waltz" [*trying again to be diplomatic*] . . . but not quite like that.

LILY [*catching his tone—laughs*][*while still playing*] [*to be funny*]: Yeah. I'm better, right?

GRAM [*a gentle reminder to concentrate on the piano*]: Lily.

ALBERT [*laughs*][*fondly remembering*][*to* Gram]: You remind me of my grandmamma, Mrs. Mollahan—always telling my sister Ruth to practice.

[Lily *finishes playing "The Blue Danube Waltz."*]

GRAM [*bit more serious*][*understandingly*]: Your aunt told me about your family, Albert.

ALBERT: Yes . . . but I will see them again—someday.

GRAM [*bit sad*]: Seems we all have someone over there we miss.

ALBERT [*smiles at her*]: But I like your American custom of putting stars in the window.

GRAM [*agreeing*][*smiles*]: Yes. A star to guide them home, hmm?

ALBERT [*bit sad but trying to cover it*]: Well, I have no home—so no window.

GRAM [*warmly, sincerely to* Albert]: Just because you have no star in a window, Albert—doesn't mean you don't miss someone. You can still let others know what you're feeling. [*pause*][*Both look at each other.*]

ALBERT [*warmly to* Gram]: My grandmamma told me I would see her again someday. [*looks at* Gram] [*warmly*] . . . Maybe today . . . I do. [Gram *warmly puts her hand on* Albert's *shoulder.*]

LILY [*breaking the mood*][*fast*][*impatient*]: Okay! I'm done! Can I go now?!

GRAM [*covering*][*changing the subject*]: Yes . . . I . . .
I think my radio show is coming on now anyway.
[*She crosses up to her overstuffed chair—sits—looking
worried.*]

LILY [*quickly*]: C'mon, Albert. We've got things to do,
right?!

ALBERT [*remembering*]: Oh . . . right. [*starts to
leave—stops—looks back at* Gram—*seeing she is sad*]
[*sincerely, warmly*][*trying to sound positive but also
sad*] . . . Don't worry, Mrs. Mollahan—soon the Allies
will march into Paris—and then Berlin . . . and everyone
we love over there is going to be okay. I know it.

GRAM [*trying to be positive, but sad*]: Yes . . . yes . . .
I-I'm sure you're right, Albert. [Gram *turns on radio—
announcer:* ". . . six thousand new casualties as the Allies push towards Paris." Gram *quickly changes the
station. She looks back at* Albert.] . . . We'll pray the
stars guide everyone safely home.

[Gram *sadly listens to* Portia Faces Life—*looking
worried, lost, sad, and alone.* Albert *and* Lily *are
looking at* Gram. Lily *had never thought of* Gram *being lost or sad. Scene change.*]

SCENE 13

Margaret's *house. The living room. Immediately following.* Lily *is watching as* Albert *is ripping open the
seam of the inside lining of his coat.* Eddie *quietly
watches the whole scene upstage.*

ALBERT [*as he is working—ripping open seam of coat
lining*]: The day I left Budapest, I found Grandmamma

sewing my coat. When she gave it back to me, it crackled. She said—when I wore it—to always remember her. [*He pulls out paper money from coat.*] See? . . . See? . . . I have money, Lily—hidden in the coat—Hungarian forints, French francs, English pounds, American dollars . . .

LILY [*amazed*]: Oh, Albert!

ALBERT: You can have some of the dollars.

LILY [*starting to protest*]: No Albert, your grand-mother . . .

ALBERT [*finishing her sentence*]: . . . would have wanted this—for Eddie.

[*Pause.* Lily *takes some of the dollar bills.*]

LILY [*grateful*]: Thank you . . . [*corrects herself*] I mean . . . [*Hungarian*] . . . "koszonom."

ALBERT [*has to smile*][*referring to her speaking Hungarian*]: You're learning. [*He puts the coat on—puts rest of money in pocket.*] . . . See? . . . Someday I will wear this coat—and I will find Ruth. [*pause*][*more serious*] . . . Lily?

LILY: Yes?

ALBERT [*again—asks*]: Teach me how to swim.

LILY [*trying to refuse*]: Albert . . .

ALBERT [*quickly*]: Please?

LILY [*avoiding*]: We . . . we have to get to the post office.

ALBERT: And after that—the ocean—for swimming lessons.

LILY: No.

ALBERT [*pleads*]: Lily.

LILY: No.

ALBERT: Lily, please.

LILY [*relenting*]: No . . . not the ocean—the bay.

ALBERT: Huh?

LILY [*explains*]: Ocean's too rough. Water on the bay side is better.

ALBERT [*not satisfied*][*impatient*]: Lily, I have no time! Summer's half over! The ocean!

LILY [*firm*]: The bay! Take it or leave it.

[*Pause. Albert* thinks, then . . .]

ALBERT [*agreeing*]: The bay. [*He celebrates.*][*hysterically happy*] Yes! I can see France now! . . . and you'll meet Ruth! . . . and she'll play "The Blue Danube Waltz!" . . . better than you! . . . [*laughs*] And we'll teach her crazy American songs, like . . . [*sings*][*being silly*] "You gotta accentuate the positive! Eliminate the negative . . ." [*He finally notices* Lily *sadly looking at* Eddie's *photo.*][*He stops, asks* . . .] Hey, what's the matter?

LILY [*sadly looking at* Eddie's *photo in her hand*]: Nothing. Just trying to say goodbye. [*to photo*] Be just a little bit missing Eddie, okay?

[*Pause.* Lily *looks sad.* Albert *tries to cheer her up.*]

ALBERT [*excited*]: Hey . . . c'mon! We're going to France!

[*Music. Scene change. Crossover during scene change.* Lily *crosses/steps up onto pier. She is calling out swimming instructions to* Albert.]

LILY [*calling out swimming instructions to* Albert] [*insistent*][*loud*]: Kick! Kick! Feet! Feet! Kick! Kick! . . . [*trying another tactic*] Maybe just try floating first! [*watching*][*He does it wrong.*] No . . . no . . . no . . . ! [*She talks to the audience.*][*referring to* Albert][*frustrated*] "Thick as a piece of wood!" . . . Sister Eileen would say. [*confides in us*] Albert was a terrible swimmer. And you could tell he was afraid of the water. [*back to* Albert] [*calls out*] No! . . . keep your head up! . . . try again! . . . every day! . . . half hour every day! [*hears herself*] [*comments to herself*][*frustrated*] Now I'm starting to sound like my grandmother! [*to audience*] We spent weeks at it! But he was never going to learn how to swim.

[*Segues into . . .*]

SCENE 14

The pier. Later in the summer. Albert *quickly enters.*

ALBERT [*entering*][*having heard her*][*insistent*]: Yes, I will! How else will I get back to Europe?!

LILY [*to* Albert][*firm*]: No, Albert! Forget it! You're not going with me! You can't swim!

ALBERT [*pleading*]: I'll get it!

LILY: No!

ALBERT: A few more lessons!

LILY: Summer's almost over, Albert!

ALBERT: I know!

LILY: I can't wait any longer!

ALBERT: I'm better than I was!

LILY: No, you're not!

ALBERT: I'll wear my lifejacket—that'll help!

LILY: And your heavy winter coat—you'll sink!

ALBERT: But I have to take my coat!

LILY: See? You are crazy!

ALBERT: You'll think of something.

LILY: I did. You're not going!

ALBERT: But I have to!

LILY: No, you don't *have* to!

ALBERT: Yes, I do!

LILY: Why?

ALBERT: Cause I have to!

LILY: Why?!

ALBERT [*practically yells*]: Cause I *lied*, okay? [*pause*][*then, finally . . . sadly . . .*] . . . I lied. [*pause*]

LILY [*slowly*][*not understanding*]: You . . . lied?

ALBERT: Yes.

LILY: About what?

ALBERT: Ruth.

LILY: She's . . . she's not in France?

ALBERT: She is.

LILY: Then . . . what?

ALBERT [*hesitant*]: If . . . if I tell you . . . you have to promise not to tell anyone.

LILY: Okay.

ALBERT [*admitting*]: It's not easy—having to live with a lie.

LILY [*feeling uneasy*]: Yeah . . . I guess.

ALBERT: How would you know? You've never lied.

LILY [*feeling guilty*][*uneasy*]: Oh . . . well . . . I . . . ah . . . I wouldn't exactly say that.

[Lily *sits down on pier. Pause.* Albert *starts his story, slowly at first.*]

ALBERT [*starts*]: Lily . . . I . . . I was afraid . . . afraid of the Nazis. They killed my mother and father. Now they were marching into France.

LILY: Well . . . did you and Ruth get to a boat?

[*Segues into flashback sequence. The docks in France, 1940. Music. Sound FX:* (*same as opening prologue*) *We hear the sound of a loud whistle blast from an ocean liner—followed by the sounds of a large crowd of people. Announcements are heard over a bad pub-*

*lic address system—first in French: "Attention, atten-
tion . . . etc. . . . ."—then in English.*]

ALBERT [*narrates*]: We made it to the docks in
France—the boat was leaving the next day—the last
one to cross the Atlantic before the Nazis arrived. But
Ruth was so sick. She had a fever, and these . . . these
spots . . .

LILY: Chicken pox?

ALBERT: No.

LILY: The measles?

ALBERT: That's it. [*continues*] I tried to hide it from
the authorities, but . . . [*The severe male* Immigration Officer *enters with clipboard—busy with papers—
brusque—he freezes.*] The immigration officer—he
said—Ruth could not get on the boat. He said she would
make everyone else sick—that he was going to call the
Sisters of Wisdom to take Ruth to the hospital! [*A Nun
enters—stands upstage—she freezes.*] I begged him to
let her go! But he said Ruth would have to stay! I . . .
I didn't know what I should do! . . . [Albert *sits on
a crate.*][*The* Immigration Officer *and the* Nun *are
upstage of* Albert. *They cannot see his face.*] That
night, I fell asleep on a bench in the waiting area. [*sitting there with his eyes open*][*worried, upset*] That's
when they came . . . they came for Ruth . . . I heard
them . . .

[Officer *and* Nun *unfreeze, just upstage of* Albert.]

OFFICER [*abrupt, rude, commanding*][*impatient*][*to*
Nun][*arguing with the* Nun][*with a slight French accent*]: The boat sails as scheduled! There's nothing to
discuss! Take the girl!

NUN [*remaining calm, in control*][*her point of view*] [*also with a slight French accent*]: I agree she should be in hospital but . . .

OFFICER [*cutting her off*] [*abrupt, rude, impatient*] [*commanding*]: Then just *do it!*—before she infects everyone!

NUN [*sympathetically explaining*]: She would be safer leaving the country.

OFFICER [*bitter*]: We all would! She stays!

NUN [*calmly resolved*]: Then I'll take her to our convent outside of Paris. [*looks at* Albert][*sympathetically*] . . . Is this the young man?

OFFICER [*nods yes, but . . .*]: So?

NUN [*concerned*]: Well, shouldn't we wake him?

OFFICER [*cold*]: Why? Why should he stay and get killed just cause of her?

NUN [*firm*]: We should at least try to tell him.

OFFICER [*begrudgingly*][*annoyed*]: All right! All right! . . . If he's awake. [*Music starts to underscore— slowly, then grows.*][Officer *crosses downstage a bit to* Albert.][Albert *has been listening—eyes open. Now he suddenly shuts his eyes on purpose—purposely pretending to be asleep.*][Officer *halfheartedly calls to* Albert.][*begrudgingly, annoyed*] Hey, boy? . . . Hey, boy, you awake? . . .

NUN [*also tries—gently*]: Young man? . . .

OFFICER [*calls, annoyed*]: Hey, boy? . . . Monsieur?! . . . hey, boy? . . . hey, boy? . . .

[*Music grows—louder, more intense.* Officer *and* Nun *freeze.*]

ALBERT [*still sitting there on the crate, his eyes are still closed*][*narrating*][*very upset*][*admitting*][*angry at/ashamed of himself*]: I . . . I . . . I kept my eyes closed! . . . I kept my eyes closed! . . . I . . . I let them take her! . . . I didn't even say goodbye! . . . [*He stands, opening his eyes—there are tears in them.*][*very agitated, upset*][*It finally pours out of him.*][*a bundle of emotions—angry, sad, upset, crying*][*rather fast*] I . . . I got on the boat! . . . I left her! . . . I abandoned her! . . . my own sister! . . . How could I do that? . . . How could I do that? . . . Grandmamma said stay together . . . But I didn't . . . I left her! . . . I abandoned her! . . . Sometimes . . . sometimes . . . when I try to go to sleep, I . . . I can hear her! . . . I can hear her calling me! . . .

[*He is listening as music, sounds, and* Ruth's *own voice calling him—all grow unbearably loud. Sound FX:* Ruth's *voice.*]

RUTH'S VOICE [*on tape*][*young girl's voice*][*calling*][*frightened*][*getting louder, more frantic*]: *Albert? . . . Albert, where are you? . . . Albert? . . . I can't find you? . . . Albert! . . .* [*screams*] *ALBERT!!!!!*

ALBERT [*can't take it anymore*][*angry, frightened, hurting*][*screams out*][*to make it all stop*]: *NOOOO!!!!!!!!*

[*Sound FX: loud boat whistle blast. Suddenly, All music, sound FX, voices end. Silence.* Officer *and* Nun *have quickly exited during boat whistle. We are back at the present. The pier.* Lily *is there.* Albert *is crying.*]

ALBERT [*continues*][*crying*][*to* Lily]: Don't you see? . . . Don't you see? . . . I . . . I have to get back there . . . I have to get back to Ruth. [*pause*]

LILY [*moved*][*at a loss for what to say*]: Oh, Albert . . .

ALBERT [*sincerely*][*to* Lily][*crying*]: When I left Hungary, I felt so alone. . . . so alone. . . . Grandmamma told me someday I would find a friend . . . a good friend . . . [*looks right at* Lily] It's almost as if she knew about you.

[*Pause.* Lily *feels terribly guilty, and ashamed of her lies. She decides to be honest with* Albert.]

LILY [*hesitant*][*ashamed*][*admitting*][*quietly*]: No . . . no, I'm not a very good friend, Albert.

ALBERT: Huh?

LILY: But I want to be.

ALBERT: Why aren't you?

LILY: Because friends shouldn't lie to each other.

ALBERT [*confused*]: What?

LILY [*finally admitting*]: Albert . . . I lied.

ALBERT: What?

LILY: I *LIED TOO*.

ALBERT [*confused*]: But . . .

LILY [*explains*]: I should never have told you we could cross the ocean.

ALBERT [*getting alarmed*]: What?

LILY [*faster*][*admitting it*]: It's impossible! I mean—there's no way for anyone to row way out into the ocean—jump into the water and swim to a ship! . . . I mean, it's crazy! I don't know why I even said it!

ALBERT [*doesn't want to believe this is true*]: No . . . no, it's not true!

LILY: Albert, listen to me . . .

ALBERT [*desperate, angry*]: No . . . no, you're lying!

LILY: I'm not!

ALBERT [*hurt, angry*]: I thought you were my friend!

LILY: I am!

ALBERT [*hurt, upset, angry*][*accusing*]: You just think I can't do it!

LILY [*trying to calm him*]: No.

ALBERT [*more and more agitated*]: You think I am a coward!

LILY: Albert . . .

ALBERT [*angry, hurt*][*fast*]: Well, I'll show you! I don't need you! I'll do it myself! I'll find Ruth! You'll see! You'll see! [Albert *runs out.*]

LILY [*calling after him*]: Albert . . . no . . . wait!

[*Music. Scene change.*]

SCENE 15

Margaret's *house. A bit later.* Lily *is there—sitting in chair—downhearted.* Eddie *enters carrying his duffel—spots* Lily—*puts down duffel—crosses over to her. He sees that she is downhearted, but uses humor to help.*

EDDIE [*upbeat, as usual*]: Hey, Mollahan . . . what's the matter?

LILY [*feeling sorry for herself*][*pouting*]: Everybody hates me.

EDDIE [*laughs*][*to tease her*]: True. But how did you finally figure it out?

LILY [*discouraged*][*pouting*]: I lied to Albert. Now he doesn't want to be my friend. I never even said goodbye to my own father. Now he hates me.

EDDIE [*not buying it*]: How do you know that?

LILY: Well . . . he never tried to tell me where he is overseas.

EDDIE [*to tease her*]: Oh . . . Well, I guess you're right.

LILY: Huh?

EDDIE [*to tease her*]: Everybody hates you.

LILY [*frustrated*][*still pouting*]: See? . . . I'm glad at least you're still around . . . even if you are a dimwit.

EDDIE [*sarcastic*]: Gee—thanks.

LILY [*feeling sorry for herself*]: At least I have someone to talk to.

EDDIE [*laughs*]: But that's just it, Mollahan—came back to tell you I'm outa here!

LILY: Huh?

EDDIE: This is goodbye.

LILY: Goodbye?

EDDIE: I won't be back.

LILY [*dismissing it*][*sarcastic*]: Yeah, right.

EDDIE: No, I mean it.

LILY [*getting worried*]: Really?

EDDIE: Yep.

LILY: Why?

EDDIE [*laughs*][*to tease her*][*playfully*]: Why? Cause you are probably the dumbest kid on all of Rockaway Beach, that's why!

LILY [*playfully*]: Am not!

EDDIE: Am too!

LILY: Take that back!

EDDIE [*playfully mocking her*]: Ooo—she's tough!

LILY: Why am I dumb?

EDDIE: Cause!

LILY: Cause why?

EDDIE: Cause lots of stuff!

LILY: Like what?

EDDIE: Like—you can't even figure out your dad's already told you where he is!

LILY: Has not!

EDDIE: Has too!

LILY: When?

EDDIE [*his list*][*quoting from* Dad's *letters*]: "Dear Lily, please read: *The Three Musketeers, The Hunchback of Nôtre Dame, Tale of Two Cities*" . . . [*quoting/mocking* Lily] . . . "Gosh, why does Poppy want me to read *Madeline*?" . . .

LILY [*seeing the light*][*excited*][*the answer*]: France!

EDDIE [*You got it.*]: Bingo!

LILY [*happily excited*]: All those books take place in France!

EDDIE [*laughs*]: About time, Mollahan!

LILY [*excited*]: He kept his promise!

EDDIE: See? *My Promise!*

LILY: He's in France!

EDDIE: You got it!

LILY: I finally figured it out!

EDDIE [*laughs*][*to tease her*]: Well, don't get too stuck on yourself!

LILY: Why?

EDDIE [*laughs*][*to tease her*]: Cause you're still dumb!

LILY [*playfully challenging him*]: Am not!

EDDIE: Am too!

LILY: Smarter than you!

EDDIE [*really egging her on*]: Oh yeah?

LILY [*right back at him*]: Yeah!

EDDIE: Really?

LILY: YEAH!

EDDIE [*laughs*][*the punch line*]: Then why haven't you figured out yet that I'm dead? [*pause*]

LILY [*shocked*]: What?

EDDIE [*laughing*][*got her*]: See? . . . You hadn't figured on that one, had you, Mollahan?

LILY [*in shock*][*trying to deny it*]: You . . . you can't be.

EDDIE: Why not?

LILY: You're . . . you're missing in action.

EDDIE [*laughs*]: All these months? C'mon! Face facts, kid! I'm not comin' back!

LILY: No . . . you . . . you have to.

EDDIE [*smiling*]: I'm out of here!

LILY: Eddie . . .

EDDIE: It's true!

LILY [*emphatic*]: But I'll *miss* you! [*pause*]

EDDIE [*bit taken aback*][*shocked she would say it out loud*][*moved*]: Really?

LILY [*bit embarrassed to say it out loud, but means it*]: Yeah . . . really.

EDDIE [*recovers*][*back to his old kidding self, but moved*]: Well, tell you what, kid—hang another star in the window. [*pause*]

LILY [*seriously*]: Eddie?

EDDIE: Yeah?

LILY [*seriously*]: I'm never going to forget you.

EDDIE [*bit embarrassed*][*trying to be lighthearted*]: Aw, sure ya will.

LILY [*seriously*][*sincerely*]: No, I mean it—I won't.

EDDIE [*smiling at her*]: Memories fade, kid. But that's okay. I'm the past. You should concentrate on the living. Like Gram says—let the people around you know how you feel. [*pause*][Lily *is thinking, then* . . .]

LILY [*slowly*][*starting to see the light*]: Hey, Eddie?

EDDIE: Yeah?

LILY [*a new resolve*][*quietly*][*slowly*]: I . . . I have to go find Albert. [*pause*][Eddie *smiles at her, happy she gets it.*]

EDDIE [*laughs*][*happy for her*][*He turns to go.*][*crosses to/picks up duffel bag*]: And I'm outa here! You don't need me hangin' around anymore!

LILY [*knowing he must leave*]: Eddie, don't go.

EDDIE [*duffel onto shoulder*]: I'm shipping out, Mollahan.

LILY [*simply smiles*][*looking straight out*]: Hey, Eddie?

EDDIE [*stops*][*looking straight out*]: Yeah? [*pause*]

LILY [*slowly*][*simply*][*sincerely*][*lovingly*]: Thanks.

EDDIE [*smiles*][*slowly*][*sincerely*]: See ya, kid.

LILY [*slowly*][*bit sad*]: Yeah . . . see ya.

[Eddie *slowly turns and exits.* Lily *sadly watches him go. Music. Scene change.*]

SCENE 16

The pier. Immediately following. Albert *enters—wearing his old coat and hat and lifejacket—carrying an old knapsack. He looks like he is getting ready for a journey. From offstage,* Lily *calls frantically to* Albert.

LILY [*offstage*][*calling frantically*]: Albert! . . . Albert, wait! . . . [*She runs on stage. She is carrying her book with her mom's bookmark.*][*She sees* Albert *is going to try to row out to sea.*][*She crosses to him.*][*frantic*][*quickly*] . . . Albert, what are you doing?

ALBERT [*continues to get ready for trip*][*stubborn, unreasoning*][*quickly*][*determined*]: Get away from me!

LILY: Albert, stop!

ALBERT [*tying on his lifejacket*][*angry*]: Get out of here! Go home!

LILY [*grabbing him by the lifejacket*]: No, Albert! Don't do it!

ALBERT [*quickly*]: I just want to see the ships, that's all! I just want to see the ships!

LILY [*pleading*]: No, wait! Don't go, Albert!

ALBERT [*hurt, determined*][*pushes her away*]: Leave me alone, will you! You're not my friend!

LILY [*grabbing him*]: But I want to be! Please!

ALBERT: Let me go! I can't wait anymore!

LILY: You could kill yourself!

ALBERT [*determined*]: I have to find Ruth! I won't just abandon her like my parents did!

LILY: They didn't abandon you!

ALBERT [*bitter, angry*]: They did!

LILY [*strong*]: They cared!

ALBERT [*yells*][*almost starting to cry*]: No! If they cared, they'd still be here!

LILY [*passionately*][*fast*][*strong*][*It finally just pours out of her.*]: No! No, you're wrong, Albert!—your parents—my dad—they left us because they wanted us to be safe. They didn't care if they died just as long as we live! Don't throw that away! You have to stay alive! [*strong*] [*passionately*][*quickly*] We have to wait, Albert! Waiting can sometimes be the hardest thing in the world to do! That's why we put stars in our windows! [*an idea*] [*quickly*] So . . . look . . . here . . . [*takes bookmark out of book*][*quickly*] . . . here, Albert . . . See? . . . this is for you!—One of the stars my mother left to me! You

can have it, see? This will be your star! So now we can
wait together. It helps to have a friend to wait with—and
I'm your friend, Albert! [*starting to cry*] Don't leave,
Albert!—I need you to be my friend!—I need you to
wait with me!—Please don't leave me, Albert!

[Lily *is crying. Moved,* Albert *is crying too—they
both hug each other—holding onto each other for life.
Meanwhile, on the other side of the stage, cue: Radio
sound FX starts. Sound FX: loudly on radio—church
bells ringing, crowds cheering, a French newsman excitedly reporting the happy news—(in French)—
Reporter:* "Yes, ladies and gentlemen! It's true! Paris
is liberated! Paris is free! Vive la France! Vive la
France! I am here—watching General Charles de
Gaulle and his army marching up the avenue! All is
pandemonium! Music playing! The French flag proudly
waving once again! People everywhere are shouting! All of Paris must be here! All are cheering!—
dancing in the streets!—singing! Paris is free! Paris
is free!" *As radio plays,* Gram *runs in—she stands
down left—she calls straight out to* Lily. *She is very
excited.*]

GRAM [*simultaneously with radio FX*][*loudly calling
straight out to be heard over radio*][*happily excited*]:
LI-LY! . . . LILY! . . . Quick! The radio! It's happened!
The news! Paris! The Allies have marched into Paris! Paris
has been liberated! It's the beginning of the end! . . . The
beginning of the end! Paris is free! Paris is free!! [Gram
happily, excitedly exits.]

[*On other side of the stage,* Lily *and* Albert *have not
reacted to the happy news—but they are holding each
other. During news,* Lily *and* Albert *have released
their hug—look at each other—* Albert *offers* Lily *his
handkerchief—she takes it, wipes her tears—they smile
at each other—a new understanding. Then, sadly,* Albert *slowly backs away—turns—exits.* Lily *is alone on-*

stage . . . Music changes—softer—underscores as Lily
crosses down stage to talk to the audience. Crossover.
Lily *crosses center, talks to audience.*]

LILY [*to the audience*][*slowly*][*bit sad, but now more
grown up—more centered—mature*]: Summer ended.
That meant Albert had to go back to his aunt's in
Canada. I went back to St. Albans. The war went on, but
at least it was the beginning of the end. [*added thought*]
I wrote to Poppy about Albert and his sister. [*thinks*][*bit-
tersweet*] So—we waited. Waiting can sometimes be the
hardest thing in the world to do. [*smiles, but not the
same little girl who gets all excited about it being the
first day of summer vacation*] Anyway, before you knew
it, it was a whole year later . . . [*crosses up to radio*] . . .
the first day of a new summer—back once again at
Rockaway Beach.

[Lily *turns on the radio.* Lily *sits in chair. Segues
into . . .*]

SCENE 17

*The Rockaway Beach house. The living room. Same as
opening, but the first Friday of the summer of 1945.*
Lily *fiddles with the radio dial. We hear short segments
of different big band songs—then a news program reporting the end of the war in Europe.*
    Like the opening, Gram *enters down left. She lis-
tens a bit to radio—noticing that* Lily *is listening to
the news—has to smile—proud. She calls straight out
to* Lily—*not angry, just a friendly reminder.*

GRAM [*calling straight out*][*instructions*]: LI-LY! . . .
no radio! Finish unpacking first!

LILY [*calls back*]: I was just checking to see if it worked.

GRAM [*same*]: We've got work to do! And the Orbans expect us at six o'clock!

LILY [*calls back*]: Okay! Just wanted to see if there was any more news!

[Gram *has to smile—exits.* Lily *turns off the radio.*]

LILY [*to the audience*][*has to smile at the irony*][*admits*]: Yeah, can you believe it? . . . me—listening to the war news! Who'd have thought, huh? [*continues*] Over in Europe, the war's just ended. In the Pacific, the war's still going on. [*worried*] Don't know if Poppy is safe. Haven't heard from him—or Albert—for a while now.

[Gram *enters—loaded down with a suitcase—happy, if a bit weary.*]

GRAM [*entering*][*putting suitcase down*][*happily*]: Well, here we are! [*smiles, thinking*] . . . As your father would say—nothing ever changes around here. Right?

LILY [*tries to smile, but thinking . . .*]: Yeah, that's what he'd say all right . . . [*thinks*] . . . but . . . you know, Gram?

GRAM: Yes?

LILY: Things do change.

GRAM [*asks*]: Like what?

LILY [*thinks*][*sadly*]: Eddie's not coming back. . . . and Margaret and her family aren't either.

GRAM [*explaining*]: Well, Mrs. Dillon said Rockaway reminds her too much of Eddie.

LILY [*bit reluctant to admit it*]: And I had sort of thought . . .

GRAM: Yes?

LILY: It's dumb, I know, but—I thought Albert would be back here, you know—waiting for us—or at least a note or something.

GRAM [*understandingly*][*a bit sad*]: I know, Sweetheart, I know. Just like I always expect to see your father here—getting ready to go fishing. I guess . . . things change. [*worried*] . . . Let's just pray they're both safe.

[Lily *has come to appreciate* Gram *in a whole new way.*]

LILY [*warmly, lovingly*]: I love you, Gram.

[Gram *is very moved to hear her say it.* Gram *and* Lily *hug each other.*]

GRAM [*while hugging* Lily][*lovingly*]: See? . . . even in the worst of times, something lovely happens. [*pause*][*then, breaking their hug—changing subject*] Well, c'mon. Let's unpack. We're expected at the Orbans' for dinner—Friday night—remember? [Gram *crosses—picks up suitcase.*][Gram *stops—looks at* Lily.] [*warmly, understanding, reassuringly*] . . . I'm sure the Orbans will have some word of Albert.

[Lily *and* Gram *smile at each other—a new bond together.* Gram *exits with suitcase.* Lily *crosses to the hat rack—she sees* Eddie's *sailor hat—picks it up—remembers him—she puts it on. Then, she picks up* Dad's *fishing pole. She crosses down stage—sadly thinking of him. She pretends to cast just like her father used to do—remembering. Meanwhile, upstage—unseen by* Lily—*her father enters. He is dressed in an army uniform and carries an army duffel. He sees*

Lily—*lovingly watches for a moment. Then he puts down duffel, crosses over to radio—and loudly turns it on to big band swing music. Sound FX: same as first scene—*Tommy Dorsey's "Opus One." *Hearing music,* Lily *quickly turns to see her father.*]

DAD [*to* Lily][*like opening*][*lovingly smiling*]: Hey lady, wanta dance?

LILY [*joyfully*]: Poppy!

[Lily *happily runs into the open arms of* Dad. *They hug each other. Hearing the radio,* Gram *starts to reenter the room.*]

GRAM [*calling*][*not angry*][*a reminder to* Lily]: LI-LY . . . no radio. We've got work to . . .

[*She stops short—seeing her son.* Lily *and* Dad *release their hug.*]

DAD [*to* Gram][*warmly*]: Hi, Mom.

GRAM [*excited*][*can hardly believe it*]: Jerry? . . . JERRY! . . . [*She runs to her son.* Gram *and* Dad *hug.*][*a bundle of questions*][*excited, happy*][*bit tongue-tied*] But how . . . how did you . . . I mean, when . . . when did you . . . ?

DAD [*laughing*][*happily*][*explains*]: Just shipped in last night—sailed right past Rockaway Beach! Man it was good to see all the lights back on again! And I knew you'd be here: first day of summer—Friday night—dinner at the Orbans'!

GRAM [*happily remembering*]: Oh my gosh, the Orbans! I almost forgot! I'd better go tell them the wonderful news—they have to set another place at the table!

[*She happily kisses* Dad, *then excitedly runs out.* Dad *and* Lily *laugh.*]

DAD [*celebrating*][*happily*]: See, LilyBilly?— What did I tell you? [*happily looking around*] Nothing ever changes around here. [*pause*]

[Lily *has to smile to herself.*]

LILY: Hey, Poppy?

DAD: Yes?

LILY [*hopefully asks*]: Remember my friend Albert? You know, we wrote you about his sister—hidden by the Daughters of Wisdom near Paris, and . . .

DAD [*stopping her*][*remembering*][*reaching inside his coat pocket*]: Oh, wait, wait . . . hold it . . . just a minute . . . just a minute . . . [*takes photo out of pocket, shows it to* Lily] . . . here, take a look.

LILY [*looking at photo*]: What's this?

DAD [*explaining photo*][*laughs*][*proud*]: Your old dad—in France—but . . . [*points at photo*] . . . guess who this is.

LILY [*catching on*][*growing excitement*][*looking at other person in photo*]: You . . . you don't mean . . . ?

DAD [*proudly explaining*]: Took that information you and Albert sent me—made my way to the convent—I've already written back to Albert—told him exactly where he can find Ruth, and . . .

[*Suddenly,* Gram *calls, then comes running back into the room all excited. She carries a letter.*]

GRAM [*offstage*][*calling*][*very excited*]: LI-LY!

DAD [*cut off*] [*confused*]: Mom?

GRAM [*entering*][*running in—all excited*]: Lily . . .

LILY: Gram? . . . What is it?

[Gram *looks happily at* Lily. *Then* Gram *holds out the letter toward* Lily.]

GRAM [*happy for* Lily][*holding letter out to* Lily][*referring to the letter*]: Even in the worst of times . . . something lovely happens.

[Lily *takes the letter from* Gram—*opens it—reads it—with* Dad *looking over her shoulder. Music underscores.* Albert *enters down right. He is dressed like he was at the beginning—old coat, hat, carrying his suitcase. Facing straight out, he recites the letter he wrote to* Lily. *He seems more confident, older.*]

ALBERT [*facing straight out*][*reciting his letter*]: "Dear Lily . . . I'm finally going back home—to start a new life—crossing back over. But don't worry. I'm not going to swim!" [*He smiles.*][*then* . . .][*remembers*] "And I'm not alone, cause . . . See? . . . I've got your star . . ." [*He turns suitcase, shows* Lily's *star pasted onto his suitcase.*] "It tells the world—I miss someone who is overseas—who plays 'The Blue Danube Waltz.' " [*more seriously*][*slowly*] "It tells the world—that I will always miss—" [*lovingly*] "—my best friend, Lily."

[*He smiles—a bit sad—but looking hopeful.* Lily *hugs* Dad *as* Gram *smiles at them both. Music builds. Blackout.*]

VARIATIONS ON THE DEATH OF TROTSKY

by David Ives

*This play is for Fred Sanders,
first appreciator of the comic possibilities
of mountain-climbers' axes.*

CHARACTERS

TROTSKY   RAMON

MRS. TROTSKY

*Trotsky's study in Coyoacan, Mexico. A desk, covered
with books and papers. A mirror hanging on the wall.
A doorway, left. Louvered windows upstage, through
which we can glimpse lush tropical fronds and green-
ery. A large wall calendar announces that today is August 21, 1940. Lights up on* Trotsky *sitting at his desk,
writing furiously. He has bushy hair and a goatee,
small glasses, a dark suit. The handle of a mountain-
climber's axe is sticking out of the back of his head.*

VARIATION 1

TROTSKY [*as he writes*]: "The proletariat is right. The
proletariat must *always* be right. And the revolution of
the proletariat against oppression must go on . . . *forever!*"

[Mrs. Trotsky *enters, grandmotherly and sweet, in an
ankle-length dress and high-button shoes. She is holding a large book.*]

MRS. TROTSKY: Leon.

TROTSKY: "And forever and forever . . . !"

MRS. TROTSKY: Leon, I was just reading the encyclopedia.

TROTSKY: The heading?

MRS. TROTSKY: "Trotsky, Leon."

TROTSKY: Good. It's about me.

MRS. TROTSKY: Listen to this. [*reads*] "On August 20th, 1940, a Spanish Communist named Ramon Mercader smashed a mountain-climber's axe into Trotsky's skull in Coyoacan, a suburb of Mexico City. Trotsky died the next day."

TROTSKY: What is the year of that encyclopedia?

MRS. TROTSKY [*checks the spine*]: 1994. [*or whatever year it happens to be right now*]

TROTSKY: Strange.

MRS. TROTSKY: Yes.

TROTSKY: But interesting. I *am* Trotsky.

MRS. TROTSKY: Yes, dear.

TROTSKY: And this is our house in Coyoacan.

MRS. TROTSKY: Yes.

TROTSKY: And we have a Spanish gardener named Ramon—?

MRS. TROTSKY: Mercader. Yes.

TROTSKY: Hmm . . . There aren't any *other* Trotskys living in Coyoacan, are there?

MRS. TROTSKY: I don't think so. Not under that name.

TROTSKY: What is the date today?

MRS. TROTSKY [*looks at the calendar*]: August 21st, 1940.

TROTSKY: Then I'm safe! That article says it happened on the twentieth, which means it would've happened yesterday.

MRS. TROTSKY: But Leon . . .

TROTSKY: And I'd be dead today, with a mountain-climber's axe in my skull!

MRS. TROTSKY: Um—Leon . . .

TROTSKY: Will the capitalist press never get things right? [*He resumes writing.*]

MRS. TROTSKY: But Leon, isn't that the handle of a mountain-climber's axe, sticking out of your skull?

TROTSKY [*looks into the mirror*]: It certainly does look like one. . . . And you know, Ramon was in here yesterday, telling me about his mountain-climbing trip. And now that I think of it, he was carrying a mountain-climber's axe. I can't remember if he had it when he left the room. . . . [Trotsky *considers all this.*] Did Ramon report to work today? [Trotsky *dies, falling face forward onto his desk.*]

[*A bell rings.*]

VARIATION 2

[Trotsky *resumes writing.*]

TROTSKY: "No one is safe. Force must be used. And the revolution of the proletariat against oppression must go on forever and forever . . ."

MRS. TROTSKY: Leon . . .

TROTSKY: "And forever!"

MRS. TROTSKY: Leon, I was just reading the encyclopedia.

TROTSKY: Is it the *Britannica*?

MRS. TROTSKY: Listen to this.

TROTSKY [*to audience*]: The universe as viewed by the victors.

MRS. TROTSKY: "On August 20th, 1940, a Spanish Communist named Ramon Mercader smashed a mountain-climber's axe into Trotsky's skull in Coyoacan, a suburb of Mexico City. Trotsky died the next day."

TROTSKY [*impatient*]: Yes? And?

MRS. TROTSKY: I *think* that there's a mountain-climber's axe in your own skull right now.

TROTSKY: I knew *that*! When I was shaving this morning, I noticed a handle sticking out of the back of my head. For a moment I thought it was an ice pick, so at first I was worried.

MRS. TROTSKY: No, it's not an ice pick.

TROTSKY: Don't even say the word! You know my recurring nightmare.

MRS. TROTSKY: Yes, dear.

TROTSKY: About the ice pick that buries itself in my skull.

MRS. TROTSKY: Yes, dear.

TROTSKY: That is why I have forbidden any of the servants to allow ice picks into the house.

MRS. TROTSKY: But Leon—

TROTSKY: No one may be seen with an ice pick in this house. *Especially* not Spanish Communists.

MRS. TROTSKY: But Leon—

TROTSKY: We'll do without ice. We'll drink our liquor neat and our Coca-Cola warm. Who cares if this *is* Coyoacan in August? Hmm. Not a bad song title, that. "Coyoacan in August." [*writes it down*] Or we'll get ice, but we just won't pick at it. Ice will be allowed into the house in blocks, but may not be picked or chipped under any circumstances—at least, not with ice picks. Ice-cube trays will also be allowed, if they've been invented yet. I'll bet this article doesn't say anything about an *ice-cube tray* in my skull, does it?

MRS. TROTSKY: No . . .

TROTSKY: Does it?

MRS. TROTSKY: No.

TROTSKY: HA! I've outsmarted destiny! [*to audience*] Which is only a capitalist explanation for the status quo!

MRS. TROTSKY: Leon . . .

TROTSKY: Also—look at this. [*opens a desk drawer and takes out a skull*] Do you know what this is?

MRS. TROTSKY: No.

TROTSKY: It's a skull.

MRS. TROTSKY: Well I knew *that*, but—

TROTSKY: *I* bought this skull. I *own* this skull. So what does that make this?

[*pause*]

MRS. TROTSKY AND TROTSKY [*together*]: Trotsky's skull.

TROTSKY: If some Spanish-Communist-posing-as-a-gardener wants to bury anything in my skull—be it a [*He is about to say "ice pick."*] you-know-what or anything else—this will be here as a decoy. He'll see this skull, recognize it as my skull, bury something in it, and he'll go his way and I'll go mine. Is that ingenious?

MRS. TROTSKY: Up to a point.

TROTSKY: Fifty more years of Trotsky!

MRS. TROTSKY: I have some very bad news for you, Leon. [*shows him the entry in the encyclopedia*]

TROTSKY: A mountain-climber's axe . . . ? Ingenious! [Trotsky *dies.*]

[*bell*]

VARIATION 3

TROTSKY: Funny. I always thought it was an ice pick.

MRS. TROTSKY: A mountain-climber's axe! *A mountain-climber's axe!* CAN'T I GET THAT THROUGH YOUR SKULL?

[Trotsky *dies.*]

[*bell*]

VARIATION 4

[Trotsky *begins to pace.*]

TROTSKY: This is very bad news. This is serious.

MRS. TROTSKY: What is serious, Leon?

TROTSKY: *I have a mountain-climber's axe buried in my skull!*

MRS. TROTSKY: Smashed, actually. It says Mercader "smashed" the axe into your skull, not "buried"—

TROTSKY: All right, all right. What am I going to do?

MRS. TROTSKY: Maybe a hat would cover the handle. You know. One of those cute little Alpine hats, with a point and a feather . . . ? [*sees the look on his face, and stops*]

TROTSKY: The encyclopedia says that I die today?

MRS. TROTSKY: The twenty-first. That's today.

TROTSKY: Does it say what time?

MRS. TROTSKY: No.

TROTSKY: So much for the usefulness of *that* encyclopedia. All right, then, I have until midnight at the latest.

MRS. TROTSKY: What should I tell Cook about supper?

TROTSKY: Well she can forget the soup course. [Trotsky *falls to the floor and dies.*]

MRS. TROTSKY: Nyet, nyet, *nyet!*

[*bell*]

VARIATION 5

TROTSKY: But this man is a gardener.

MRS. TROTSKY: Yes.

TROTSKY: At least he's been *posing* as a gardener.

MRS. TROTSKY: Yes.

TROTSKY: Doesn't that make him a member of the proletariat?

MRS. TROTSKY: I'd say so.

TROTSKY: Then what's he doing smashing a mountain-climber's axe into my skull?

MRS. TROTSKY: I don't know. Have you been oppressing him?

TROTSKY: Why would Ramon have done this to me? [*He holds up the skull, Hamlet-like.*]

MRS. TROTSKY: Maybe he's a literalist.

TROTSKY: A what?

MRS. TROTSKY: A literalist. Maybe Ramon ran into Manuel yesterday. You know—Manuel? The head gardener?

TROTSKY: I know who Manuel is.

MRS. TROTSKY: I know you know who Manuel is.

TROTSKY [*Ralph Kramden*]: One of these days, Mrs. Trotsky . . . *Bang! Zoom!*

MRS. TROTSKY: Maybe Ramon asked him, "Will Mr. Trotsky have time to look at the nasturtiums today?"

And maybe Manuel said, "I don't know—*axe* Mr. Trotsky." HA HA HA HA HA HA!

TROTSKY: Very funny.

MRS. TROTSKY: Or maybe he was just hot-to-trotsky.

TROTSKY: Oh very, very funny.

MRS. TROTSKY: Or maybe he just wanted to *pick your brain*! HOO HOO HEE HEE HAA HAA!

TROTSKY: Stop it! *Stop it!* [*He dies.*]

MRS. TROTSKY: HA HA HA HA HA HA!

[*bell*]

VARIATION 6

TROTSKY: Call Ramon in here.

MRS. TROTSKY: Ramon!

TROTSKY: You'd better get him quickly. I have a mountain-climber's axe in my skull.

MRS. TROTSKY: *Ramon! Come quickly!*

[Ramon *enters: sombrero, serape, huaraches, and guitar.*]

TROTSKY: Good morning, Ramon.

RAMON: Good morning, señor. [*They shake hands.*]

TROTSKY: Have a seat, please. [*to* Mrs. Trotsky] You see? We have very good employer-employee relations here. [*to* Ramon] Ramon, did you bury this mountain-climber's axe in my skull?

RAMON: I did not bury it, señor. I *smashed* it into your skull.

TROTSKY: Excuse me?

RAMON: You see? You can still see the handle.

MRS. TROTSKY: It's true, Leon. The axe is not entirely out of sight.

RAMON: So we cannot say "buried," we can only say "smashed," or perhaps "jammed"—

TROTSKY: All right, all right. But *why* did you do this?

RAMON: I think I read about it in an encyclopedia.

TROTSKY [*to audience*]: The power of the printed word!

RAMON: I wanted to use an ice pick, but there weren't any around the house.

TROTSKY: But why? Do you realize who I am? Do you realize that you smashed this axe into the skull of a major historical figure? I helped run the Russian Revolution! I fought Stalin! I was a major political theorist! Why did you do this? Was it political disaffection? Anti-counterrevolutionary backlash?

RAMON: Actually—it was love, señor.

MRS. TROTSKY: It's true, Leon. [*She and* Ramon *join hands.*] I'm only sorry you had to find out about it this way.

TROTSKY: No.

MRS. TROTSKY: Yes.

TROTSKY: No.

RAMON: Sí!

TROTSKY: Oh God! What a fool I've been! [*He dies.*]

[*bell*]

VARIATION 7

TROTSKY: Why did you really do this, Ramon?

RAMON: *You* will never know, Señor Trotsky.

TROTSKY: This is a nightmare!

RAMON: But luckily for you—your night will soon be over. [Trotsky *dies.*]

[*bell*]

VARIATION 8

TROTSKY: All right, Ramon. Thank you. You may go.

[Ramon *starts out. Stops.*]

RAMON: Señor Trotsky—?

TROTSKY: Yes?

RAMON: Do you think you will have time to look at the nasturtiums today? They are really very beautiful.

TROTSKY: I don't think so, Ramon. But I'll try.

RAMON: Thank you, señor. *Hasta la vista.* Or should I say, *buenas noches.* [*exits*]

TROTSKY: Well. All right then. The twenty-first of August, 1940. The day I'm going to die. Interesting. And to think that I've gone over so many twenty-firsts of August in my life, like a man walking over his own grave. . . .

MRS. TROTSKY: It's been wonderful being married to you, Leon.

TROTSKY: Thank you, Mrs. Trotsky.

MRS. TROTSKY: Though it was a burden at times, being married to a major historical figure.

TROTSKY: I'm sorry I was away from home so often, tending the revolution.

MRS. TROTSKY: I understand.

TROTSKY: And I'm sorry I couldn't have been more in touch with my feelings.

MRS. TROTSKY [*gentle protest*]: No . . . please . . .

TROTSKY: And that I often had such trouble expressing my emotions.

MRS. TROTSKY: Oh, I haven't been everything I should have been.

TROTSKY: Well it's a little late for regrets, with a mountain-climber's axe buried in one's skull.

MRS. TROTSKY: Smashed, actually.

TROTSKY: So it wasn't old age, or cancer, or even the ice pick that I feared for years. It was an axe wielded by a Spanish Communist posing as a gardener.

MRS. TROTSKY: You really couldn't have guessed that, Leon.

TROTSKY: So even an assassin can make the flowers grow. The gardener was false, and yet the garden that he tended was real. How was I to know he was my killer when I passed him every day? How was I to know that the man tending the nasturtiums would keep me from seeing what the weather will be like tomorrow? How was I to know I'd never get to see *Casablanca,* which wouldn't be made until 1942 and which I would have despised anyway? How was I to know I'd never get to know about the bomb, or the eighty thousand dead at Hiroshima? Or rock and roll, or Gorbachev, or the state of Israel? How was I supposed to know I'd be erased from the history books of my own land . . . ?

MRS. TROTSKY: But reinstated, at least partially, someday.

TROTSKY: Sometime, for everyone, there's a room that you go into, and it's the room that you never leave. Or else you go out of a room and it's the last room that you'll *ever* leave. [*He looks around.*] This is my last room.

MRS. TROTSKY: But you aren't even here, Leon.

TROTSKY: This desk, these books, that calendar . . .

MRS. TROTSKY: You're not even here, my love.

TROTSKY: The sunshine coming through the blinds . . .

MRS. TROTSKY: That was yesterday. You're in a hospital, unconscious.

TROTSKY: The flowers in the garden. You, standing there . . .

MRS. TROTSKY: This is yesterday you're seeing.

TROTSKY: What does that entry say? Would you read it again?

MRS. TROTSKY: "On August 20th, 1940, a Spanish Communist named Ramon Mercader smashed a mountain-climber's axe into Trotsky's skull in Coyoacan, a suburb of Mexico City. Trotsky died the next day."

TROTSKY: It gives you a little hope about the world, doesn't it? That a man could have a mountain-climber's axe smashed into his skull, and yet live on for one whole day . . . ? Maybe I'll go look at the nasturtiums.

[Trotsky *dies. The garden outside the louvered window begins to glow.*]

COMING THROUGH THE RYE

by William Saroyan

CHARACTERS

The Voice

Butch

Carroll

Steve

Miss Quickly

Roosevelt

Alice

Larry

Pedro Gonzalez

Johnny Gallanti

Henrietta

Ralph Hastings

Peggy

A large room, beyond which is visible, in varying degrees of light and movement, infinite space. Sun, moon, planets, stars, constellations, and so on.

The room is one of many. It is The American Room, and is so marked.

Each person here has been conceived and is waiting to be born. Each possesses his ultimate physical form and ego. Ultimate, that is, in the sense that here, in this waiting room, he is the way he shall be the day he begins to die, or the day he dies, in the world.

The faces of the unconceived appear to be a white cloud of a summer afternoon.

A solemn but witty Voice *speaks.*

THE VOICE: O.K., people. Your time has come. You are now going to enter the world. You'll find it a strange place. There are no instructions. You know your destiny now, but the moment you are in the world, breathing, you shall forget it. You can thank God for that, let me tell you. Good things, and bad, are ahead for each of you. The world is still new, and the idea of sending you out there for a visit has not yet proved itself to be a good one. It may in time, though. Your destination is America. [*a phrase of patriotic music*] It's an interesting place. No better and no worse than any other place, except of course superficially, which the Americans make a good deal of, one way or the other. The climate's fair everywhere, excellent here and there. Everything you do, you shall imagine is your own doing. You can thank God for that, too. You shall live as long as you shall. No more. You will find noise and confusion everywhere, even in your sleep. Sometimes in sleep, however, you shall almost, but not quite, return to this place. Nothing in the world is important. Nothing is unimportant. Many things shall *seem* important. Many shall seem *unimportant*. In a moment you shall begin to be human. You have waited here nine months of the world's time. A few of you a little less. From now on you shall be alone in body, apparently cut off from everything. You shall also *seem* to be alone in spirit. That, however, is an illusion. Each of you is the continuation of two others, each of whom was a continuation of two others, each of whom—and so on. [*blithely*] I could go on talking for two or three years, but it wouldn't mean anything. O.K., now, here you go! Take a deep breath! [*dramatically*] Hold it! You will exhale in the world. O.K., Joe, let 'em out!

[*A few chords of music. Some* People *go out.* Butch, *a boy of nine, and* Mr. Carroll, *a man of seventy, come in.* Butch *is thoughtfully bouncing an old tennis ball.*]

BUTCH: Well, we're next, Mr. Carroll. Do you like the idea of being born?

CARROLL: Why, yes, of course, Butch. There's nothing like getting born and being alive.

BUTCH: I don't know whether I'm lucky or unlucky. Steve says I'm lucky because I don't have to stay in the world very long, and Miss Quickly—she says it ain't fair.

CARROLL: What *ain't*?

BUTCH: Me having to get born, just for nine years. Before I get a chance to turn around I'll have to come back, so what's the use going? I'm the way I'm going to be when I die, and you're the way you're going to be when you die. I'm nine, and you're an old man.

CARROLL: Butch, my boy, those nine years are going to be wonderful.

BUTCH: Maybe. Miss Quickly says it'll take me five or six years just to begin. Gosh, that only leaves three. I won't even get a chance to see any big-league baseball games.

CARROLL: Maybe you will.

BUTCH: Heck no. How am I going to get from a little town in Texas to New York?

CARROLL: It may happen.

BUTCH: Boy, I *hope* it does, but Miss Quickly—she told Steve it wasn't fair.

CARROLL: What wasn't?

BUTCH: My father dying before I'm born and my mother being poor, and dying a year later. She says I may have to go to an institution. What the heck's an institution?

CARROLL: That's an orphanage, I guess. Now, listen, Butch, don't you go worrying about anything. Everything's wonderful out there.

BUTCH: How's it really going to be?

CARROLL: Well, the minute you're out there you're alive, the same as here, only different. Out there you begin right away.

BUTCH: Begin what?

CARROLL: Living—and dying. They're both beautiful, Butch. [*happily*] Living and dying in the world. That great big little tiny place. And from the first breath you take you begin being somebody: *yourself.*

BUTCH: I'm myself right now.

CARROLL: That's because you're here waiting. You've started at last. It takes a long time to get started. It took me—well, I don't know how long exactly in the world's time—but it was a long time.

BUTCH: Steve says the world stinks.

CARROLL: Now, Steve is a young fellow with ideas. He's a nice boy, but he's wrong about the world. It's the only place for us, and any of us who get to go out there are mighty lucky.

BUTCH: What happens when we leave the world?

CARROLL: We come back.

BUTCH: Here? And wait some more?

CARROLL: Not *here,* exactly. We wait *here, after* we've started. When we leave the world we go back to where we were before we came here.

BUTCH: Where the heck's that?

CARROLL: It's not exactly *any* place, Butch. And it's not exactly waiting either. *This* is where we *wait.*

BUTCH: Oh, well, I guess it'll be all right. But nine years. What the heck chance will I have to see anything?

CARROLL: Butch, one day out there is a long time, let alone nine years. Twenty-four hours every day. Sixty minutes every hour.

BUTCH: What are you going to be out there, Mr. Carroll?

CARROLL [*laughing*]: Oh, a lot of things, one after another.

BUTCH: Well, *what*?

CARROLL: Well, let's see. [*He brings out a paper and studies it.*] It says here, Thomas Carroll. Mother: Amy Wallace Carroll. Father: Jonathan Carroll. Will be, at birth: son, brother, nephew, cousin, grandson, and so on.

BUTCH: Brother?

CARROLL: Yes. I guess I've got a sister or a brother out there, maybe a couple of sisters and a couple of brothers.

BUTCH: I thought we were all brothers. I thought everybody was related to everybody else.

CARROLL: Oh, yes, of course, but this kind of brotherhood is closer. Whoever my brother is, he has my father and mother for *his* father and mother.

BUTCH: Well, what the heck's the difference? I thought we were all the same.

CARROLL: Oh, we are, really, but in the world there are families. They're still all really one family, but in the world the family is broken down to the people you come from, and the people that come from you. It gets pretty complicated.

BUTCH: But everybody *is* one family just the same, though, ain't they?

CARROLL: Well, yes, but in the world everybody forgets that for a while.

BUTCH [*bringing out his paper, which is a good deal smaller than* Carroll's]: What the heck. I never looked at this. What do I get to be? [*reading the card*] James Nelson, also called Butch. By gosh, there it is right there. Also called Butch, but my real name is James Nelson. Let's see what I get to be. [*reading*] Son. Newsboy. Schoolboy. [*reflectively*] Son. No brothers?

CARROLL: Well, I guess not, Butch.

BUTCH: Why the heck not?

CARROLL: There will be all sorts of kids out there in Texas. They'll *all* be your brothers.

BUTCH: Honest?

CARROLL: Sure.

BUTCH [*reading*]: Newsboy. What's that?

CARROLL: Well, I guess you'll sell papers.

BUTCH: Is that good?

CARROLL: Now don't you worry about anything, Butch.

BUTCH: O.K. The heck with it. [*He puts the paper away.*]

CARROLL [*affectionately*]: Give me a catch, Butch.

BUTCH [*delighted*]: No fooling?

CARROLL: Why, sure, I'm going to play second base for the New Haven Orioles.

BUTCH [*throwing the ball, which* Carroll *tries to catch*]: Who the heck are they?

CARROLL: A bunch of kids in my neighborhood. [*He throws the ball back.*]

[Steve *comes in. About twenty-seven, sober, serious, but a drunkard.* Butch *holds the ball and watches* Steve. *Then goes to him.*]

BUTCH: Steve? Tell him about the war—and all that stuff.

STEVE [*scarcely noticing* Butch, *absorbed in thought*]: Tell *who, what*?

BUTCH: Mr. Carroll. About the war.

STEVE [*looking at* Carroll, *smiling*]: I was talking to the old lady—

BUTCH: He means Miss Quickly.

STEVE: Yeah.

BUTCH [*to* Carroll]: If everybody is everybody else's brother, what the heck do they have a war for?

CARROLL: Well, now, Butch—

STEVE [*laughing solemnly*]: I'm afraid you won't be able to find a good answer for that question, Doc.

BUTCH [*delighted*]: Honest, Steve?

CARROLL: Now, Steve, you know the world is a wonderful place.

STEVE [*simply*]: I'm sorry, but I think it stinks. I think the human race is unholy and disgusting. I think putting people in the world is a dirty trick.

CARROLL: No. No. No, it isn't, Steve.

STEVE: What is it, then? You're called out, everybody's a stranger, you suffer every kind of pain there is, and then you crawl back. A little tiny place that got sidetracked in space and began to fill up with terrible unclean animals in clothes.

CARROLL: Those *animals* have created several magnificent civilizations, and right now they're creating another one. It's a privilege to participate.

BUTCH [*delighted*]: You mean the World Series?

STEVE [*wearily*]: O.K., Doc. Anything you say.

CARROLL: Excuse me, Steve. Can I ask you a question?

STEVE: Anything at all.

CARROLL: What's ahead for you?

STEVE: A number of things.

CARROLL: Won't you tell me what they are?

STEVE [*to* Butch]: How about it, kid? Come back in a few minutes.

BUTCH: Ah, shucks. I want to listen. I'm not born yet.

STEVE: This is nothing. I'll be seeing you.

BUTCH [*obedient, going to one side*]: O.K., Steve.

CARROLL: What is your destiny, Steve?

STEVE [*pause*]: Murder.

CARROLL [*amazed*]: Murder?

STEVE [*slowly*]: Yes. *I am going to murder* another human being.

CARROLL: Oh, I'm sorry, Steve.

STEVE: He's here, too.

CARROLL: Here? Who is he?

STEVE: I don't know if you've noticed him. *I* have. His name is Hastings.

CARROLL [*shocked*]: Ralph Hastings?

STEVE: That's right.

CARROLL: Why, he's a nice young fellow. Are you sure it's not a mistake?

STEVE: No, it's not a mistake.

CARROLL: Well, good Lord. This is awful. But why? Why do you do it?

STEVE: It's a lot of nonsense.

CARROLL: What do you mean, Steve?

STEVE: You know he's rich. Well, he does a number of things that I think wreck the lives of poor people, so I— If he's going to wreck the lives of people, what's he born for? If all I'm supposed to do is kill him, what am *I* born for?

CARROLL: I'm sorry, Steve. Of course you'll never know once you're out there.

STEVE: That'll help some, of course, but I just don't like the idea. What do *you* do, Doc?

CARROLL: Oh, nothing really.

STEVE: Do *you* kill anybody?

CARROLL: No, I don't, Steve. I do a lot of ordinary things.

STEVE: Do you raise a family?

CARROLL [*delighted, but shyly*]: Oh, yes. Three sons. Three daughters. All kinds of grandchildren.

STEVE [*sincerely*] : That's swell. That'll help a little.

CARROLL: Help? Help what?

STEVE: Help balance things.

CARROLL: Do *you* marry, Steve?

STEVE: Not exactly.

CARROLL [*a little shocked but sympathetic*]: Oh?

STEVE: I get a lot of women, but not a *lot* of them. I get a year of one, though. That's toward the end. She's here. [*smiling*] I'm a little ashamed of myself.

CARROLL: Why should you be ashamed?

STEVE: Well, she's Peggy.

CARROLL [*shocked*]: Peggy?

STEVE: She'll probably be all right for me by that time.

CARROLL: Peggy's really a good girl, I suppose, but she seems so—

STEVE: I don't know her very well.

[Miss Quickly *enters, with* Seven Kids, *ranging in age from three to thirteen:* Roosevelt, *colored, aged 3.* Alice, *aged 5.* Larry, *aged 7.* Pedro Gonzalez, *Mexican, aged 8.* Johnny Gallanti, *Italian, aged 9.* Butch. Henrietta, *aged 13.*]

MISS QUICKLY: Now, children, what'll it be? Singing or playacting?

SOME: Singing.

SOME: Playacting.

ROOSEVELT [*emphatically, as if with a grudge*]: Nothing.

MISS QUICKLY: Nothing, Roosevelt? Now, really, you want to sing, don't you?

ROOSEVELT: No.

MISS QUICKLY: You want to act in a play, don't you?

ROOSEVELT: No.

MISS QUICKLY: You want to—

ROOSEVELT: No. I don't want to do nothing.

MISS QUICKLY: But *why,* Roosevelt?

ROOSEVELT: Because.

MISS QUICKLY: Because, what?

ROOSEVELT: Because I don't.

MISS QUICKLY: Don't you want to have fun?

ROOSEVELT: No.

MISS QUICKLY [*patiently*]: But why, child?

ROOSEVELT: Because.

MISS QUICKLY: Oh, dear.

STEVE [*calling*]: Come here, Roosevelt.

ROOSEVELT [*going to* Steve]: She's always making us do stuff.

MISS QUICKLY [*gaily, to* Steve]: Oh, thank you, Steve. All right, children, we'll sing.

ROOSEVELT [*getting up into* Steve's *arms*]: They're going to sing! She's *always* making people sing, or something. [*looking at* Miss Quickly] Shame on you!

STEVE: You stick with me, pardner.

ROOSEVELT: Wants 'em to playact.

MISS QUICKLY [*sharply*]: All right, children! [*She blows the pitch.*] "Beautiful Dreamer" by Stephen Foster. Ready. One, two, three: Sing!

[Miss Quickly *and the* Children *sing the song.*]

That was fine, children. Now, Roosevelt, don't you want to sing?

ROOSEVELT [*opening his eyes*]: Shame on you—talk to me that way!

MISS QUICKLY: My gracious! Come along, children!

[*They go to one side.* Ralph Hastings *comes in, looks around. He is a well-dressed, decent sort of fellow, same age as* Steve, *but younger looking. He looks at the colored boy, runs his hand through the kid's hair.*]

HASTINGS: How's the boy?

ROOSEVELT: No.

HASTINGS [*laughing*]: No, what?

ROOSEVELT: No, everything.

STEVE [*comforting him*]: O.K., kid.

ROOSEVELT [*with anger*]: Only Steve's *my* pardner.

HASTINGS: Sure.

ROOSEVELT: Steve's the best man everywhere.

HASTINGS [*smiling at Steve*]: Sure, he is.

CARROLL [*studying the two young men sadly*]: Well, Mr. Hastings, here we are.

HASTINGS: By the grace of God, here we wait for the first mortal breath. Are you pleased, Mr. Carroll?

CARROLL: I can't wait to begin.

HASTINGS: You, Steve?

STEVE [*simply*]: I'm here.

HASTINGS: And so am I. [*pause*] Well—

STEVE: Look. I don't know if you know, but if you do—

HASTINGS: As a matter of fact, I *do* know, but what the hell—!

STEVE: I want you to know—

HASTINGS [*cheerfully*]: It's all right.

CARROLL [*thoughtfully*]: There must be some mistake.

HASTINGS: No, there's no mistake. Everything's in order. I'm sorry, Steve. I'll have it coming to me, I suppose.

STEVE: I don't think so.

HASTINGS: These things all balance. I *must* have it coming to me.

STEVE: That's why I say the world stinks.

HASTINGS: It depends, I guess.

STEVE [*sincerely*]: Thanks. [*to* Carroll] Right now he's the way he is the day he dies, and I'm the way I am that day. It's obvious it's not him, and not me, so it *must* be the world.

HASTINGS: We're not human yet.

STEVE: You mean we're not inhuman yet.

CARROLL: Now, boys.

HASTINGS [*cheerfully*]: Of course, Mr. Carroll. [*to* Steve] I have a lot of fun, after a fashion, as long as it lasts. How about you?

STEVE [*laughs, stops*]: It's O.K.

[Peggy *comes in, looks around, comes over to the three men. She simply stands near them.*]

You know—I like you, Peggy. Even here, you're lost.

PEGGY: Oh, it's boring—that's what burns me up. Nothing to do. No excitement. I want to get started, so

I can get it over with. I want to dance— I just heard a new one— [*singing*] "I don't want to set the world on fire."

[Carroll *and* Hastings *move away*.]

STEVE: Ah, now, Peggy—sure you do.

PEGGY: All I want to do is get it over with. I'm in a hurry. When do we start?

STEVE [*He puts* Roosevelt *with the other kids*.]: Any time, now—any minute. They just got rid of another mob. We're next. [*pause, while he smiles at her*] Near you, Peggy, I'm in a hurry myself. [*He takes her by the shoulders*.]

PEGGY [*shocked a little*]: Here?

STEVE: What's the difference? I've waited a long time for you. [*He takes her and kisses her*.] You see, Peggy, you're no good, and I love you for it. Because I'm no good, too. I don't know why, but it's so. Now, before we know it, we'll be separated and I won't be seeing you again for a long time. Remember me, so that when we *do* meet again, you'll know who I am.

PEGGY: I've got a poor memory, but I guess I'll know you just the same.

STEVE [*kissing her again*]: You'll remember, don't worry.

[*They stand, kissing*.]

THE VOICE: O.K., people! Here we go again! I'm not going to go through the whole speech. You're going out whether you like it or not, so get going, and good luck to you!

[*Everybody goes. Only* Steve *and* Peggy *stand together, kissing.*]

O.K., you two—get going!

[Peggy *tries to move, but* Steve *won't let her go.*]

Come on, come on, you American lovers, get going!

[Peggy *struggles.* Steve *holds her. She falls. He holds her terribly.*]

PEGGY [*whispering*]: Let me go—please let me go!

[*They struggle passionately for some time.*]

THE VOICE: What's *this*? What goes on around here?

[*A whistle is blown, like a police whistle, but* Steve *clings to* Peggy. *At last* Peggy *breaks away from him, gets to her feet, turns and runs.* Steve *gets up and looks around, smiling wisely. He straightens out. As he stands, a newborn babe begins to bawl, as if it were himself being born. He looks around, turns easily, and walks out.*]

STEVE: O.K. O.K. I'm going.

No Skronking

—◦◦◦—

by Shel Silverstein

CHARACTERS

ARNOLD
BERTHA

A lunch counter. Bertha *stands behind counter.* Arnold *sits at counter eating pie. A sign on the wall says* NO SKRONKING. Arnold *looks at sign.*

ARNOLD: Is that . . . spelled right? [Bertha *looks.*]

BERTHA: Uh-huh.

ARNOLD: Skronking?

BERTHA: That's right— Warm that up? [*She pours more coffee.*]

ARNOLD: Skronking?

BERTHA: No skronking.

ARNOLD: What . . . is *skronking*?

BERTHA: *Skronking?*

ARNOLD: Am I *skronking*?

BERTHA: If you were, we'd let you know. Believe me. We don't allow it.

ARNOLD: I don't know what it is.

BERTHA: You're better off. Stay in your safe secure little world.

ARNOLD: I'm—curious.

BERTHA: About—skronking.

ARNOLD: About things I don't understand.

BERTHA: Oh, aren't you the little scientist. Mr. Thirst-for-Knowledge.

ARNOLD: You don't permit skronking.

BERTHA: We don't allow it—not for a minute.

ARNOLD: So you don't want me to—*skronk*—is that the word?

BERTHA: We'd frown upon it.

ARNOLD: So—if I *know* what it is, I can be aware—make sure I don't do it—by *mistake*.

BERTHA: One does *not* skronk—inadvertently. Oh no—no, no, no. Not by mistake.

ARNOLD: But I *might*—if I had no idea what . . .

BERTHA: Look, this sign is not for you, all right? It is meant for—*others*—don't dwell on it—enjoy your—pie?—Pie—Enjoy your banana cream pie.

ARNOLD [*eats—pauses*]: That *skronking* has got to me.

BERTHA: I hope not—for *your* sake.

ARNOLD: It's meant—the sign—is meant for—

BERTHA: Skronkers—they know who they are.

ARNOLD: They see the sign.

BERTHA: We hope they do. They can't miss it.

ARNOLD: And they don't—skronk.

BERTHA: They'd better not. The sign *warns* them that there will be . . . *consequences*.

ARNOLD [*Puts finger in his ear, crosses eyes and sticks out tongue. Pause. He rolls eyes, wags tongue, and makes a gurgling sound.*]: Is *this* skronking?

BERTHA: Not by a long shot. [Arnold *twists arm behind head, pushes up nostrils and does Bugs Bunny stutter.*] No—please don't pursue this. You could go on all week, you're not going to get it. [Arnold *squeezes cheeks, crosses eyes and squeaks.*]

ARNOLD: No—?

BERTHA: No.

ARNOLD: Supposing . . .

BERTHA: Please—I have work.

ARNOLD: Supposing—I *did* . . . skronk . . . by mistake—what would you do?

BERTHA: You see, you *won't*— That question proves that you won't. You're not a *skronker*. A skronker would never ask that question. He—or she—would *know*.

ARNOLD: Things can be done—*unawares*. Someone has a bit too much to drink, okay?— They lose control— do things one would never imagine them doing—they sing bawdy songs, put on female clothing—pour ketchup on their—

BERTHA: You think skronking is something you do when you're *drunk*? Ho-ho— Think again, my friend. *Skronking* is . . .

ARNOLD: What? What? Why is it such a deep dark secret?

BERTHA: It is not a dark secret. Why would we put up a public sign if it were such a dark secret?

ARNOLD: Then what *is* it? What?

BERTHA: Tell me, do you have a good life?

ARNOLD: Do I have . . . ?

BERTHA: A pleasant life? Reasonably content?

ARNOLD: I—suppose I . . .

BERTHA: No major problems—health—work—love—sex—drugs—alcohol—no major neuroses?

ARNOLD: I think I'm all right—except for my curiosity—that always—

BERTHA: You're all right. *Stay* all right, all right? Don't go opening cans of beans. You're not a skronker—you don't skronk—be grateful—thank God— You're skronkless— Why borrow trouble?

ARNOLD: How is it borrowing trouble?— Being aware?— Understanding the meaning of a—

BERTHA: Being aware puts it into your mind. You discover there *is* skronking—you learn the *process* of skronking— You become curious as to the *effect* of

skronking, the *pleasures* of skronking? You *skronk*—
once—just to try it—it's skronk-skronk-skronk-skronk-
skronk-skronk all the way home.

ARNOLD: So there are pleasures—

BERTHA: You *see*?— You *see*?— You're already nib-
bling at the pleasure part. You'd better *watch out*— I tell
you this—seriously— *You*—*could* be a skronker—quite
easily— You *could*— I've observed you— You've got
the potential—you're in *danger*— Quit *now*—get off
this train before it picks up steam.

ARNOLD: I'm not frightened—of something I don't
understand.

BERTHA: If you understood—and recognized within
yourself—the *potential*—you might be truly frightened.

ARNOLD: So—frighten me.

BERTHA: I won't—you frighten me—you do—that
sign—it *does* apply to you—it does—you *are*— [*points*]
Just heed that sign.

ARNOLD: Hey, I just . . .

BERTHA: [*frightened—points to sign*] Not *here*— Not
in *here*.

ARNOLD: Look, I'm not a skron—

BERTHA: *Whatever* you are—or *aren't*—whatever you
do—not here, all right—not here— [*She backs slowly
away as lights fade.*]

VISIT TO A SMALL PLANET

by Gore Vidal

CHARACTERS

ROGER SPELDING

ELLEN SPELDING

MRS. SPELDING

TWO TECHNICIANS

JOHN RANDOLPH

KRETON

GENERAL POWERS

AIDE

PRESIDENT OF PARAGUAY

PAUL LAURENT

SECOND VISITOR

ACT 1

Stock Shot: The night sky, stars. Then slowly a luminous object arcs into view. As it is almost upon us, dissolve to the living room of the Spelding house in Maryland:

Superimpose card: THE TIME: THE DAY AFTER TO-MORROW

The room is comfortably balanced between the expensively decorated and the homely. Roger Spelding *is concluding his TV broadcast. He is middle-aged, unctuous, resonant. His wife, bored and vague, knits passively while he talks at his desk. Two technicians are on hand, operating the equipment. His daughter,* Ellen, *a lively girl of twenty, fidgets as she listens.*

SPELDING [*into microphone*]: . . . and so, according to General Powers . . . who should know if anyone does . . . the flying object which has given rise to so much irresponsible conjecture is nothing more than a meteor passing through the earth's orbit. It is not, as many believe, a secret weapon of this country. Nor is it a space ship as certain lunatic elements have suggested. General Powers has assured me that it is highly doubtful there is any form of life on other planets capable of building a space ship. "If any traveling is to be done in space, we will do it first." And those are his exact words. . . .

Which winds up another week of news. [*crosses to pose with wife and daughter*] This is Roger Spelding, saying good night to Mother and Father America, from my old homestead in Silver Glen, Maryland, close to the warm pulse-beat of the nation.

TECHNICIAN: Good show tonight, Mr. Spelding.

SPELDING: Thank you.

TECHNICIAN: Yes, sir, you were right on time.

[Spelding *nods wearily, his mechanical smile and heartiness suddenly gone.*]

MRS. SPELDING: Very nice, dear. Very nice.

TECHNICIAN: See you next week, Mr. Spelding.

SPELDING: Thank you, boys.

[Technicians *go.*]

SPELDING: Did you like the broadcast, Ellen?

ELLEN: Of course I did, Daddy.

SPELDING: Then what did I say?

ELLEN: Oh, that's not fair.

SPELDING: It's not very flattering when one's own daughter won't listen to what one says while millions of people . . .

ELLEN: I always listen, Daddy, you know that.

MRS. SPELDING: We love your broadcasts, dear. I don't know what we'd do without them.

SPELDING: Starve.

ELLEN: I wonder what's keeping John?

SPELDING: Certainly not work.

ELLEN: Oh, Daddy, stop it! John works very hard and you know it.

MRS. SPELDING: Yes, he's a perfectly nice boy, Roger. I like him.

SPELDING: I know. I know: he has every virtue except the most important one: he has no get-up-and-go.

ELLEN [*precisely*]: He doesn't want to get up and he doesn't want to go because he's already where he wants to be on his own farm which is exactly where *I'm* going to be when we're married.

SPELDING: More thankless than a serpent's tooth is an ungrateful child.

ELLEN: I don't think that's right. Isn't it "more deadly . . ."

SPELDING: Whatever the exact quotation is, I stand by the sentiment.

MRS. SPELDING: Please don't quarrel. It always gives me a headache.

SPELDING: I never quarrel. I merely reason, in my simple way, with Miss Know-it-all here.

ELLEN: Oh, Daddy! Next you'll tell me I should marry for money.

SPELDING: There is nothing wrong with marrying a wealthy man. The horror of it has always eluded me.

However, my only wish is that you marry someone hard-working, ambitious, a man who'll make his mark in the world. Not a boy who plans to sit on a farm all his life, growing peanuts.

ELLEN: English walnuts.

SPELDING: Will you stop correcting me?

ELLEN: But, Daddy, John grows walnuts . . .

[John *enters, breathlessly.*]

JOHN: Come out! Quickly. It's coming this way. It's going to land right here!

SPELDING: *What's* going to land?

JOHN: The space ship. Look!

SPELDING: Apparently you didn't hear my broadcast. The flying object in question is a meteor, not a space ship.

[John *has gone out with* Ellen. Spelding *and* Mrs. Spelding *follow.*]

MRS. SPELDING: Oh, my! Look! Something *is* falling! Roger, you don't think it's going to hit the house, do you?

SPELDING: The odds against being hit by a falling object that size are, I should say, roughly, ten million to one.

JOHN: Ten million to one or not it's going to land right here and it's *not* falling.

SPELDING: I'm sure it's a meteor.

MRS. SPELDING: Shouldn't we go down to the cellar?

SPELDING: If it's not a meteor, it's an optical illusion . . . mass hysteria.

ELLEN: Daddy, it's a real space ship. I'm sure it is.

SPELDING: Or maybe a weather balloon. Yes, that's what it is. General Powers said only yesterday . . .

JOHN: It's landing!

SPELDING: I'm going to call the police . . . the army! [*bolts inside*]

ELLEN: Oh look how it shines!

JOHN: Here it comes!

MRS. SPELDING: Right in my rose garden!

ELLEN: Maybe it's a balloon.

JOHN: No, it's a space ship and right in your own backyard.

ELLEN: What makes it shine so?

JOHN: I don't know but I'm going to find out. [*runs off toward the light*]

ELLEN: Oh, darling, don't! John, please! John, John, come back!

[Spelding, *wide-eyed, returns.*]

MRS. SPELDING: Roger, it's landed right in my rose garden.

SPELDING: I got General Powers. He's coming over. He said they've been watching this thing. They . . . they don't know what it is.

ELLEN: You mean it's nothing of ours?

SPELDING: They believe it . . . [*swallows hard*] . . . it's from outer space.

ELLEN: And John's down there! Daddy, get a gun or something.

SPELDING: Perhaps we'd better leave the house until the army gets here.

ELLEN: We can't leave John.

SPELDING: I can. [*peers nearsightedly*] Why, it's not much larger than a car. I'm sure it's some kind of meteor.

ELLEN: Meteors are blazing hot.

SPELDING: This is a cold one . . .

ELLEN: It's opening . . . the whole side's opening! [*shouts*] John! Come back! Quick. . . .

MRS. SPELDING: Why, there's a man getting out of it! [*sighs*] I feel much better already. I'm sure if we ask him, he'll move that thing for us. Roger, you ask him.

SPELDING [*ominously*]: If it's really a man?

ELLEN: John's shaking hands with him. [*calls*] John darling, come on up here . . .

MRS. SPELDING: And bring your friend . . .

SPELDING: There's something wrong with the way that creature looks . . . if it is a man and not a . . . not a monster.

MRS. SPELDING: He looks perfectly nice to me.

[John *and the* Visitor *appear. The* Visitor *is in his for-
ties, a mild, pleasant-looking man with side whiskers
and dressed in the fashion of 1860. He pauses when
he sees the three people, in silence for a moment. They
stare back at him, equally interested.*]

VISITOR: I seem to've made a mistake. I *am* sorry. I'd
better go back and start over again.

SPELDING: My dear sir, you've only just arrived.
Come in, come in. I don't need to tell you what a pleasure this is . . . Mister . . . Mister . . .

VISITOR: Kreton . . . This *is* the wrong costume, isn't it?

SPELDING: Wrong for what?

KRETON: For the country, and the time.

SPELDING: Well, it's a trifle old-fashioned.

MRS. SPELDING: But really awfully handsome.

KRETON: Thank you.

MRS. SPELDING: [*to husband*] Ask him about moving
that thing off my rose bed.

[Spelding *leads them all into living room.*]

SPELDING: Come on in and sit down. You must be
tired after your trip.

KRETON: Yes, I am a little. [*looks around delightedly*]
Oh, it's better than I'd hoped!

SPELDING: Better? What's better?

KRETON: The house . . . that's what you call it? Or is
this an apartment?

SPELDING: This is a house in the State of Maryland, U.S.A.

KRETON: In the late twentieth century! To think this is really the twentieth century. I must sit down a moment and collect myself. The *real* thing! [*He sits down.*]

ELLEN: You . . . you're not an American, are you?

KRETON: What a nice thought! No, I'm not.

JOHN: You sound more English.

KRETON: Do I? Is my accent very bad?

JOHN: No, it's quite good.

SPELDING: Where *are* you from, Mr. Kreton?

KRETON [*evasively*]: Another place.

SPELDING: On this earth of course.

KRETON: No, not on this planet.

ELLEN: Are you from Mars?

KRETON: Oh dear no, not Mars. There's nobody on Mars . . . at least no one I know.

ELLEN: I'm sure you're testing us and this is all some kind of publicity stunt.

KRETON: No, I really am from another place.

SPELDING: I don't suppose you'd consent to my interviewing you on television?

KRETON: I don't think your authorities will like that. They are terribly upset as it is.

SPELDING: How do you know?

KRETON: Well, I . . . pick up things. For instance, I know that in a few minutes a number of people from your Army will be here to question me and they . . . like you . . . are torn by doubt.

SPELDING: How extraordinary!

ELLEN: Why did you come here?

KRETON: Simply a visit to your small planet. I've been studying it for years. In fact, one might say, you people are my hobby. Especially, this period of your development.

JOHN: Are you the first person from your . . . your planet to travel in space like this?

KRETON: Oh my no! Everyone travels who wants to. It's just that no one wants to visit you. I can't think why. *I* always have. You'd be surprised what a thorough study I've made. [*recites*] The planet, Earth, is divided into five continents with a number of large islands. It is mostly water. There is one moon. Civilization is only just beginning. . . .

SPELDING: Just beginning! My dear sir, we have had. . . .

KRETON [*blandly*]: You are only in the initial stages, the most fascinating stage as far as I'm concerned . . . I do hope I don't sound patronizing.

ELLEN: Well, we are very proud.

KRETON: I know and that's one of your most endearing, primitive traits. Oh, I can't believe I'm here at last!

[General Powers, *a vigorous product of the National Guard, and his* Aide *enter.*]

POWERS: All right, folks. The place is surrounded by troops. Where is the monster?

KRETON: I, my dear General, am the monster.

POWERS: What are you dressed up for, a fancy-dress party?

KRETON: I'd hoped to be in the costume of the period. As you see I am about a hundred years too late.

POWERS: Roger, who is this joker?

SPELDING: This is Mr. Kreton . . . General Powers. Mr. Kreton arrived in that thing outside. He is from another planet.

POWERS: I don't believe it.

ELLEN: It's true. We saw him get out of the flying saucer.

POWERS [*to* Aide]: Captain, go down and look at that ship. But be careful. Don't touch anything. And don't let anybody else near it. [Aide *goes.*] So you're from another planet.

KRETON: Yes. My, that's a very smart uniform but I prefer the ones made of metal, the ones you used to wear, you know: with the feathers on top.

POWERS: That was five hundred years ago . . . Are you *sure* you're not from the earth?

KRETON: Yes.

POWERS: Well, I'm not. You've got some pretty tall explaining to do.

KRETON: Anything to oblige.

POWERS: All right, which planet?

KRETON: None that you have ever heard of.

POWERS: Where is it?

KRETON: You wouldn't know.

POWERS: This solar system?

KRETON: No.

POWERS: Another system?

KRETON: Yes.

POWERS: Look, Buster, I don't want to play games: I just want to know where you're from. The law requires it.

KRETON: It's possible that I could explain it to a mathematician but I'm afraid I couldn't explain it to you, not for another five hundred years and by then of course *you'd* be dead because you people do die, don't you?

POWERS: What?

KRETON: Poor fragile butterflies, such brief little moments in the sun. . . . You see *we* don't die.

POWERS: You'll die all right if it turns out you're a spy or a hostile alien.

KRETON: I'm sure you wouldn't be so cruel.

[Aide *returns; he looks disturbed.*]

POWERS: What did you find?

AIDE: I'm not sure, General.

POWERS [*heavily*]: Then do your best to describe what the object is like.

AIDE: Well, it's elliptical, with a fourteen-foot diameter. And it's made of an unknown metal which shines and inside there isn't anything.

POWERS: Isn't anything?

AIDE: There's nothing inside the ship: no instruments, no food, nothing.

POWERS [*to* Kreton]: What did you do with your instrument board?

KRETON: With my what? Oh, I don't have one.

POWERS: How does the thing travel?

KRETON: I don't know.

POWERS: You don't know. Now look, mister, you're in pretty serious trouble. I suggest you do a bit of cooperating. You claim you traveled here from outer space in a machine with no instruments . . .

KRETON: Well, these cars are rather common in my world and I suppose, once upon a time, I must've known the theory on which they operate but I've long since forgotten. After all, General, we're not mechanics, you and I.

POWERS: Roger, do you mind if we use your study?

SPELDING: Not at all. Not at all, General.

POWERS: Mr. Kreton and I are going to have a chat. [*to* Aide] Put in a call to the Chief of Staff.

AIDE: Yes, General.

[Spelding *rises, leads* Kreton *and* Powers *into next room, a handsomely furnished study, many books and a globe of the world.*]

SPELDING: This way, gentlemen.

[Kreton *sits down comfortably beside the globe, which he twirls thoughtfully. At the door,* Spelding *speaks in a low voice to* Powers.]

I hope I'll be the one to get the story first, Tom.

POWERS: There isn't any story. Complete censorship. I'm sorry but this house is under martial law. I've a hunch we're in trouble.

[*He shuts the door.* Spelding *turns and rejoins his family.*]

ELLEN: I think he's wonderful, whoever he is.

MRS. SPELDING: I wonder how much damage he did to my rose garden . . .

JOHN: It's sure hard to believe he's really from outer space. No instruments, no nothing . . . boy, they must be advanced scientifically.

MRS. SPELDING: Is he spending the night, dear?

SPELDING: What?

MRS. SPELDING: Is he spending the night?

SPELDING: Oh yes, yes, I suppose he will be.

MRS. SPELDING: Then I'd better go make up the bedroom. He seems perfectly nice to me. I like his whiskers. They're so very . . . comforting. Like Grandfather Spelding's. [*She goes.*]

SPELDING [*bitterly*]: I *know* this story will leak out before I can interview him. I just know it.

ELLEN: What does it mean, we're under martial law?

SPELDING: It means we have to do what General Powers tells us to do. [*He goes to the window as a soldier passes by.*] See?

JOHN: I wish I'd taken a closer look at that ship when I had the chance.

ELLEN: Perhaps he'll give us a ride in it.

JOHN: Traveling in space! Just like those stories. You know: intergalactic drive stuff.

SPELDING: *If* he's not an imposter.

ELLEN: I have a feeling he isn't.

JOHN: Well, I better call the family and tell them I'm all right.

[*He crosses to telephone by the door, which leads into hall.*]

AIDE: I'm sorry, sir, but you can't use the phone.

SPELDING: He certainly can. This is my house . . .

AIDE [*mechanically*]: This house is a military reservation until the crisis is over: Order General Powers. I'm sorry.

JOHN: How am I to call home to say where I am?

AIDE: Only General Powers can help you. You're also forbidden to leave this house without permission.

SPELDING: You can't do this!

AIDE: I'm afraid, sir, we've done it.

ELLEN: Isn't it exciting!

[*Cut to study.*]

POWERS: Are you deliberately trying to confuse me?

KRETON: Not deliberately, no.

POWERS: We have gone over and over this for two hours now and all that you've told me is that you're from another planet in another solar system . . .

KRETON: In another dimension. I think that's the word you use.

POWERS: In another dimension and you have come here as a tourist.

KRETON: Up to a point, yes. What did you expect?

POWERS: It is my job to guard the security of this country.

KRETON: I'm sure that must be very interesting work.

POWERS: For all I know, you are a spy, sent here by an alien race to study us, preparatory to invasion.

KRETON: Oh, none of my people would *dream* of invading you.

POWERS: How do I know that's true?

KRETON: You don't, so I suggest you believe me. I should also warn you: I can tell what's inside.

POWERS: What's inside?

KRETON: What's inside your mind.

POWERS: You're a mind reader?

KRETON: I don't really read it. I hear it.

POWERS: What am I thinking?

KRETON: That I am either a lunatic from the earth or a spy from another world.

POWERS: Correct. But then you could've guessed that. [*frowns*] What am I thinking now?

KRETON: You're making a picture. Three silver stars. You're pinning them on your shoulder, instead of the two stars you now wear.

POWERS [*startled*]: That's right. I was thinking of my promotion.

KRETON: If there's anything I can do to hurry it along, just let me know.

POWERS: You can. Tell me why you're here.

KRETON: Well, we don't travel much, my people. We used to but since we see everything through special monitors and recreators, there is no particular need to travel. However, *I* am a hobbyist. I love to gad about.

POWERS [*taking notes*]: Are you the first to visit us?

KRETON: Oh, no! We started visiting you long before there were people on the planet. However, we are seldom noticed on our trips. I'm sorry to say I slipped up, coming in the way I did . . . but then this visit was all rather impromptu. [*laughs*] I am a creature of impulse, I fear.

[Aide *looks in.*]

AIDE: Chief of Staff on the telephone, General.

POWERS [*picks up phone*]: Hello, yes, sir. Powers speaking. I'm talking to him now. No, sir. No, sir. No, we can't determine what method of power was used. He won't talk. Yes, sir. I'll hold him there. I've put the house under martial law . . . belongs to a friend of mine, Roger Spelding, the TV commentator. Roger Spelding, the TV . . . What? Oh, no, I'm sure he won't say anything. Who . . . oh, yes, sir. Yes, I realize the importance of it. Yes, I will. Good-by. [*hangs up*] The President of the United States wants to know all about you.

KRETON: How nice of him! And I want to know all about him. But I do wish you'd let me rest a bit first. Your language is still not familiar to me. I had to learn them all, quite exhausting.

POWERS: You speak *all* our languages?

KRETON: Yes, all of them. But then it's easier than you might think since I can see what's inside.

POWERS: Speaking of what's inside, we're going to take your ship apart.

KRETON: Oh, I wish you wouldn't.

POWERS: Security demands it.

KRETON: In that case *my* security demands you leave it alone.

POWERS: You plan to stop us?

KRETON: I already have . . . Listen.

[*Far-off shouting.* Aide *rushes into the study.*]

AIDE: Something's happened to the ship, General. The door's shut and there's some kind of wall all around it, an invisible wall. We can't get near it.

KRETON [*to camera*]: I hope there was no one inside.

POWERS [*to* Kreton]: How did you do that?

KRETON: I couldn't begin to explain. Now if you don't mind, I think we should go in and see our hosts.

[*He rises, goes into living room.* Powers *and* Aide *look at each other.*]

POWERS: Don't let him out of your sight.

[*Cut to living room as* Powers *picks up phone.* Kreton *is with* John *and* Ellen.]

KRETON: I don't mind curiosity but I really can't permit them to wreck my poor ship.

ELLEN: What do you plan to do, now you're here?

KRETON: Oh, keep busy. I have a project or two . . . [*sighs*] I can't believe you're real!

JOHN: Then we're all in the same boat.

KRETON: Boat? Oh, yes! Well, I should have come ages ago but I . . . I couldn't get away until yesterday.

JOHN: Yesterday? It only took you a *day* to get here?

KRETON: One of *my* days, not yours. But then you don't know about time yet.

JOHN: Oh, you mean relativity.

KRETON: No, it's much more involved than that. You won't know about time until . . . now let me see if I remember . . . no, I don't, but it's about two thousand years.

JOHN: What do we do between now and then?

KRETON: You simply go on the way you are, living your exciting primitive lives . . . You have no idea how much fun you're having now.

ELLEN: I hope you'll stay with us while you're here.

KRETON: That's very nice of you. Perhaps I will. Though I'm sure you'll get tired of having a visitor underfoot all the time.

ELLEN: Certainly not. And Daddy will be deliriously happy. He can interview you by the hour.

JOHN: What's it like in outer space?

KRETON: Dull.

ELLEN: I should think it would be divine!

[Powers *enters.*]

KRETON: No, General, it won't work.

POWERS: What won't work?

KRETON: Trying to blow up my little force field. You'll just plough up Mrs. Spelding's garden.

[Powers *snarls and goes into study.*]

ELLEN: Can you tell what we're *all* thinking?

KRETON: Yes. As a matter of fact, it makes me a bit giddy. Your minds are not at all like ours. You see we control our thoughts while you . . . well, it's extraordinary the things you think about!

ELLEN: Oh, how awful! You can tell *everything* we think?

KRETON: Everything! It's one of the reasons I'm here, to intoxicate myself with your primitive minds . . . with the wonderful rawness of your emotions! You have no idea how it excites me! You simply seethe with unlikely emotions.

ELLEN: I've never felt so sordid.

JOHN: From now on I'm going to think about agriculture.

SPELDING [*entering*]: You would.

ELLEN: Daddy!

KRETON: No, no. You must go right on thinking about Ellen. Such wonderfully *purple* thoughts!

SPELDING: Now see here, Powers, you're carrying this martial law thing too far . . .

POWERS: Unfortunately, until I have received word from Washington as to the final disposition of this problem, you must obey my orders: no telephone calls, no communication with the outside.

SPELDING: This is unsupportable.

KRETON: Poor Mr. Spelding! If you like, I shall go. That would solve everything, wouldn't it?

POWERS: You're not going anywhere, Mr. Kreton, until I've had my instructions.

KRETON: I sincerely doubt if you could stop me. However, I put it up to Mr. Spelding. Shall I go?

SPELDING: Yes! [Powers *gestures a warning.*] Do stay. I mean, we want you to get a good impression of us . . .

KRETON: And of course you still want to be the first journalist to interview me. Fair enough. All right, I'll stay on for a while.

POWERS: Thank you.

KRETON: Don't mention it.

SPELDING: General, may I ask our guest a few questions?

POWERS: Go right ahead, Roger. I hope you'll do better than I did.

SPELDING: Since you read our minds, you probably already know what our fears are.

KRETON: I do, yes.

SPELDING: We are afraid that you represent a hostile race.

KRETON: And I have assured General Powers that my people are not remotely hostile. Except for me, no one is interested in this planet's present stage.

SPELDING: Does this mean you might be interested in a *later* stage?

KRETON: I'm not permitted to discuss your future. Of course my friends think me perverse to be interested in a primitive society but there's no accounting for tastes, is there? You are my hobby. I love you. And that's all there is to it.

POWERS: So you're just here to look around . . . sort of going native.

KRETON: What a nice expression! That's it exactly. I am going native.

POWERS [*grimly*]: Well, it is my view that you have been sent here by another civilization for the express purpose of reconnoitering prior to invasion.

KRETON: That *would* be your view! The wonderfully primitive assumption that all strangers are hostile. You're almost too good to be true, General.

POWERS: You deny your people intend to make trouble for us?

KRETON: I deny it.

POWERS: Then are they interested in establishing communication with us? Trade? That kind of thing?

KRETON: We have always had communication with you. As for trade, well, we do not trade . . . that is something peculiar only to your social level. [*quickly*] Which I'm not criticizing! As you know, I approve of everything you do.

POWERS: I give up.

SPELDING: You have no interest then in . . . well, trying to dominate the earth.

KRETON: Oh, yes!

POWERS: I thought you just said your people weren't interested in us.

KRETON: *They're* not, but *I* am.

POWERS: You!

KRETON: Me . . . I mean I. You see I've come here to take charge.

POWERS: Of the United States?

KRETON: No, of the whole world. I'm sure you'll be much happier and it will be great fun for me. You'll get used to it in no time.

POWERS: This is ridiculous. How can one man take over the world?

KRETON [*gaily*]: Wait and see!

POWERS [*to* Aide]: Grab him!

[Powers *and* Aide *rush* Kreton *but within a foot of him, they stop, stunned.*]

KRETON: You can't touch me. That's part of the game. [*He yawns.*] Now, if you don't mind, I shall go up to my room for a little lie-down.

SPELDING: I'll show you the way.

KRETON: That's all right, I know the way. [*touches his brow*] Such savage thoughts! My head is vibrating like a drum. I feel quite giddy, all of you thinking away. [*He starts to the door; he pauses beside* Mrs. Spelding.] No, it's not a dream, dear lady. I shall be here in the morning when you wake up. And now, good night, dear, wicked children. . . .

[*He goes as we fade out.*]

ACT 2

Fade in on Kreton's *bedroom next morning. He lies fully clothed on bed with cat on his lap.*

KRETON: Poor cat! Of course I sympathize with you. Dogs *are* distasteful. What? Oh, I can well believe they do: yes, yes, how disgusting. They don't ever groom their fur! But you do *constantly,* such a fine coat. No, no, I'm not just saying that. I really mean it: exquisite texture. Of course, I wouldn't say it was *nicer* than skin but even so. . . . What? Oh, no! They *chase* you! Dogs chase you for no reason at all except pure malice? You poor creature. Ah, but you *do* fight back! That's right! Give it to them: slash, bite, scratch! Don't let them get away with a trick. . . . No! Do dogs really do that? Well, I'm sure *you* don't. What . . . oh, well, yes I completely agree about mice. They *are* delicious! (Ugh!) Pounce, snap and there is a heavenly dinner. No, I don't know any mice yet . . . they're not very amusing? But after all think how you must terrify them because you are so bold, so cunning, so beautifully predatory!

[*knock at door*]

Come in.

ELLEN [*enters*]: Good morning. I brought you your breakfast.

KRETON: How thoughtful! [*examines bacon*] Delicious, but I'm afraid my stomach is not like yours, if you'll pardon me. I don't eat. [*removes pill from his pocket and swallows it*] This is all I need for the day. [*indicates cat*] Unlike this creature, who would eat her own weight every hour, given a chance.

ELLEN: How do you know?

KRETON: We've had a talk.

ELLEN: You can *speak* to the cat?

KRETON: Not speak exactly but we communicate. I look inside and the cat cooperates. Bright red thoughts, very exciting, though rather on one level.

ELLEN: Does kitty like us?

KRETON: No, I wouldn't say she did. But then she has very few thoughts not connected with food. Have you, my quadruped criminal? [*He strokes the cat, which jumps to the floor.*]

ELLEN: You know you've really upset everyone.

KRETON: I supposed that I would.

ELLEN: Can you really take over the world, just like that?

KRETON: Oh, yes.

ELLEN: What do you plan to do when you *have* taken over?

KRETON: Ah, that is my secret.

ELLEN: Well, I think you'll be a very nice President, *if* they let you of course.

KRETON: What a sweet girl you are! Marry him right away.

ELLEN: Marry John?

KRETON: Yes. I see it in your head *and* in his. He wants you very much.

ELLEN: Well, we plan to get married this summer, if father doesn't fuss too much.

KRETON: Do it before then. I shall arrange it all if you like.

ELLEN: How?

KRETON: I can convince your father.

ELLEN: That sounds awfully ominous. I think you'd better leave poor Daddy alone.

KRETON: Whatever you say. [*sighs*] Oh, I love it so! When I woke up this morning I had to pinch myself to prove I was really here.

ELLEN: We were all doing a bit of pinching too. Ever since dawn we've had nothing but visitors and phone calls and troops outside in the garden. No one has the faintest idea what to do about you.

KRETON: Well, I don't think they'll be confused much longer.

ELLEN: How do you plan to conquer the world?

KRETON: I confess I'm not sure. I suppose I must make some demonstration of strength, some colorful trick that will frighten everyone . . . though I much prefer taking charge quietly. That's why I've sent for the President.

ELLEN: The President? *Our* President?

KRETON: Yes, he'll be along any minute now.

ELLEN: But the President just doesn't go around visiting people.

KRETON: He'll visit me. [*chuckles*] It may come as a surprise to him, but he'll be in this house in a very few minutes. I think we'd better go downstairs now. [*to cat*]

No, I will not give you a mouse. You must get your own. Be self-reliant. Beast!

[*Dissolve to the study.* Powers *is reading book entitled:* The Atom and You. *Muffled explosions offstage.*]

AIDE [*entering*]: Sir, nothing seems to be working. Do we have the General's permission to try a fission bomb on the force field?

POWERS: No . . . no. We'd better give it up.

AIDE: The men are beginning to talk.

POWERS [*thundering*]: Well, keep them quiet! [*contritely*] I'm sorry, Captain. I'm on edge. Fortunately, the whole business will soon be in the hands of the World Council.

AIDE: What will the World Council do?

POWERS: It will be interesting to observe them.

AIDE: You don't think this Kreton can really take over the world, do you?

POWERS: Of course not. Nobody can.

[*Dissolve to living room.* Mrs. Spelding *and* Spelding *are talking.*]

MRS. SPELDING: You still haven't asked Mr. Kreton about moving that thing, have you?

SPELDING: There are too many *important* things to ask him.

MRS. SPELDING: I hate to be a nag but you know the trouble I have had getting anything to grow in that part of the garden . . .

JOHN [*enters*]: Good morning.

MRS. SPELDING: Good morning, John.

JOHN: Any sign of your guest?

MRS. SPELDING: Ellen took his breakfast up to him a few minutes ago.

JOHN: They don't seem to be having much luck, do they? I sure hope you don't mind my staying here like this.

[Spelding *glowers*.]

MRS. SPELDING: Why, we love having you! I just hope your family aren't too anxious.

JOHN: One of the G.I.'s finally called them, said I was staying here for the weekend.

SPELDING: The rest of our *lives,* if something isn't done soon.

JOHN: Just how long do you think that'll be, Dad?

SPELDING: Who knows?

[Kreton *and* Ellen *enter.*]

KRETON: Ah, how wonderful to see you again! Let me catch my breath. . . . Oh, your minds! It's not easy for me, you know. So many crude thoughts blazing away! Yes, Mrs. Spelding, I will move the ship off your roses.

MRS. SPELDING: That's awfully sweet of you.

KRETON: Mr. Spelding, if any interviews are to be granted you will be the first. I promise you.

SPELDING: That's very considerate, I'm sure.

KRETON: So you can stop thinking *those* particular thoughts. And now where is the President?

SPELDING: The President?

KRETON: Yes, I sent for him. He should be here. [*He goes to the terrace window.*] Ah, that must be he.

[*A swarthy man in uniform with a sash across his chest is standing, bewildered, on the terrace.* Kreton *opens the glass doors.*]

Come in, sir, come in, Your Excellency. Good of you to come on such short notice.

[Man *enters.*]

MAN [*in Spanish accent*]: Where am I?

KRETON: You *are* the President, aren't you?

MAN: Of course I am the President. What am I doing here? I was dedicating a bridge and I find myself . . .

KRETON [*aware of his mistake*]: Oh, dear! *Where* was the bridge?

MAN: Where do you think, you idiot, in Paraguay!

KRETON [*to others*]: I seem to've made a mistake. Wrong President. [*He gestures and the* Man *disappears.*] Seemed rather upset, didn't he?

JOHN: You can make people come and go just like that?

KRETON: Just like that.

[Powers *looks into room from the study.*]

POWERS: Good morning, Mr. Kreton. Could I see you for a moment?

KRETON: By all means. [*He crosses to the study.*]

SPELDING: I believe I am going mad.

[*Cut to study. The* Aide *stands at attention while* Powers *addresses* Kreton.]

POWERS: . . . and so we feel, the government of the United States feels, that this problem is too big for any one country, therefore we are turning the whole affair over to Paul Laurent, the Secretary-General of the World Council.

KRETON: Very sensible. I should've thought of that myself.

POWERS: Mr. Laurent is on his way here now. And I may add, Mr. Kreton, you've made me look singularly ridiculous.

KRETON: I'm awfully sorry. [*pause*] No, you can't kill me.

POWERS: You were reading my mind again.

KRETON: I can't really help it, you know. And such *black* thoughts today, but intense, very intense.

POWERS: I regard you as a menace.

KRETON: I know you do and I think it's awfully unkind. I do mean well.

POWERS: Then go back where you came from and leave us alone.

KRETON: I'm afraid I can't do that just yet . . .

[Phone rings; the Aide *answers it.]*

AIDE: He's outside? Sure, let him through. *[to* Powers] The Secretary-General of the World Council is here sir.

POWERS *[to* Kreton]: I hope you'll listen to *him.*

KRETON: Oh, I shall, of course. I love listening.

[The door opens and Paul Laurent, *middle-aged and serene, enters.* Powers *and his* Aide *stand to attention.* Kreton *goes forward to shake hands.]*

LAURENT: Mr. Kreton?

KRETON: At your service, Mr. Laurent.

LAURENT: I welcome you to this planet in the name of the World Council.

KRETON: Thank you, sir, thank you.

LAURENT: Could you leave us alone for a moment, General?

POWERS: Yes, sir.

[Powers *and* Aide *go.* Laurent *smiles at* Kreton.]

LAURENT: Shall we sit down?

KRETON: Yes, yes, I love sitting down. I'm afraid my manners are not quite suitable, yet.

[They sit down.]

LAURENT: Now, Mr. Kreton, in violation of all the rules of diplomacy, may I come to the point?

KRETON: You may.

LAURENT: Why are you here?

KRETON: Curiosity. Pleasure.

LAURENT: You are a tourist then in this time and place?

KRETON [*nods*]: Yes. Very well put.

LAURENT: We have been informed that you have extraordinary powers.

KRETON: By your standards, yes, they must seem extraordinary.

LAURENT: We have also been informed that it is your intention to . . . to take charge of this world.

KRETON: That is correct. . . . What a remarkable mind you have! I have difficulty looking inside it.

LAURENT [*laughs*]: Practice. I've attended so many conferences. . . . May I say that your conquest of our world puts your status of tourist in a rather curious light?

KRETON: Oh, I said nothing about *conquest.*

LAURENT: Then how else do you intend to govern? The people won't allow you to direct their lives without a struggle.

KRETON: But I'm sure they will if I ask them to.

LAURENT: You believe you can do all this without, well, without violence?

KRETON: Of course I can. One or two demonstrations and I'm sure they'll do as I ask. [*smiles*] Watch this.

[*Pauses, then shouting.* Powers *bursts into room.*]

POWERS: Now what've you done?

KRETON: Look out the window, your Excellency. [*Laurent goes to window. A rifle floats by, followed by an alarmed soldier.*] Nice, isn't it? I confess I worked out a number of rather melodramatic tricks last night. Incidentally, all the rifles of all the soldiers in all the world are now floating in the air. [*gestures*] Now they have them back.

POWERS [*to* Laurent]: You see, sir, I didn't exaggerate in my report.

LAURENT [*awed*]: No, no, you certainly didn't.

KRETON: You were skeptical, weren't you?

LAURENT: Naturally. But now I . . . now I think it's possible.

POWERS: That this . . . this gentleman is going to run everything?

LAURENT: Yes, yes, I do. And it might be wonderful.

KRETON: You *are* more clever than the others. You begin to see that I mean only good.

LAURENT: Yes, only good. General, do you realize what this means? We can have one government . . .

KRETON: With innumerable bureaus, and intrigue. . . .

LAURENT [*excited*]: And the world could be incredibly prosperous, especially if he'd help us with his superior knowledge.

KRETON [*delighted*]: I will, I will. I'll teach you to look into one another's minds. You'll find it devastating but enlightening: all that self-interest, those *lurid* emotions . . .

LAURENT: No more countries. No more wars . . .

KRETON [*startled*]: What? Oh, but I like a lot of countries. Besides, at this stage of your development you're supposed to have lots of countries and lots of wars . . . innumerable wars . . .

LAURENT: But you can help us change all that.

KRETON: *Change* all that! My dear sir, I am your friend.

LAURENT: What do you mean?

KRETON: Why, your deepest pleasure is violence. How can you deny that? It is the whole point to you, the whole point to my hobby . . . and you are my hobby, all mine.

LAURENT: But our lives are devoted to *controlling* violence, and not creating it.

KRETON: Now, don't take me for an utter fool. After all, I can see into your minds. My dear fellow, don't you *know* what you are?

LAURENT: What are we?

KRETON: You are savages. I have returned to the dark ages of an insignificant planet simply because I want the glorious excitement of being among you and reveling in your savagery! There is murder in all your hearts and I love it! It intoxicates me!

LAURENT [*slowly*]: You hardly flatter us.

KRETON: I didn't mean to be rude but you did ask me why I am here and I've told you.

LAURENT: You have no wish then to . . . to help us poor savages.

KRETON: I couldn't even if I wanted to. You won't be civilized for at least two thousand years and you won't reach the level of my people for about a million years.

LAURENT [*sadly*]: Then you have come here only to . . . to observe?

KRETON: No, more than that. I mean to regulate your pastimes. But don't worry: I won't upset things too much. I've decided I don't want to be known to the people. You will go right on with your countries, your squabbles, the way you always have, while I will *secretly* regulate things through you.

LAURENT: The World Council does not govern. We only advise.

KRETON: Well, I shall advise you and you will advise the governments and we shall have a lovely time.

LAURENT: I don't know what to say. You obviously have the power to do as you please.

KRETON: I'm glad you realize that. Poor General Powers is now wondering if a hydrogen bomb might destroy me. It won't, General.

POWERS: Too bad.

KRETON: Now, Your Excellency, I shall stay in this house until you have laid the groundwork for my first project.

LAURENT: And what is that to be?

KRETON: A war! I want one of your really splendid wars, with all the trimmings, all the noise and the fire . . .

LAURENT: A war! You're joking. Why at this moment we are working as hard as we know how *not* to have a war.

KRETON: But secretly you want one. After all, it's the one thing your little race does well. You'd hardly want me to deprive you of your simple pleasures, now would you?

LAURENT: I think you must be mad.

KRETON: Not mad, simply a philanthropist. Of course I myself shall get a great deal of pleasure out of a war (the vibrations must be incredible!) but I'm doing it mostly for you. So, if you don't mind, I want you to arrange a few incidents, so we can get one started spontaneously.

LAURENT: I refuse.

KRETON: In that event, I shall select someone else to head the World Council. Someone who *will* start a war. I suppose there exist a few people here who might like the idea.

LAURENT: How can you do such a horrible thing to us? Can't you see that we don't want to be savages?

KRETON: But you have no choice. Anyway, you're just pulling my leg! I'm sure you want a war as much as the rest of them do and that's what you're going to get: the biggest war you've ever had!

LAURENT [*stunned*]: Heaven help us!

KRETON [*exuberant*]: Heaven won't! Oh, what fun it will be! I can hardly wait! [*He strikes the globe of the world a happy blow as we fade out.*]

ACT 3

Fade in on the study, two weeks later. Kreton is sitting at desk on which a map is spread out. He has a pair of dividers, some models of jet aircraft. Occasionally he pretends to dive-bomb, imitating the sound of a bomb going off. Powers *enters.*

POWERS: You wanted me, sir?

KRETON: Yes, I wanted those figures on radioactive fallout.

POWERS: They're being made up now, sir. Anything else?

KRETON: Oh, my dear fellow, why do you dislike me so?

POWERS: I am your military aide, sir: I don't have to answer that question. It is outside the sphere of my duties.

KRETON: Aren't you at least happy about your promotion?

POWERS: Under the circumstances, no, sir.

KRETON: I find your attitude baffling.

POWERS: Is that all, sir?

. KRETON: You have never once said what you thought of my war plans. Not once have I got a single word of encouragement from you, a single compliment . . . only black thoughts.

POWERS: Since you read my mind, sir, you know what I think.

KRETON: True, but I can't help but feel that deep down inside of you there is just a twinge of professional jealousy. You don't like the idea of an outsider playing your game better than you do. Now confess!

POWERS: I am acting as your aide only under duress.

KRETON [*sadly*]: Bitter, bitter . . . and to think I chose you especially as my aide. Think of all the other generals who would give anything to have your job.

POWERS: Fortunately, they know nothing about my job.

KRETON: Yes, I do think it wise not to advertise my presence, don't you?

POWERS: I can't see that it makes much difference, since you seem bent on destroying our world.

KRETON: I'm not going to destroy it. A few dozen cities, that's all, and not very nice cities either. Think of the fun you'll have building new ones when it's over.

POWERS: How many millions of people do you plan to kill?

KRETON: Well, quite a few, but they love this sort of thing. You can't convince me they don't. Oh, I know what Laurent says. But he's a misfit, out of step with this time. Fortunately, my new World Council is more reasonable.

POWERS: Paralyzed is the word, sir.

KRETON: You don't think they like me either?

POWERS: You *know* they hate you, sir.

KRETON: But love and hate are so confused in your savage minds and the vibrations of the one are so very like those of the other that I can't always distinguish. You see, we neither love nor hate in my world. We simply have hobbies. [*He strokes the globe of the world ten-*

derly.] But now to work. Tonight's the big night: first, the sneak attack, then: boom! [*He claps his hands gleefully.*]

[*Dissolve to the living room, to* John *and* Ellen.]

ELLEN: I've never felt so helpless in my life.

JOHN: Here we all stand around doing nothing while he plans to blow up the world.

ELLEN: Suppose we went to the newspapers.

JOHN: He controls the press. When Laurent resigned they didn't even print his speech.

[*a gloomy pause*]

ELLEN: What are you thinking about, John?

JOHN: Walnuts.

[*They embrace.*]

ELLEN: Can't we do anything?

JOHN: No, I guess there's nothing.

ELLEN [*vehemently*]: Oh! I could kill him!

[Kreton *and* Powers *enter.*]

KRETON: Very good, Ellen, *very* good! I've never felt you so violent.

ELLEN: You heard what I said to John?

KRETON: Not in words, but you were absolutely bathed in malevolence.

POWERS: I'll get the papers you wanted, sir. [Powers *exits.*]

KRETON: I don't think he likes me very much but your father does. Only this morning he offered to handle my public relations and I said I'd let him. Wasn't that nice of him?

JOHN: I think I'll go get some fresh air. [*He goes out through the terrace door.*]

KRETON: Oh, dear! [*sighs*] Only your father is really entering the spirit of the game. He's a much better sport than you, my dear.

ELLEN [*exploding*]: Sport! That's it! You think we're sport. You think we're animals to be played with: well, we're not. We're people and we don't want to be destroyed.

KRETON [*patiently*]: But *I* am not destroying you. You will be destroying one another of your own free will, as you have always done. I am simply a . . . a kibitzer.

ELLEN: No, you are a vampire!

KRETON: A vampire? You mean I drink blood? Ugh!

ELLEN: No, you drink emotions, our emotions. You'll sacrifice us all for the sake of your . . . your vibrations!

KRETON: Touché. Yet what harm am I really doing? It's true I'll enjoy the war more than anybody; but it will be *your* destructiveness after all, not mine.

ELLEN: You could stop it.

KRETON: So could you.

ELLEN: I?

KRETON: Your race. They could stop altogether but they won't. And I can hardly intervene in their natural development. The most I can do is help out in small, practical ways.

ELLEN: We are not what you think. We're not so . . . so primitive.

KRETON: My dear girl, just take this one household: your mother dislikes your father but she is too tired to do anything about it so she knits and she gardens and she tries not to think about him. Your father, on the other hand, is bored with all of you. Don't look shocked: he doesn't like you any more than you like him . . .

ELLEN: Don't say that!

KRETON: I am only telling you the truth. Your father wants you to marry someone important; therefore he objects to John while you, my girl . . .

ELLEN [*With a fierce cry,* Ellen *grabs vase to throw.*]: You devil! [*Vase breaks in her hand.*]

KRETON: You see? That proves my point perfectly. [*gently*] Poor savage, I cannot help what you are. [*briskly*] Anyway, you will soon be distracted from your personal problems. Tonight is the night. If you're a good girl, I'll let you watch the bombing.

[*Dissolve to study: eleven forty-five.* Powers *and the* Aide *gloomily await the war.*]

AIDE: General, isn't there anything we can do?

POWERS: It's out of our hands.

[Kreton, *dressed as a Hussar with shako, enters.*]

KRETON: Everything on schedule?

POWERS: Yes, sir. Planes left for their targets at twenty-two hundred.

KRETON: Good . . . good. I myself shall take off shortly after midnight to observe the attack first hand.

POWERS: Yes, sir.

[Kreton *goes into the living room where the family is gloomily assembled.*]

KRETON [*enters from study*]: And now the magic hour approaches! I hope you're all as thrilled as I am.

SPELDING: You still won't tell us who's attacking whom?

KRETON: You'll know in exactly . . . fourteen minutes.

ELLEN [*bitterly*]: Are we going to be killed too?

KRETON: Certainly not! You're quite safe, at least in the early stages of the war.

ELLEN: Thank you.

MRS. SPELDING: I suppose this will mean rationing again.

SPELDING: Will . . . will we see anything from here?

KRETON: No, but there should be a good picture on the monitor in the study. Powers is tuning in right now.

JOHN [*at window*]: Hey look, up there! Coming this way!

[Ellen *joins him.*]

ELLEN: What is it?

JOHN: Why . . . it's *another* one! And it's going to land.

KRETON [*surprised*]: I'm sure you're mistaken. No one would dream of coming here. [*He has gone to the window, too.*]

ELLEN: It's landing!

SPELDING: Is it a friend of yours, Mr. Kreton?

KRETON [*slowly*]: No, no, not a friend . . . [*Kreton retreats to the study; he inadvertently drops a lace handkerchief beside the sofa.*]

JOHN: Here he comes.

ELLEN [*suddenly bitter*]: Now we have two of them.

MRS. SPELDING: My poor roses.

[*The new Visitor enters in a gleam of light from his ship. He is wearing a most futuristic costume. Without a word, he walks past the awed family into the study. Kreton is cowering behind the globe. Powers and the Aide stare, bewildered, as the Visitor gestures sternly and Kreton reluctantly removes shako and sword. They communicate by odd sounds.*]

VISITOR [*to Powers*]: Please leave us alone.

[*Cut to living room as Powers and the Aide enter from the study.*]

POWERS [*to Ellen*]: Who on earth was that?

ELLEN: It's another one, another visitor.

POWERS: Now we're done for.

ELLEN: I'm going in there.

MRS. SPELDING: Ellen, don't you dare!

ELLEN: I'm going to talk to them. [*starts to door*]

JOHN: I'm coming, too.

ELLEN [*grimly*]: No, alone. I know what I want to say.

[*Cut to interior of the study, to* Kreton *and the other* Visitor *as* Ellen *enters.*]

ELLEN: I want you both to listen to me . . .

VISITOR: You don't need to speak. I know what you will say.

ELLEN: That you have no right here? That you mustn't . . .

VISITOR: I agree. Kreton has no right here. He is well aware that it is forbidden to interfere with the past.

ELLEN: The past?

VISITOR [*nods*]: You are the past, the dark ages: we are from the future. In fact, we are *your* descendants on another planet. We visit you from time to time but we never interfere because it would change *us* if we did. Fortunately, I have arrived in time.

ELLEN: There won't be a war?

VISITOR: There will be no war. And there will be no memory of any of this. When we leave here you will forget Kreton and me. Time will turn back to the moment before his arrival.

ELLEN: Why did you want to hurt us?

KRETON [*heartbroken*]: Oh, but I didn't! I only

wanted to have . . . well, to have a little fun, to indulge my hobby . . . against the rules of course.

VISITOR [*to* Ellen]: Kreton is a rarity among us. Mentally and morally he is retarded. He is a child and he regards your period as his toy.

KRETON: A child, now really!

VISITOR: He escaped from his nursery and came back in time to you . . .

KRETON: And *every*thing went wrong, everything! I wanted to visit 1860 . . . that's my *real* period but then something happened to the car and I ended up here, not that I don't find you nearly as interesting but . . .

VISITOR: We must go, Kreton.

KRETON [*to* Ellen]: You did like me just a bit, didn't you?

ELLEN: Yes, yes I did, until you let your hobby get out of hand. [*to* Visitor] What is the future like?

VISITOR: Very serene, very different . . .

KRETON: Don't believe him: it is dull, dull, dull beyond belief! One simply floats through eternity: no wars, no excitement . . .

VISITOR: It is forbidden to discuss these matters.

KRETON: I can't see what difference it makes since she's going to forget all about us anyway.

ELLEN: Oh, how I'd love to see the future . . .

VISITOR: It is against . . .

KRETON: Against the rules: how tiresome you are. [*to* Ellen] But, alas, you can never pay us a call because you aren't born yet! I mean where we are you are not. Oh, Ellen, dear, think kindly of me, until you forget.

ELLEN: I will.

VISITOR: Come. Time has begun to turn back. Time is bending.

[*He starts to door. Kreton turns conspiratorially to* Ellen.]

KRETON: Don't be sad, my girl. I shall be back one bright day, but a bright day in 1860. I dote on the Civil War, so exciting . . .

VISITOR: Kreton!

KRETON: Only next time I think it'll be more fun if the *South* wins! [*He hurries after the* Visitor.]

[*Cut to clock as the hands spin backwards. Dissolve to the living room, exactly the same as the first scene:* Spelding, Mrs. Spelding, Ellen.]

SPELDING: There is nothing wrong with marrying a wealthy man. The horror of it has always eluded me. However, my only wish is that you marry someone hard-working, ambitious, a man who'll make his mark in the world. Not a boy who is content to sit on a farm all his life, growing peanuts . . .

ELLEN: English walnuts! And he won't just sit there.

SPELDING: Will you stop contradicting me?

ELLEN: But, Daddy, John grows walnuts . . .

[John *enters.*]

JOHN: Hello, everybody.

MRS. SPELDING: Good evening, John.

ELLEN: What kept you, darling? You missed Daddy's broadcast.

JOHN: I saw it before I left home. Wonderful broadcast, sir.

SPELDING: Thank you, John.

[John *crosses to window.*]

JOHN: That meteor you were talking about, well, for a while it looked almost like a space ship or something. You can just barely see it now.

[Ellen *joins him at window. They watch, arms about one another.*]

SPELDING: Space ship! Nonsense! Remarkable what some people will believe, *want* to believe. Besides, as I said in the broadcast: if there's any traveling to be done in space we'll do it first.

[*He notices* Kreton's *handkerchief beside the sofa and picks it up. They all look at it, puzzled, as we cut to stock shot of the starry night against which two space ships vanish in the distance, one serene in its course, the other erratic, as we fade out.*]

TENDER OFFER

by Wendy Wasserstein

CHARACTERS

PAUL
LISA

A girl of around nine is alone in a dance studio. She is dressed in traditional leotards and tights. She begins singing to herself, "Nothing Could Be Finer Than to Be in Carolina." She maps out a dance routine, including parts for the chorus. She builds to a finale. A man, Paul, around thirty-five, walks in. He has a sweet, though distant, demeanor. As he walks in, Lisa notices him and stops.

PAUL: You don't have to stop, sweetheart.

LISA: That's okay.

PAUL: Looked very good.

LISA: Thanks.

PAUL: Don't I get a kiss hello?

LISA: Sure.

PAUL [*embraces her*]: Hi, Tiger.

LISA: Hi, Dad.

PAUL: I'm sorry I'm late.

LISA: That's okay.

PAUL: How'd it go?

LISA: Good.

PAUL: Just good?

LISA: Pretty good.

PAUL: "Pretty good." You mean you got a lot of applause or "pretty good" you could have done better.

LISA: Well, Courtney Palumbo's mother thought I was pretty good. But you know the part in the middle when everybody's supposed to freeze and the big girl comes out. Well, I think I moved a little bit.

PAUL: I thought what you were doing looked very good.

LISA: Daddy, that's not what I was doing. That was tap-dancing. I made that up.

PAUL: Oh. Well it looked good. Kind of sexy.

LISA: Yuch!

PAUL: What do you mean "yuch"?

LISA: Just yuch!

PAUL: You don't want to be sexy?

LISA: I don't care.

PAUL: Let's go, Tiger. I promised your mother I'd get you home in time for dinner.

LISA: I can't find my leg warmers.

PAUL: You can't find your what?

LISA: Leg warmers. I can't go home till I find my leg warmers.

PAUL: I don't see you looking for them.

LISA: I was waiting for you.

PAUL: Oh.

LISA: Daddy.

PAUL: What?

LISA: Nothing.

PAUL: Where do you think you left them?

LISA: Somewhere around here. I can't remember.

PAUL: Well, try to remember, Lisa. We don't have all night.

LISA: I told you. I think somewhere around here.

PAUL: I don't see them. Let's go home now. You'll call the dancing school tomorrow.

LISA: Daddy, I can't go home till I find them. Miss Judy says it's not professional to leave things.

PAUL: Who's Miss Judy?

LISA: She's my ballet teacher. She once danced the lead in *Swan Lake,* and she was a June Taylor dancer.

PAUL: Well, then, I'm sure she'll understand about the leg warmers.

LISA: Daddy, Miss Judy wanted to know why you were late today.

PAUL: Hmmmmmmmm?

LISA: Why were you late?

PAUL: I was in a meeting. Business. I'm sorry.

LISA: Why did you tell Mommy you'd come instead of her if you knew you had business?

PAUL: Honey, something just came up. I thought I'd be able to be here. I was looking forward to it.

LISA: I wish you wouldn't make appointments to see me.

PAUL: Hmmmmmmm.

LISA: You shouldn't make appointments to see me unless you know you're going to come.

PAUL: Of course I'm going to come.

LISA: No, you're not. Talia Robbins told me she's much happier living without her father in the house. Her father used to come home late and go to sleep early.

PAUL: Lisa, stop it. Let's go.

LISA: I can't find my leg warmers.

PAUL: Forget your leg warmers.

LISA: Daddy.

PAUL: What is it?

LISA: I saw this show on television. I think it was WPIX Channel 11. Well, the father was crying about his daughter.

PAUL: Why was he crying? Was she sick?

LISA: No. She was at school. And he was at business. And he just missed her, so he started to cry.

PAUL: What was the name of this show?

LISA: I don't know. I came in in the middle.

PAUL: Well, Lisa, I certainly would cry if you were sick or far away, but I know that you're well and you're home. So no reason to get maudlin.

LISA: What's maudlin?

PAUL: Sentimental, soppy. Frequently used by children who make things up to get attention.

LISA: I am sick! I am sick! I have Hodgkin's disease and a bad itch on my leg.

PAUL: What do you mean you have Hodgkin's disease? Don't say things like that.

LISA: Swoosie Kurtz, she had Hodgkin's disease on a TV movie last year, but she got better and now she's on *Love Sidney*.

PAUL: Who is Swoosie Kurtz?

LISA: She's an actress named after an airplane. I saw her on *Live at Five*.

PAUL: You watch too much television; you should do your homework. Now, put your coat on.

LISA: Daddy, I really do have a bad itch on my leg. Would you scratch it?

PAUL: Lisa, you're procrastinating.

LISA: Why do you use words I don't understand? I hate it. You're like Daria Feldman's mother. She always talks in Yiddish to her husband so Daria won't understand.

PAUL: Procrastinating is not Yiddish.

LISA: Well, I don't know what it is.

PAUL: Procrastinating means you don't want to go about your business.

LISA: I don't go to business. I go to school.

PAUL: What I mean is you want to hang around here until you and I are late for dinner and your mother's angry and it's too late for you to do your homework.

LISA: I do not.

PAUL: Well, it sure looks that way. Now put your coat on and let's go.

LISA: Daddy.

PAUL: Honey, I'm tired. Really, later.

LISA: Why don't you want to talk to me?

PAUL: I do want to talk to you. I promise when we get home we'll have a nice talk.

LISA: No, we won't. You'll read the paper and fall asleep in front of the news.

PAUL: Honey, we'll talk on the weekend, I promise. Aren't I taking you to the theater this weekend? Let me look. [*He takes out appointment book.*] Yes. Sunday. *Joseph and the Amazing Technicolor Raincoat* with Lisa. Okay, Tiger?

LISA: Sure. It's Dreamcoat.

PAUL: What?

LISA: Nothing. I think I see my leg warmers. [*She goes to pick them up, and an odd-looking trophy.*]

PAUL: What's that?

LISA: It's stupid. I was second best at the dance recital, so they gave me this thing. It's stupid.

PAUL: Lisa.

LISA: What?

PAUL: What did you want to talk about?

LISA: Nothing.

PAUL: Was it about my missing your recital? I'm really sorry, Tiger. I would have liked to have been here.

LISA: That's okay.

PAUL: Honest?

LISA: Daddy, you're prostrastinating.

PAUL: I'm procrastinating. Sit down. Let's talk. So. How's school?

LISA: Fine.

PAUL: You like it?

LISA: Yup.

PAUL: You looking forward to camp this summer?

LISA: Yup.

PAUL: Is Daria Feldman going back?

LISA: Nope.

PAUL: Why not?

LISA: I don't know. We can go home now. Honest, my foot doesn't itch anymore.

PAUL: Lisa, you know what you do in business when it seems like there's nothing left to say? That's when you really start talking. Put a bid on the table.

LISA: What's a bid?

PAUL: You tell me what you want and I'll tell you what I've got to offer. Like Monopoly. You want Boardwalk, but I'm only willing to give you the Railroads. Now, because you are my daughter I'd throw in Water Works and Electricity. Understand, Tiger?

LISA: No. I don't like board games. You know, Daddy, we could get Space Invaders for our home for thirty-five dollars. In fact, we could get an Osborne System for two thousand. Daria Feldman's parents . . .

PAUL: Daria Feldman's parents refuse to talk to Daria, so they bought a computer to keep Daria busy so they won't have to speak in Yiddish. Daria will probably grow up to be a homicidal maniac lesbian prostitute.

LISA: I know what that word prostitute means.

PAUL: Good. [*pause*] You still haven't told me about school. Do you still like your teacher?

LISA: She's okay.

PAUL: Lisa, if we're talking try to answer me.

LISA: I am answering you. Can we go home now, please?

PAUL: Damn it, Lisa, if you want to talk to me . . . talk to me!

LISA: I can't wait till I'm old enough so I can make my own money and never have to see you again. Maybe I'll become a prostitute.

PAUL: Young lady, that's enough.

LISA: I hate you, Daddy! I hate you! [*She throws her trophy into the trash bin.*]

PAUL: What'd you do that for?

LISA: It's stupid.

PAUL: Maybe I wanted it.

LISA: What for?

PAUL: Maybe I wanted to put it where I keep your dinosaur and the picture you made of Mrs. Kimbel with the chicken pox.

LISA: You got mad at me when I made that picture. You told me I had to respect Mrs. Kimbel because she was my teacher.

PAUL: That's true. But she wasn't my teacher. I liked her better with the chicken pox. [*pause*] Lisa, I'm sorry. I was very wrong to miss your recital, and you don't have to become a prostitute. That's not the type of profession Miss Judy has in mind for you.

LISA [*mumbles*]: No.

PAUL: No. [*pause*] So Talia Robbins is really happy her father moved out?

LISA: Talia Robbins picks open the eighth-grade lockers during gym period. But she did that before her father moved out.

PAUL: You can't always judge someone by what they do or what they don't do. Sometimes you come home from dancing school and run upstairs and shut the door, and when I finally get to talk to you, everything is "okay" or "fine." Yup or nope?

LISA: Yup.

PAUL: Sometimes, a lot of times, I come home and fall asleep in front of the television. So you and I spend a lot of time being a little scared of each other. Maybe?

LISA: Maybe.

PAUL: Tell you what. I'll make you a tender offer.

LISA: What?

PAUL: I'll make you a tender offer. That's when one company publishes in the newspaper that they want to buy another company. And the company that publishes is called the Black Knight because they want to gobble up the poor little company. So the poor little company needs to be rescued. And then a White Knight comes along and makes a bigger and better offer so the shareholders won't have to tender shares to the Big Black Knight. You with me?

LISA: Sort of.

PAUL: I'll make you a tender offer like the White Knight. But I don't want to own you. I just want to make a much better offer. Okay?

LISA [*sort of understanding*]: Okay. [*Pause. They sit for a moment.*] Sort of. Daddy, what do you think about? I mean, like when you're quiet what do you think about?

PAUL: Oh, business usually. If I think I made a mistake or if I think I'm doing okay. Sometimes I think about what I'll be doing five years from now and if it's what I hoped it would be five years ago. Sometimes I think about what your life will be like, if Mount Saint Helens will erupt again. What you'll become if you'll study penmanship or word processing. If you speak kindly of me to your psychiatrist when you are in graduate school. And how the hell I'll pay for your graduate school. And sometimes I try and think what it was I thought about when I was your age.

LISA: Do you ever look out your window at the clouds and try to see which kinds of shapes they are? Like one time, honest, I saw the head of Walter Cronkite in a flower vase. Really! Like look don't those kinda look like if you turn it upside down, two big elbows or two elephant trunks dancing?

PAUL: Actually still looks like Walter Cronkite in a flower vase to me. But look up a little. See the one that's still moving? That sorta looks like a whale on a thimble.

LISA: Where?

PAUL: Look up. To your right.

LISA: I don't see it. Where?

PAUL: The other way.

LISA: Oh, yeah! There's the head and there's the stomach. Yeah! [Lisa *picks up her trophy.*] Hey, Daddy.

PAUL: Hey, Lisa.

·

LISA: You can have this thing if you want it. But you have to put it like this, because if you put it like that it is gross.

PAUL: You know what I'd like? So I can tell people who come into my office why I have this gross stupid thing on my shelf, I'd like it if you could show me your dance recital.

LISA: Now?

PAUL: We've got time. Mother said she won't be home till late.

LISA: Well, Daddy, during a lot of it I freeze and the big girl in front dances.

PAUL: Well, how 'bout the number you were doing when I walked in?

LISA: Well, see, I have parts for a lot of people in that one, too.

PAUL: I'll dance the other parts.

LISA: You can't dance.

PAUL: Young lady, I played Yvette Mimieux in a *Hasty Pudding Show*.

LISA: Who's Yvette Mimieux?

PAUL: Watch more television. You'll find out. [*Paul stands up.*] So I'm ready. [*He begins singing.*] "Nothing could be finer than to be in Carolina."

LISA: Now I go. In the morning. And now you go. Dum-da.

PAUL [*obviously not a tap dancer*]: Da-da-dum.

LISA [*whines*]: Daddy!

PAUL [*mimics her*]: Lisa! Nothing could be finer . . .

LISA: That looks dumb.

PAUL: Oh, yeah? You think they do this better in *The Amazing Minkcoat*? No way! Now you go—da da da dum.

LISA: Da da da dum.

PAUL: If I had Aladdin's lamp for only a day, I'd make a wish. . . .

LISA: Daddy, that's maudlin!

PAUL: I know it's maudlin. And here's what I'd say:

LISA AND PAUL: I'd say that "nothing could be finer than to be in Carolina in the mooooooooooornin'."

THE HAPPY JOURNEY TO
TRENTON AND CAMDEN

by Thornton Wilder

CHARACTERS

THE STAGE MANAGER   CAROLINE KIRBY
MA KIRBY   ELMER KIRBY (PA)
ARTHUR KIRBY   BEULAH

No scenery is required for this play. Perhaps a few dusty flats may be seen leaning against the brick wall at the back of the stage.

The five members of the Kirby family and The Stage Manager *compose the cast. The Stage Manager not only moves forward and withdraws the few properties that are required, but he reads from a typescript the lines of all the minor characters. He reads them clearly, but with little attempt at characterization, scarcely troubling himself to alter his voice, even when he responds in the person of a child or a woman.*

As the curtain rises The Stage Manager *is leaning lazily against the proscenium pillar at the audience's left. He is smoking.*

Arthur *is playing marbles in the center of the stage.*

Caroline *is at the remote back, right, talking to some girls who are invisible to us.*

Ma Kirby *is anxiously putting on her hat before an imaginary mirror.*

MA: Where's your pa? Why isn't he here? I declare we'll never get started.

ARTHUR: Ma, where's my hat? I guess I don't go if I can't find my hat.

MA: Go out into the hall and see if it isn't there. Where's Caroline gone to now, the plagued child?

317

ARTHUR: She's out waitin' in the street talkin' to the Jones girls.—I just looked in the hall a thousand times, Ma, and it isn't there. [*He spits for good luck before a difficult shot and mutters.*] Come on, baby.

MA: Go and look again, I say. Look carefully.

[Arthur *rises, runs to the right, turns around swiftly, returns to his game, flinging himself on the floor with a terrible impact, and starts shooting an aggie.*]

ARTHUR: No. Ma, it's not there.

MA [*serenely*]: Well, you don't leave Newark without that hat, make up your mind to that. I don't go no journeys with a hoodlum.

ARTHUR: Aw, Ma!

[Ma *comes down to the footlights and talks toward the audience as through a window.*]

MA: Oh, Mrs. Schwartz!

THE STAGE MANAGER [*consulting his script*]: Here I am, Mrs. Kirby. Are you going yet?

MA: I guess we're going in just a minute. How's the baby?

THE STAGE MANAGER: She's all right now. We slapped her on the back and she spat it up.

MA: Isn't that fine!—Well now, if you'll be good enough to give the cat a saucer of milk in the morning and the evening, Mrs. Schwartz, I'll be ever so grateful to you.—Oh, good afternoon, Mrs. Hobmeyer!

THE STAGE MANAGER: Good afternoon, Mrs. Kirby, I hear you're going away.

MA [*modest*]: Oh, just for three days, Mrs. Hobmeyer, to see my married daughter Beulah, in Camden. Elmer's got his vacation week from the laundry
early this year, and he's just the best driver in the
world.

[Caroline *comes "into the house" and stands by her
mother.*]

THE STAGE MANAGER: Is the whole family going?

MA: Yes, all four of us that's here. The change ought
to be good for the children. My married daughter was
downright sick a while ago—

THE STAGE MANAGER: Tchk—tchk—tchk! Yes. I remember you tellin' us.

MA: And I just want to go down and see the child. I
ain't seen her since then. I just won't rest easy in my
mind without I see her. [*to* Caroline] Can't you say good
afternoon to Mrs. Hobmeyer?

CAROLINE [*blushes and lowers her eyes and says
woodenly*]: Good afternoon, Mrs. Hobmeyer.

THE STAGE MANAGER: Good afternoon, dear.—Well,
I'll wait and beat these rugs until after you're gone, because I don't want to choke you. I hope you have a good
time and find everything all right.

MA: Thank you, Mrs. Hobmeyer, I hope I will.—
Well, I guess that milk for the cat is all, Mrs. Schwartz,
if you're sure you don't mind. If anything should
come up, the key to the back door is hanging by the
icebox.

ARTHUR AND CAROLINE: Ma! Not so loud. Everybody
can hear yuh.

MA: Stop pullin' my dress, children. [*in a loud whisper*] The key to the back door I'll leave hangin' by the icebox and I'll leave the screen door unhooked.

THE STAGE MANAGER: Now have a good trip, dear, and give my love to Loolie.

MA: I will, and thank you a thousand times. [*She returns "into the room."*] What can be keeping your pa?

ARTHUR: I can't find my hat, Ma.

[*Enter* Elmer *holding a hat.*]

ELMER: Here's Arthur's hat. He musta left it in the car Sunday.

MA: That's a mercy. Now we can start.—Caroline Kirby, what you done to your cheeks?

CAROLINE [*defiant, abashed*]: Nothin'.

MA: If you've put anything on 'em, I'll slap you.

CAROLINE: No, Ma, of course I haven't. [*hanging her head*] I just rubbed'm to make'm red. All the girls do that at high school when they're goin' places.

MA: Such silliness I never saw. Elmer, what kep' you?

ELMER [*always even-voiced and always looking out a little anxiously through his spectacles*]: I just went to the garage and had Charlie give a last look at it, Kate.

MA: I'm glad you did. I wouldn't like to have no breakdown miles from anywhere. Now we can start. Arthur, put those marbles away. Anybody'd think you didn't want to go on a journey to look at yuh.

[*They go out "through the hall," take the short steps that denote going downstairs, and find themselves in the street.*]

ELMER: Here, you boys, you keep away from that car.

MA: Those Sullivan boys put their heads into everything.

[*The Stage Manager has moved forward four chairs and a low platform. This is the automobile. It is in the center of the stage and faces the audience. The platform slightly raises the two chairs in the rear. Pa's hands hold an imaginary steering wheel and continually shift gears.* Caroline *sits beside him.* Arthur *is behind him and* Ma *behind* Caroline.]

CAROLINE [*self-consciously*]: Good-by, Mildred. Good-by, Helen.

THE STAGE MANAGER: Good-by, Caroline. Good-by, Mrs. Kirby. I hope y' have a good time.

MA: Good-by, girls.

THE STAGE MANAGER: Good-by, Kate. The car looks fine.

MA [*looking upward toward a window*]: Oh, good-by, Emma! [*modestly*] We think it's the best little Chevrolet in the world.—Oh, good-by, Mrs. Adler!

THE STAGE MANAGER: What, are you going away, Mrs. Kirby?

MA: Just for three days, Mrs. Adler, to see my married daughter in Camden.

THE STAGE MANAGER: Have a good time.

[*Now* Ma, Caroline, *and* The Stage Manager *break out into a tremendous chorus of good-bys. The whole street is saying good-by.* Arthur *takes out his pea-shooter and lets fly happily into the air. There is a lurch or two and they are off.*]

ARTHUR [*in sudden fright*]: Pa! Pa! Don't go by the school. Mr. Biedenbach might see us!

MA: I don't care if he does see us. I guess I can take my children out of school for one day without having to hide down back streets about it. [Elmer *nods to a passer-by.* Ma *asks without sharpness.*] Who was that you spoke to, Elmer?

ELMER: That was the fellow who arranges our banquets down to the Lodge, Kate.

MA: Is he the one who had to buy four hundred steaks? [Pa *nods.*] I declare, I'm glad I'm not him.

ELMER: The air's getting better already. Take deep breaths, children.

[*They inhale noisily.*]

ARTHUR: Gee, it's almost open fields already. *"Weber and Heilbronner Suits for Well-dressed Men."* Ma, can I have one of them someday?

MA: If you graduate with good marks perhaps your father'll let you have one for graduation.

CAROLINE [*whining*]: Oh, Pa! Do we have to wait while that whole funeral goes by?

[Pa *takes off his hat.* Ma *cranes forward with absorbed curiosity.*]

MA: Take off your hat, Arthur. Look at your father.—Why, Elmer, I do believe that's a Lodge brother of yours. See the banner? I suppose this is the Elizabeth branch.

[Elmer *nods.* Ma *sighs: Tchk—tchk—tchk. They all lean forward and watch the funeral in silence, growing momentarily more solemnized. After a pause,* Ma *continues almost dreamily.*]

Well, we haven't forgotten the one that we went on, have we? We haven't forgotten our good Harold. He gave his life for his country, we mustn't forget that. [*She passes her finger from the corner of her eye across her cheek. There is another pause.*] Well, we'll all hold up the traffic for a few minutes someday.

THE CHILDREN [*very uncomfortable*]: Ma!

MA [*without self-pity*]: Well I'm "ready," children. I hope everybody in this car is "ready." [*She puts her hand on* Pa's *shoulder.*] And I pray to go first, Elmer. Yes. [Pa *touches her hand.*]

THE CHILDREN: Ma, everybody's looking at you. Everybody's laughing at you.

MA: Oh, hold your tongues! I don't care what a lot of silly people in Elizabeth, New Jersey, think of me.—Now we can go on. That's the last. [*There is another lurch and the car goes on.*]

CAROLINE: *"Fit-Rite Suspenders. The Working Man's Choice."* Pa, why do they spell "Rite" that way?

ELMER: So that it'll make you stop and ask about it, missy.

CAROLINE: Papa, you're teasing me.—Ma, why do they say *"Three Hundred Rooms Three Hundred Baths"*?

ARTHUR: *"Miller's Spaghetti: The Family's Favorite Dish."* Ma, why don't you ever have spaghetti?

MA: Go along, you'd never eat it.

ARTHUR: Ma, I like it now.

CAROLINE [*with a gesture*]: Yum-yum. It looks wonderful up there. Ma, make some when we get home?

MA [*dryly*]: "The management is always happy to receive suggestions. We aim to please."

[*The whole family finds this exquisitely funny. The children scream with laughter. Even* Elmer *smiles.* Ma *remains modest.*]

ELMER: Well, I guess no one's complaining, Kate. Everybody knows you're a good cook.

MA: I don't know whether I'm a good cook or not, but I know I've had practice. At least I've cooked three meals a day for twenty-five years.

ARTHUR: Aw, Ma, you went out to eat once in a while.

MA: Yes. That made it a leap year.

[*This joke is no less successful than its predecessor. When the laughing dies down,* Caroline *turns around in an ecstasy of well-being and, kneeling on the cushions, says.*]

CAROLINE: Ma, I love going out in the country like this. Let's do it often, Ma.

MA: Goodness, smell that air, will you! It's got the whole ocean in it.—Elmer, drive careful over that bridge. This must be New Brunswick we're coming to.

ARTHUR [*jealous of his mother's successes*]: Ma, when is the next comfort station?

MA [*unruffled*]: You don't want one. You just said that to be awful.

CAROLINE [*shrilly*]: Yes, he did, Ma. He's terrible. He says that kind of thing right out in school and I want to sink through the floor, Ma. He's terrible.

MA: Oh, don't get so excited about nothing, Miss Proper! I guess we're all yewman beings in this car, at least as far as I know. And Arthur, you try and be a gentleman.—Elmer, don't run over that collie dog. [*She follows the dog with her eyes.*] Looked kinda peakèd to me. Needs a good honest bowl of leavings. Pretty dog, too. [*Her eyes fall on a billboard.*] That's a pretty advertisement for Chesterfield cigarettes, isn't it? Looks like Beulah, a little.

ARTHUR: Ma?

MA: Yes.

ARTHUR [*"Route" rhymes with "out."*]: Can't I take a paper route with the *Newark Daily Post*?

MA: No, you cannot. No, sir. I hear they make the paper boys get up at four-thirty in the morning. No son of mine is going to get up at four-thirty every morning, not if it's to make a million dollars. Your *Saturday Evening Post* route on Thursday mornings is enough.

ARTHUR: Aw, Ma.

MA: No, sir. No son of mine is going to get up at four-thirty and miss the sleep God meant him to have.

ARTHUR [*sullenly*]: Hhm! Ma's always talking about God. I guess she got a letter from him this morning.

[Ma *rises, outraged.*]

MA: Elmer, stop that automobile this minute. I don't
go another step with anybody that says things like that.
Arthur, you get out of this car. Elmer, you give him another dollar bill. He can go back to Newark by himself. I
don't want him.

ARTHUR: What did I say? There wasn't anything terrible about that.

ELMER: I didn't hear what he said, Kate.

MA: God has done a lot of things for me and I won't
have him made fun of by anybody. Go away. Go away
from me.

CAROLINE: Aw, Ma—don't spoil the ride.

MA: No.

ELMER: We might as well go on, Kate, since we've got
started. I'll talk to the boy tonight.

MA [*slowly conceding*]: All right, if you say so, Elmer.
But I won't sit beside him. Caroline, you come and sit
by me.

ARTHUR [*frightened*]: Aw, Ma, that wasn't so terrible.

MA: I don't want to talk about it. I hope your father
washes your mouth out with soap and water.—Where'd
we all be if I started talking about God like that, I'd like
to know! We'd be in the speakeasies and night clubs and
places like that, that's where we'd be.—All right, Elmer,
you can go on now.

CAROLINE: What did he say, Ma? I didn't hear what
he said.

MA: I don't want to talk about it.

[*They drive on in silence for a moment, the shocked silence after a scandal.*]

ELMER: I'm going to stop and give the car a little water, I guess.

MA: All right, Elmer. You know best.

ELMER [*to a garage hand*]: Could I have a little water in the radiator—to make sure?

THE STAGE MANAGER [*In this scene alone he lays aside his script and enters into a role seriously.*]: You sure can. [*He punches the tires.*] Air all right? Do you need any oil or gas?

ELMER: No, I think not. I just got fixed up in Newark.

MA: We're on the right road for Camden, are we?

THE STAGE MANAGER: Yes, keep straight ahead. You can't miss it. You'll be in Trenton in a few minutes. [*He carefully pours some water into the hood.*] Camden's a great town, lady, believe me.

MA: My daughter likes it fine—my married daughter.

THE STAGE MANAGER: Ye'? It's a great burg all right. I guess I think so because I was born near there.

MA: Well, well. Your folks live there?

THE STAGE MANAGER: No, my old man sold the farm and they built a factory on it. So the folks moved to Philadelphia.

MA: My married daughter Beulah lives there because her husband works in the telephone company.—Stop pokin' me, Caroline!—We're all going down to see her for a few days.

THE STAGE MANAGER: Ye'?

MA: She's been sick, you see, and I just felt I had to go and see her. My husband and my boy are going to stay at the Y.M.C.A. I hear they've got a dormitory on the top floor that's real clean and comfortable. Had you ever been there?

THE STAGE MANAGER: No. I'm Knights of Columbus myself.

MA: Oh.

THE STAGE MANAGER: I used to play basketball at the Y, though. It looked all right to me. [*He has been standing with one foot on the rung of* Ma's *chair. They have taken a great fancy to one another. He reluctantly shakes himself out of it and pretends to examine the car again, whistling.*] Well, I guess you're all set now, lady. I hope you have a good trip; you can't miss it.

EVERYBODY: Thanks. Thanks a lot. Good luck to you.

[*jolts and lurches*]

MA [*with a sigh*]: The world's full of nice people.— That's what I call a nice young man.

CAROLINE [*earnestly*]: Ma, you oughtn't to tell'm all everything about yourself.

MA: Well, Caroline, you do your way and I'll do mine.—He looked kinda thin to me. I'd like to feed him up for a few days. His mother lives in Philadelphia and I expect he eats at those dreadful Greek places.

CAROLINE: I'm hungry. Pa, there's a hot-dog stand. K'n I have one?

ELMER: We'll all have one, eh, Kate? We had such an early lunch.

MA: Just as you think best, Elmer.

ELMER: Arthur, here's half a dollar.—Run over and see what they have. Not too much mustard, either.

[Arthur *descends from the car and goes off stage right.* Ma *and* Caroline *get out and walk a bit.*]

MA: What's that flower over there?—I'll take some of those to Beulah.

CAROLINE. It's just a weed, Ma.

MA: I like it.—My, look at the sky, wouldya! I'm glad I was born in New Jersey. I've always said it was the best state in the Union. Every state has something no other state has got.

[*They stroll about humming. Presently* Arthur *returns with his hands full of imaginary hot dogs, which he distributes. He is still very much cast down by the recent scandal. He finally approaches his mother and says falteringly.*]

ARTHUR: Ma, I'm sorry. I'm sorry for what I said. [*He bursts into tears and puts his forehead against her elbow.*]

MA: There. There. We all say wicked things at times. I know you didn't mean it like it sounded.

[*He weeps still more violently than before.*]

Why, now, now! I forgive you, Arthur, and tonight before you go to bed you . . . [*She whispers.*] You're a good boy at heart, Arthur, and we all know it.

[Caroline *starts to cry too.* Ma *is suddenly joyously alive and happy.*]

Sakes alive, it's too nice a day for us all to be cryin'. Come now, get in. You go up in front with your father, Caroline. Ma wants to sit with her beau. I never saw such children. Your hot dogs are all getting wet. Now chew them fine, everybody.—All right, Elmer, forward march.—Caroline, whatever are you doing?

CAROLINE: I'm spitting out the leather, Ma.

MA: Then say "Excuse me."

CAROLINE: Excuse me, please.

MA: What's this place? Arthur, did you see the post office?

ARTHUR: It said Lawrenceville.

MA: Hhn. School kinda nice. I wonder what that big yellow house set back was.—Now it's beginning to be Trenton.

CAROLINE: Papa, it was near here that George Washington crossed the Delaware. It was near Trenton, Mamma. He was first in war and first in peace and first in the hearts of his countrymen.

MA [*surveying the passing world, serene and didactic*]: Well, the thing I like about him best was that he never told a lie.

[*The children are duly cast down. There is a pause.*]

There's a sunset for you. There's nothing like a good sunset.

ARTHUR: There's an Ohio license in front of us. Ma, have you ever been to Ohio?

MA: No.

[*A dreamy silence descends upon them.* Caroline *sits closer to her father.* Ma *puts her arm around* Arthur.]

ARTHUR: Ma, what a lotta people there are in the world, Ma. There must be thousands and thousands in the United States. Ma, how many are there?

MA: I don't know. Ask your father.

ARTHUR: Pa, how many are there?

ELMER: There are a hundred and twenty-six million, Kate.

MA [*giving a pressure about* Arthur's *shoulder*]: And they all like to drive out in the evening with their children beside'm. [*another pause*] Why doesn't somebody sing something? Arthur, you're always singing something; what's the matter with you?

ARTHUR: All right. What'll we sing? [*He sketches.*]

> In the Blue Ridge mountains of Virginia,
> On the trail of the lonesome pine . . .

No, I don't like that anymore. Let's do:

> I been workin' on de railroad
> All de liblong day.
> I been workin' on de railroad
> Just to pass de time away.

[Caroline *joins in at once. Finally even* Ma *is singing. Even* Pa *is singing.* Ma *suddenly jumps up with a wild cry.*]

MA: Elmer, that signpost said Camden. I saw it.

ELMER: All right, Kate, if you're sure.

[*much shifting of gears, backing, and jolting*]

MA: Yes, there it is. Camden—five miles. Dear old
Beulah.—Now, children, you be good and quiet during
dinner. She's just got out of bed after a big sorta opera-
tion, and we must all move around kinda quiet. First you
drop me and Caroline at the door and just say hello, and
then you menfolk go over to the Y.M.C.A. and come
back for dinner in about an hour.

CAROLINE [*shutting her eyes and pressing her fists
passionately against her nose*]: I see the first star.
Everybody make a wish.

> Star light, star bright,
> First star I seen tonight,
> I wish I may, I wish I might
> Have the wish I wish tonight.

[*then solemnly*] Pins. Mamma, you say "needles." [*She
interlocks little fingers with her mother.*]

MA: Needles.

CAROLINE: Shakespeare. Ma, you say "Longfellow."

MA: Longfellow.

CAROLINE: Now it's a secret and I can't tell it to anybody. Ma, you make a wish.

MA [*with almost grim humor*]: No, I can make wishes
without waiting for no star. And I can tell my wishes
right out loud too. Do you want to hear them?

CAROLINE [*resignedly*]: No, Ma, we all know'm already. We've heard'm. [*She hangs her head affectedly
on her left shoulder and says with unmalicious*

mimicry.] You want me to be a good girl and you want Arthur to be honest-in-word-and-deed.

MA [*majestically*]: Yes. So mind yourself.

ELMER: Caroline, take out that letter from Beulah in my coat pocket by you and read aloud the places I marked with a red pencil.

CAROLINE [*working*]: *"A few blocks after you pass the two big oil tanks on your left . . ."*

EVERYBODY [*pointing backward*]: There they are!

CAROLINE: *" . . . you come to a corner where there's an A and P store on the left and a firehouse kitty-corner to it . . .* [*They all jubilantly identify these landmarks.*] *. . . turn right, go two blocks, and our house is Weyerhauser St. Number 471."*

MA: It's an even nicer street than they used to live in. And right handy to an A and P.

CAROLINE [*whispering*]: Ma, it's better than our street. It's richer than our street.—Ma, isn't Beulah richer than we are?

MA [*looking at her with a firm and glassy eye*]: Mind yourself, missy. I don't want to hear anybody talking about rich or not rich when I'm around. If people aren't nice I don't care how rich they are. I live in the best street in the world because my husband and children live there. [*She glares impressively at* Caroline *a moment to let this lesson sink in, then looks up, sees* Beulah *and waves.*] There's Beulah standing on the steps lookin' for us.

[Beulah *has appeared and is waving. They all call out: "Hello, Beulah—Hello." Presently they are all getting out of the car.* Beulah *kisses her father long and affectionately.*]

BEULAH: Hello, Papa. Good old Papa. You look tired, Pa.—Hello, Mamma.—Lookit how Arthur and Caroline are growing!

MA: They're bursting all their clothes!—Yes, your pa needs a rest. Thank heaven his vacation has come just now. We'll feed him up and let him sleep late. Pa has a present for you, Loolie. He would go and buy it.

BEULAH: Why, Pa, you're terrible to go and buy anything for me. Isn't he terrible?

MA: Well, it's a secret. You can open it at dinner.

ELMER: Where's Horace, Loolie?

BEULAH: He was kep' over a little at the office. He'll be here any minute. He's crazy to see you all.

MA: All right. You men go over to the Y and come back in about an hour.

BEULAH [*As her father returns to the wheel, she stands out in the street beside him.*]: Go straight along, Pa, you can't miss it. It just stares at yuh. [*She puts her arm around his neck and rubs her nose against his temple.*] Crazy old Pa, goin' buyin' things! It's me that ought to be buyin' things for you, Pa.

ELMER: Oh no! There's only one Loolie in the world.

BEULAH [*whispering, as her eyes fill with tears*]: Are you glad I'm still alive, Pa?

[*She kisses him abruptly and goes back to the house steps.* The Stage Manager *removes the automobile with the help of* Elmer *and* Arthur, *who go off waving their good-bys.*]

Well, come on upstairs, Ma, and take off your things. Caroline, there's a surprise for you in the backyard.

CAROLINE: Rabbits?

BEULAH: No.

CAROLINE: Chickins?

BEULAH: No. Go and see. [Caroline *runs offstage.* Beulah *and* Ma *gradually go upstairs.*] There are two new puppies. You be thinking over whether you can keep one in Newark.

MA: I guess we can. It's a nice house, Beulah. You just got a *lovely* home.

BEULAH: When I got back from the hospital, Horace had moved everything into it, and there wasn't anything for me to do.

MA: It's lovely.

[The Stage Manager *pushes out a bed from the left. Its foot is toward the right.* Beulah *sits on it, testing the springs.*]

BEULAH: I think you'll find the bed comfortable, Ma.

MA [*taking off her hat*]: Oh, I could sleep on a heapa shoes, Loolie! I don't have no trouble sleepin'. [*She sits down beside her.*] Now let me look at my girl. Well, well, when I last saw you, you didn't know me. You kep' saying: "When's Mamma comin'? When's Mamma comin'?" But the doctor sent me away.

BEULAH [*puts her head on her mother's shoulder and weeps*]: It was awful, Mamma. It was awful. She didn't even live a few minutes, Mamma. It was awful.

MA [*looking far away*]: God thought best, dear. God thought best. We don't understand why. We just go on, honey, doin' our business. [*then almost abruptly— passing the back of her hand across her cheek*] Well, now, what are we giving the men to eat tonight?

BEULAH: There's a chicken in the oven.

MA: What time didya put it in?

BEULAH [*restraining her*]: Aw, Ma, don't go yet. I like to sit here with you this way. You always get the fidgets when we try and pet yuh, Mamma.

MA [*ruefully, laughing*]: Yes, it's kinda foolish. I'm just an old Newark bag o' bones. [*She glances at the backs of her hands.*]

BEULAH [*indignantly*]: Why, Ma, you're good-lookin'! We always said you were good-lookin'.—And besides, you're the best ma we could ever have.

MA [*uncomfortable*]: Well, I hope you like me. There's nothin' like being liked by your family.—Now I'm going downstairs to look at the chicken. You stretch out here for a minute and shut your eyes.—Have you got everything laid in for breakfast before the shops close?

BEULAH: Oh, you know! Ham and eggs.

[*They both laugh.*]

MA: I declare I never could understand what men see in ham and eggs. I think they're horrible.—What time did you put the chicken in?

BEULAH: Five o'clock.

MA: Well, now, you shut your eyes for ten minutes. [Beulah *stretches out and shuts her eyes*. Ma *descends the stairs absentmindedly singing.*]

> There were ninety and nine that safely lay
> In the shelter of the fold,
> But one was out on the hills away,
> Far off from the gates of gold. . . .

THE CASE OF THE CRUSHED PETUNIAS

A LYRICAL FANTASY

———∽∾∽———

by Tennessee Williams

CHARACTERS

DOROTHY SIMPLE
POLICE OFFICER

YOUNG MAN
MRS. DULL

The action of the play takes place in the Simple Notion Shop, owned and operated by Miss Dorothy Simple, *a New England maiden of twenty-six, who is physically very attractive but has barricaded her house and her heart behind a double row of petunias.*

The town is Primanproper, Massachusetts, which lies within the cultural orbit of Boston.

The play starts in the early morning. Miss Simple, *very agitated for some reason, has just opened her little shop. She stands in the open door in a flood of spring sunlight, but her face expresses grief and indignation. She is calling to a* Police Officer *on the corner.*

DOROTHY: Officer?—Officer!

OFFICER [*strolling up to her*]: Yes, Miss Simple?

DOROTHY: I wish to report a case of deliberate and malicious sabotage!

OFFICER: Sabotage of what, Miss Simple?

DOROTHY: Of my petunias!

OFFICER: Well, well, well. Now what do you mean by that?

341

DOROTHY: Exactly what I said. You can see for yourself. Last night this house was surrounded by a beautiful
double row of pink and lavender petunias. Look at them
now! When I got up this morning I discovered them in
this condition. Every single little petunia deliberately
and maliciously crushed underfoot!

OFFICER: My goodness! Well, well, well!

DOROTHY: "Well, well, well" is not going to catch the
culprit!

OFFICER: What do you want me to do, Miss Simple?

DOROTHY: I want you to apprehend a petuniacidal maniac with a size eleven D foot.

OFFICER: Eleven D?

DOROTHY: Yes. That is the size of the footprints that
crushed my petunias. I just now had them measured by a
shoe clerk.

OFFICER: That's a pretty large foot, Miss Simple, but
lots of men have got large feet.

DOROTHY: Not in Primanproper, Massachusetts. Mr.
Knowzit, the shoe clerk, assured me that there isn't a
man in town who wears a shoe that size. Of course you
realize the danger of allowing this maniac to remain at
large. Any man who would crush a sweet petunia is
equally capable in my opinion of striking a helpless
woman or kicking an innocent child!

OFFICER: I'll do my best, Miss Simple. See yuh later.

DOROTHY [*curtly*]: Yes. Good-by. [*Slams door. She
returns behind her notion counter and drums restively
with her pale pink-polished nails. The canary cheeps
timidly. Then tries an arpeggio. Dorothy, to canary.*] Oh,

hush up! [*then contritely*] Excuse me, please. My nerves
are all to pieces!

[*Blows her nose. The doorbell tinkles as a customer
enters. He is a* Young Man, *shockingly large and aggressive looking in the flower-papered cubicle of the
shop.*]

Gracious, please be careful. You're bumping your head
against my chandelier.

YOUNG MAN [*good-humoredly*]: Sorry, Miss Simple.
I guess I'd better sit down. [*The delicate little chair col-
lapses beneath him.*]

DOROTHY: Heaven have mercy upon us! You seem to
have a genius for destruction! You've broken that little
antique chair to smithereens!

YOUNG MAN: Sorry, Miss Simple.

DOROTHY: I appreciate your sorrow, but that won't
mend my chair.—Is there anything I can show you in the
way of notions?

YOUNG MAN: I'd like to see that pair of wine-colored
socks you have in the window.

DOROTHY: What size socks do you wear?

YOUNG MAN: I keep forgetting. But my shoes are
eleven D.

DOROTHY [*sharply*]: What size did you say? Eleven?
Eleven D?

YOUNG MAN: That's right, Miss Simple. Eleven D.

DOROTHY: Oh. Your shoes are rather muddy, aren't
they?

YOUNG MAN: That's right, Miss Simple, I believe they are.

DOROTHY: Quite muddy. It looks like you might have stepped in a freshly watered flower bed last night.

YOUNG MAN: Come to think of it, that's what I did.

DOROTHY: I don't suppose you've heard about that horrible case of petunia crushing which occurred last night?

YOUNG MAN: As a matter of fact, I have heard something about it.

DOROTHY: From the policeman on the corner?

YOUNG MAN: No, ma'am. Not from him.

DOROTHY: Who from, then? He's the only man who knows about it except—except—except—the man who *did* it! [*Pause. The canary cheeps inquiringly.*] You—you—*you*—are the man who *did* it!

YOUNG MAN: Yes, Miss Simple. I am the man who did it.

DOROTHY: Don't try to get away!

YOUNG MAN: I won't, Miss Simple.

DOROTHY: Stand right where you are till the officer comes!

YOUNG MAN: You're going to call the officer?

DOROTHY: Yes, I am, I certainly am.—In a minute. First I'd like to ask you *why* you *did* it? Why did you crush my petunias?

YOUNG MAN: Okay. I'll tell you why. First, because you'd barricaded your house—and also your heart—behind that silly little double row of petunias!

DOROTHY: Barricaded? My house—my heart—behind them? That's absurd. I don't know what you mean.

YOUNG MAN: I know. They're apparently such delicate, fragile creatures, these petunias, but they have a terrible resistance.

DOROTHY: Resistance to what, may I ask?

YOUNG MAN: Anything big or important that happens to come by your house. Nothing big or important can ever get by a double row of petunias! That is the reason why you are living alone with your canary and beginning to dislike it.

DOROTHY: Dislike my canary? I love it!

YOUNG MAN: Secretly, Miss Simple, you wish the birdseed would choke it! You dislike it nearly as much as you secretly disliked your petunias.

DOROTHY: Why should I, why should you, why should anybody dislike petunias!

YOUNG MAN: Our animosity and its resultant action is best explained by a poem I once composed on the subject of petunias—and similar flora. Would you like to hear it?

DOROTHY: I suppose I should, if it's relevant to the case.

YOUNG MAN: Extremely relevant. It goes like this:

[*light music:*]

How grimly do petunias look
on things not listed in the book,

For these dear creatures never move
outside the academic groove.
They mark with sharp and moral eye
phenomena that pass them by
And classify as good or evil
mammoth whale or tiny weevil.
They note with consummate disdain
all that is masculine or plain.
They blush down to their tender roots
when men pass by in working boots.
All honest language shocks them so
they cringe to hear a rooster crow.
Of course they say that good clean fun's
permissible for *every* one
But find that even Blindman's Bluff
is noisy and extremely rough
and—[*stage whisper*]
—Not quite innocent enough!

What do you think of it?

DOROTHY: Unfair! Completely unfair!

YOUNG MAN [*laughing*]: To organized petunias?

DOROTHY: Yes, and besides, I don't think anyone has the right to impose his opinions in the form of footprints on other people's petunias!

YOUNG MAN [*removing small package from pocket*]: I'm prepared to make complete restitution.

DOROTHY: What with?

YOUNG MAN: With these.

DOROTHY: What are they?

YOUNG MAN: Seeds.

DOROTHY: Seeds of what? Sedition?

YOUNG MAN: No. Wild roses.

DOROTHY: Wild? I couldn't use them!

YOUNG MAN: Why not, Miss Simple?

DOROTHY: Flowers are like human beings. They can't be allowed to grow wild. They have to be—

YOUNG MAN: Regimented? Ahhh. I see. You're a horticultural fascist!

DOROTHY [*with an indignant gasp*]: I ought to call the policeman about those petunias!

YOUNG MAN: Why don't you, then?

DOROTHY: Only because you made an honest confession.

YOUNG MAN: That's not why, Miss Simple.

DOROTHY: No?

YOUNG MAN: The actual reason is that you are fascinated.

DOROTHY: *Am* I? Indeed!

YOUNG MAN: Indeed you are, Miss Simple. In spite of your late unlamented petunias, you're charmed, you're intrigued—you're frightened!

DOROTHY: You're very conceited!

YOUNG MAN: Now, if you please, I'd like to ask you a question.

DOROTHY: You may. But I may not answer.

YOUNG MAN: You will if you can. But you probably won't be able. The question is this: what do you make of it all?

DOROTHY: I don't understand— All *what*?

YOUNG MAN: The world? The universe? And your position in it? This miraculous accident of being alive! [*soft music background*] Has it ever occurred to you how much the living are outnumbered by the dead? Their numerical superiority, Miss Simple, is so tremendous that you couldn't possibly find a ratio with figures vast enough *above* the line, and small enough *below* to represent it.

DOROTHY: You sound like you were trying to sell me something.

YOUNG MAN: I am, I am, just wait!

DOROTHY: I'm not in the market for—

YOUNG MAN: Please! One minute of your infinitely valuable time!

DOROTHY: All right. One minute.

YOUNG MAN: *Look!*

DOROTHY: At what?

YOUNG MAN: Those little particles of dust in the shaft of April sunlight through that window.

DOROTHY: What about them?

YOUNG MAN: Just think. You might have been one of those instead of what you are. You might have been any one of those infinitesimal particles of dust. Or any one of millions and billions and trillions of other particles of mute, unconscious matter. Never capable of asking any questions. Never capable of giving any answers. Never capable of doing, thinking, feeling anything at all! But instead, dear lady, by the rarest and most improbable of accidents, you happened to be what you are. Miss Dorothy Simple from Boston! Beautiful. Human. Alive. Capable of thought and feeling and action. Now here comes the vital part of my question. What are you going to *do* about it, Miss Simple?

DOROTHY [*who is somewhat moved, in spite of her crushed petunias*]: Well, goodness—gracious—sakes alive! I thought you came in here to buy some socks?

YOUNG MAN: Yes, but I've got to sell *you* something first.

DOROTHY: Sell me what?

YOUNG MAN: A wonderful bill of goods.

DOROTHY: I'll have to see it before I sign the order.

YOUNG MAN: That's impossible. I can't display my samples in this shop.

DOROTHY: Why not?

YOUNG MAN: They're much too precious. You have to make an appointment.

DOROTHY [*retreating*]: Sorry. But I do all my business in here.

YOUNG MAN: Too bad for you.—In fact, too bad for us both. Maybe you'll change your mind?

DOROTHY: I don't think so.

YOUNG MAN: Anyway, here's my card.

DOROTHY [*reading it, bewildered*]:—LIFE—INCOR-PORATED. [*looks up slowly*]

YOUNG MAN: Yes. I represent that line.

DOROTHY: I see. You're a magazine salesman?

YOUNG MAN: No. It isn't printed matter.

DOROTHY: But it's matter, though?

YOUNG MAN: Oh, yes, and it's matter of tremendous importance, too. But it's neglected by people. Because of their ignorance they've been buying cheap substitute products. And lately a rival concern has sprung up outside the country. This firm is known as "Death, Unlimited." Their product comes in a package labeled "War." They're crowding us out with new aggressive methods of promotion. And one of their biggest sales points is "Excitement." Why does it work so well? Because you little people surround your houses and also your hearts with rows of tiresome, trivial little things like petunias! If we could substitute wild roses, there wouldn't be wars! No, there'd be excitement enough in the world *without* having wars! That's why we've started this petunia-crushing campaign, Miss Simple. "Life, Incorporated" has come to the realization that we have to use the same aggressive methods of promotion used by "Death, Unlimited," over there! We've got to show people that the malignantly trivial little petunias of the world can be eliminated more cleanly, permanently and completely by "Life, Incorporated" than by "Death, Unlimited!" Now what do you say, Miss Simple? Won't you try our product?

DOROTHY [*nervously*]: Well, you see it's like this—I do all my buying in Boston and—

YOUNG MAN: What do you buy in Boston?

DOROTHY: You can see for yourself. Look over the stock.

YOUNG MAN [*examining the shelves*]: Thimbles—threads—ladies' needlework—white gloves—

DOROTHY: Notions. Odds and ends.

YOUNG MAN: Odds and ends—of existence?

DOROTHY: Yes, that's it exactly.

YOUNG MAN: What do you do after hours?

DOROTHY: I carry on a lot of correspondence.

YOUNG MAN: Who with?

DOROTHY: With wholesale firms in Boston.

YOUNG MAN: How do you sign your letters?

DOROTHY: "Sincerely." "As ever." "Very truly yours."

YOUNG MAN: But never with love?

DOROTHY: Love? To firms in Boston?

YOUNG MAN: I guess not. I think you ought to enlarge your correspondence. I'll tell you what I'll do. I'll meet you tonight on Highway No. 77!

DOROTHY: Oh, no! I have my correspondence!

YOUNG MAN: Delay your correspondence. Meet me there. We'll have a couple of beers at the Starlight Casino.

DOROTHY [*with frantic evasion*]: But I don't drink!

YOUNG MAN: Then *eat*. Swiss cheese on rye. It doesn't matter. Afterwards I'll take you for a ride in an open car.

DOROTHY: Where to?

YOUNG MAN: To Cypress Hill.

DOROTHY: Why, that's the cemetery.

YOUNG MAN: Yes, I know.

DOROTHY: Why there?

YOUNG MAN: Because dead people give the best advice.

DOROTHY: Advice on what?

YOUNG MAN: The problems of the living.

DOROTHY: What advice do they give?

YOUNG MAN: Just one word: *Live*!

DOROTHY: Live?

YOUNG MAN: Yes, live, live, live! It's all they know, it's the only word left in their vocabulary!

DOROTHY: I don't see how—?

YOUNG MAN: I'll tell you how. There's one thing in Death's favor. It's a wonderful process of simplification. It rids the heart of all inconsequentials. For instance, it goes through the dictionary with an absolutely merciless blue pencil. Finally all that you've got left's one page—and on that page one word!

DOROTHY: The word you hear at night on Cypress Hill?

YOUNG MAN: The word you hear at night on Cypress Hill!

DOROTHY: Ohhh. Oh, oh!

YOUNG MAN: But no one hears it till they deal with *me*. I have a secret patented device that makes it audible to them. Something never processed by Du Pont. But none the less a marvelous invention. It's absolutely weightless and transparent. It fits inside the ear. Your friends won't even know you have it on. But this I guarantee: you'll hear that word, that sound much like the long, sweet sound of leaves in motion!

DOROTHY: Leaves?

YOUNG MAN: Yes, willow leaves or leaves of cypresses or leaves of windblown grass! And afterwards you'll never be the same. No, you'll be changed forever!

DOROTHY: In what way?

YOUNG MAN: You'll live, live, *live*!—And not behind petunias. How about it, Miss Simple? Dorothy? Is it a date? Tonight at half-past eight on No. 77?

DOROTHY: Whereabouts on Highway No. 77?

YOUNG MAN: By the wild plum tree—at the broken place in the long stone wall—where roots have cleft the rocks and made them crumble.

DOROTHY: It sounds so far. It sounds—uncivilized.

YOUNG MAN: It is uncivilized, but it isn't far.

DOROTHY: How would I get out there? What means of transportation?

YOUNG MAN: Borrow your kid brother's bike.

DOROTHY: Tonight's Scout meeting night; he wouldn't let me.

YOUNG MAN: Then walk, it wouldn't kill you!

DOROTHY: How do you know? It might. I come from Boston.

YOUNG MAN: Listen, lady. Boston's a state of mind that you'll grow out of.

DOROTHY: Not without some insulin shock treatments.

YOUNG MAN: Stop evading! Will you or will you not?

DOROTHY: I've got so much to do. I have to return some books to the public library.

YOUNG MAN: Just one more time—will you or will you not?

DOROTHY: I can't give definite answers—I'm from Boston!

YOUNG MAN: Just one more mention of Boston's apt to be fatal! Well, Miss Simple? I can't wait forever!

DOROTHY: I guess I—might.

YOUNG MAN: You guess you *might*?

DOROTHY: I mean I guess I will.

YOUNG MAN: You *guess* you will?

DOROTHY: I mean I will—I *will*!

YOUNG MAN: That's better.—So long, Dorothy. [*He grins and goes out, slamming door.*]

DOROTHY: Good-by. [*She stares dreamily into space for a moment.* Mrs. Dull *comes in.*]

MRS. DULL [*sharply*]: Miss Simple!

DOROTHY: Oh! Excuse me. What do you want?

MRS. DULL: I want a pair of wine-colored socks for my husband.

DOROTHY: I'm terribly sorry but the only pair in stock have been reserved.

MRS. DULL: Reserved for whom, Miss Simple?

DOROTHY: A gentleman who represents this line. [*showing card*]

MRS. DULL: "Life, Incorporated"? Huh, I never heard of it.

DOROTHY: Neither had I before. But now I have. And tomorrow the store will be closed for extensive alterations.

MRS. DULL: Alterations of what kind, Miss Simple?

DOROTHY: I'm going to knock out all four walls.

MRS. DULL: Knock out—what—? Incredible!

DOROTHY: Yes, to accommodate some brand-new merchandise. Things I never kept in stock before.

MRS. DULL: What kind of things? Things in bottles, Miss Simple, or things in boxes?

DOROTHY: Neither one nor the other, Mrs. Dull.

MRS. DULL: But everything comes in bottles or in boxes.

DOROTHY: Everything but "Life, Incorporated."

MRS. DULL: What does it come in, then?

DOROTHY: I'm not sure yet. But I suspect it's something unconfined, something wild and open as the sky is!—Also I'm going to change the name of the store. It isn't going to be "Simple Notions" anymore, it's going to be "Tremendous Inspirations!"

MRS. DULL: Gracious! In that case you'll certainly lose my custom.

DOROTHY: I rather expected to.

MRS. DULL: And you're not sorry?

DOROTHY: Not the least bit sorry. I think I caught a slight skin rash from dealing with your silver. Also you sniff too much. You ought to blow your nose. Or better still, you ought to trim it down. I've often wondered how you get your nose through traffic.

[Mrs. Dull *gasps, looks desperately about her, rushes out.*]

You forgot your groceries, Mrs. Dull! [*heaves them out the door*]

[*Loud impact, sharp outcry. Music up.*]

Officer?—Officer!

OFFICER: Did you say size eleven D, Miss Simple?

DOROTHY: Never mind that now, that's all been settled.

OFFICER: Amicably? Out of court, you mean?

DOROTHY: Amicably and out of court. The saboteur has made full restitution and the case is dropped. Now what I want to ask of you is this: how do I get out to No. 77?

OFFICER: Highway No. 77? That road's abandoned.

DOROTHY: Not by me. Where is it?

OFFICER: It's in an awful condition, it's overgrown by brambles!

DOROTHY: I don't care! Where is it?

OFFICER: They say the rain has loosened half the stones. Also the wind has taken liberties with it. The moon at night makes such confusing shadows people lose their way, go dangerous places, do outrageous things!

DOROTHY: Things such as what?

OFFICER: Oh—senseless acrobatics, cartwheels in mid-air, unheard of songs they sing, distil the midnight vapors into wine—do pagan dances!

DOROTHY: Marvelous! How do I get there?

OFFICER: I warn you, Miss Simple, once you go that way you can't come back to Primanproper, Massachusetts!

DOROTHY: Who wants to come back here? Not I! Never was anyone a more willing candidate for expatriation than I am tonight! All I want to know is where it is.— Is it north, south, or east or west of town?

OFFICER: That's just it, ma'am. It's in all four directions.

DOROTHY: Then I don't suppose that I could possibly miss it.

OFFICER: Hardly possibly, if you want to find it. Is that all?

DOROTHY: Yes, sir, that's all.—Thanks very much.—Good-by! [*Music up*. Dorothy *softly*.] Good-by forever!

Playwright Biographies

Kia Corthron has received many honors, including a National Endowment for the Arts/TCG residency, a Kennedy Center Fund grant for New American Playwrights, and a Van Lier Fellowship. She has worked with several theater organizations, including the National Playwrights Conference, the Aubrey Skirball-Kennis Theater Projects, the Delaware Theatre Company, Crossroads Theatre Company's Genesis Festival, the Public Theatre's New Work Now! Festival, and the Circle Rep Lab.

A Harlem resident, Ms. Corthron is developing plays for the Children's Theatre in Minneapolis and the Royal Court Theatre.

Among her plays are: *Force Continuum*; *Breath, Boom*; *Safe Box*; *Up*; *Light Raise the Roof*; *Digging Eleven*; *Anchor Aria*; *Come Down Burning*; *Slide Glide the Slippery Slope*, and *Moot the Messenger*, which premiered at the Humana Festival of New American Plays in Louisville, Kentucky.

Daisy Foote is the recipient of the Roger L. Stevens Award, in association with the Kennedy Center Fund for New American Plays.

Her plays have been developed and produced by such prestigious groups as the Women's Project, the Eugene O'Neill National Playwrights Conference, the American Conservatory in San Francisco, and Primary Stages.

Among her plays are *Living with Mary*; *God's Pictures*; *Farley and Betsy*; *Darcy and Clara*; *The Hand of God*; and *When They Speak of Rita*.

Horton Foote's writings include stage plays, television scripts, and screenplays. He wrote for such successful programs as *Playhouse 90* and *U.S. Steel Hour*. His screenplays for *To Kill a Mockingbird* (1962) and *Tender Mercies* (1983) earned him Academy Awards, and in 1995 he received a Pulitzer Prize for his play *The Young Man from Atlanta*.

Mr. Foote has also been honored with the William Inge Award for Lifetime Achievement in the American Theater; the Academy of Arts and Letters Gold Medal for Drama; the Writer's Guild of America Lifetime Achievement Award; and the Pen American Center's Master American Dramatist Award.

Among his popular plays are *The Traveling Lady*; *The Trip to Bountiful*; *Six O'Clock Theatre*; *The Conquerors*; and *The Carpetbagger's Children*.

Having written several short stories and novels, **Susan Keating Glaspell** (1876–1948) became interested in dramatic writing when her husband, George Cram Cook, with other artists, developed the Provincetown Players in 1915. Eugene O'Neill joined the group the following year.

Her first success was *Trifles*, a one-act play, followed by *Suppressed Desires*, which she wrote in collaboration with Cook. Before the death of her husband in 1924, she had written several other short dramas and three full-length plays. She collaborated with Norman H. Matson on the Pulitzer Prize winner *Alison's House*, in 1930, and then went on to write four novels. Among her other plays are *Close the Book*; *Bernice*; *The Inheritors*; and *The Verge*.

Greg Gunning has written, among other works, the plays *Salem Justice*, the story of the Salem witch trials, and *Fourscore and Seven Years Ago*, a Civil War musical. He has written the book and lyrics for adaptations of Lois Lowry's *Anastasia Krupnik*, Judy Blume's *Otherwise Known as Sheila the Great*, and E. L. Konigsburg's *From the Mixed-up Files of Mrs. Basil E. Frankweiler*. His plays and musicals have played to an estimated four million people across the U.S. *Lily's Crossing*, based on the Newbery Medal of Honor book by Patricia Reilly Giff, has toured the country under the auspices of Arts-Power National Touring Theatre. Gunning resides in New York City.

David Ives (1919–2003), a popular on-air personality for WGBH public television and radio, held many executive positions at that station, including chairman of the board of directors.

Mr. Ives was instrumental in the development of several new productions for WGBH, including *Masterpiece Theatre*, *Mystery*, Julia Child's cooking program, and *This Old House*. He was most interested in promoting multicultural awareness through the station's programs.

His collection of fourteen plays, *All in the Timing*, shows Mr. Ives's great humor and intelligence.

Before turning to writing plays, **William Saroyan** (1908–81) was an extremely successful short story writer, beginning with the collection *The Daring Young Man on the Flying Trapeze*. His first full-length play was *The Time of Your Life*, for which he was offered the Pulitzer Prize and the New York Drama Critics Award (1939–40). He refused the Pulitzer Prize on the grounds that he didn't feel the play was better than anything else he had written.

Among his short plays are *My Heart's in the Highlands* and *Hello, Out There*, both of which are performed extensively. He collaborated with a cousin to write the hit song "Come on-a My House." He went on to write many novels, of which *The Human Comedy* was his most successful, as well as many scripts for *Candid Camera*.

Shel Silverstein (1932–99) is well known as a cartoonist, children's author, poet, and songwriter, as well as a playwright.

He got his start in the military publication *Stars and Stripes* while he was stationed in Japan and Korea. Several years later he turned to writing for children such works as *Uncle Shelby's ABC Book: A Primer for Young Minds* and *Who Wants a Cheap Rhinoceros?* He went on to write such classics as *Lafcadio, The Lion Who Shot Back* and *The Giving Tree.*

His poetry collections, which have sold in the millions, include *Where the Sidewalk Ends*, a winner of the Michigan Writers Award; *A Light in the Attic*, which won a *School Library Journal* Best Books Award; and his last collection, *Falling Up*, published in 1996.

After 1980, Mr. Silverstein devoted himself to writing plays for adults. *The Lady or the Lion Show*, the story of a television producer who will try anything to raise the ratings of his show, is still widely produced throughout the country. He also wrote a collection of one-act plays published in 1983, *Wild Life*. He collaborated in 1988 with David Mamet on the screenplay *Things Change*.

At the age of 21, **Gore Vidal** published his first novel, *Williwaw*. He went on to write several other successful novels, television scripts, and screenplays. *Visit to a Small Planet*, a TV play written in 1955, was extremely well received. He was encouraged by a producer to turn this into a full-length Broadway play, and it was a tremendous hit.

He went on to write *The Best Man*, a 1960 political drama, which was another great success. A new production of the play was produced in 2000 in New York.

Wendy Wasserstein enjoys writing with humor and keen insight about modern intelligent women who are concerned with their equal rights in American society. She points out that bright, well-educated women can and should have careers, if they want them.

Her play *The Heidi Chronicles*, produced in 1989, won both a Pulitzer Prize and a Tony Award. Other plays by Ms. Wasserstein include: *Any Woman Can't*; *The Sisters Rosenzweig*; and *Isn't It Romantic*. She also wrote a well-received children's book, *Pamela's First Musical*, published in 1996.

Thornton Wilder (1897–1975) is the only writer to win the Pulitzer Prize for both fiction and drama: for his novel *The Bridge of San Luis Rey* (1927) and two plays, *Our Town* (1938) and *The Skin of Our Teeth* (1942). His other novels include *The Women of Andros*, *Heaven's My Destination*, *The Ides of March*, and *Theophilus North*. His other major dramas include *The Matchmaker* (which was adapted as the internationally acclaimed musical comedy *Hello Dolly!*) and *The Alcestiad*. *The Happy Journey to Trenton and Camden*, *the Long Christmas Dinner*, and his series on the *Seven Ages of Man* and *Seven Deadly Sins* are among his best-known shorter plays. Among Wilder's many honors are the Gold Medal for Fiction of the American Academy of Arts and Letters, the Presidential Medal of Freedom, the National Book Committee's National Medal for Literature, the National Book Award, the Order of Merit (Peru), the Order pour Le Merit, and the Goethe-Plakette (Germany).

In addition to his talents as playwright and novelist, Wilder was an accomplished essayist, translator, scholar, teacher and lecturer, librettist, and screenwriter. In 1942, he teamed with Alfred Hitchcock to write the screenplay for the classic psychothriller *Shadow of a Doubt*. Well versed in four languages, he translated and adapted plays by such varied authors as Henrik Ibsen, Jean-Paul Sartre, and Andre Obey. Wilder enjoyed acting and played major roles in several of his plays in summer theater productions. He also possessed a lifelong love of music—reading musical scores was a hobby—and he wrote the librettos for operas based on *The Long Christmas Dinner* (with composer Paul Hindemith) and *The Alcestiad* (with Louise Talma).

Tennessee Williams (1911–83) first received recognition as a dramatist from the Group Theater in 1939 for *American Blues*, four short plays. Next came *Battle of Angels* and, in 1944, *The Glass Menagerie*, which won the New York Drama Critics Award. His next big achievement was *A Streetcar Named Desire*, for which he won both the New York Drama Critics Award and the Pulitzer Prize for the 1947–48 season. In 1955 he won these two awards again for *Cat on a Hot Tin Roof. Battle Of Angels*, revised and retitled *Orpheus Descending*, met with wide approval. Other plays by Mr. Williams include *Period Of Adjustment*; *The Night of the Iguana*; *The Rose Tattoo*; *Sweet Bird of Youth*; and *Summer and Smoke*.

M. Jerry Weiss is a distinguished professor of communications emeritus at New Jersey City University. He currently lives in Upper Montclair, New Jersey.

READ THE TOP 20 SIGNET CLASSICS